The Choice Modelling Approach to Environmental Valuation

NEW HORIZONS IN ENVIRONMENTAL ECONOMICS

General Editors: Wallace E. Oates, *Professor of Economics, University of Maryland, USA* and Henk Folmer, *Professor of General Economics, Wageningen University and Professor of Environmental Economics, Tilburg University, The Netherlands*

This important series is designed to make a significant contribution to the development of the principles and practices of environmental economics. It includes both theoretical and empirical work. International in scope, it addresses issues of current and future concern in both East and West and in developed and developing countries.

The main purpose of the series is to create a forum for the publication of high quality work and to show how economic analysis can make a contribution to understanding and resolving the environmental problems confronting the world in the twenty-first century.

Recent titles in the series include:

Game Theory and International Environmental Cooperation
Michael Finus

Sustainable Small-scale Forestry
Socio-economic Analysis and Policy
Edited by S.R. Harrison, J.L. Herbohn and K.F. Herbohn

Environmental Economics and Public Policy
Selected Papers of Robert N. Stavins, 1988-1999
Robert N. Stavins

International Environmental Externalities and the Double Dividend
Sebastian Killinger

Global Emissions Trading
Key Issues for Industrialized Countries
Edited by Suzi Kerr

The Choice Modelling Approach to Environmental Valuation
Edited by Jeff Bennett and Russell Blamey

Uncertainty and the Environment
Implications for Decision Making and Environmental Policy
Richard A. Young

Global Warming and the American Economy
A Regional Assessment of Climate Change Impacts
Edited by Robert Mendelsohn

The International Yearbook of Environmental and Resource Economics
2001/2002
A Survey of Current Issues
Edited by Henk Folmer and Tom Tietenberg

Sustainable Farm Forestry in the Tropics
Social and Economic Analysis and Policy
Edited by S.R. Harrison and J.L. Herbohn

The Economic Value of Water Quality
Edited by John C. Bergstrom, Kevin J. Boyle and Gregory L. Poe

The Choice Modelling Approach to Environmental Valuation

Edited by

Jeff Bennett
Professor of Environmental Management, National Centre for Development Studies, The Australian National University, Australia

Russell Blamey
Programme Visitor, Research School of Social Sciences, The Australian National University, Australia

NEW HORIZONS IN ENVIRONMENTAL ECONOMICS

Edward Elgar
Cheltenham, UK • Northampton, MA, USA

Published by
Edward Elgar Publishing Limited
The Lypiatts
15 Lansdown Road
Cheltenham
Glos GL50 2JA
UK

Edward Elgar Publishing, Inc.
William Pratt House
9 Dewey Court
Northampton
Massachusetts 01060
USA

Reprinted 2009, 2010, 2015

A catalogue record for this book
is available from the British Library

Library of Congress Cataloguing in Publication Data
The choice modelling approach to environmental valuation / edited by Jeff Bennett, Russell Blamey
      p. cm.—(New horizons in environmental economics)
   Includes bibliographical references and index.
      1. Environmental economics. 2. Environmental policy—Costs. 3. Environmental policy—Evaluation. I. Bennett, Jeff. II. Blamey, Russell. III. Series.

HC79.E5 C4865 2001   00-049082

ISBN 978 1 84064 304 6

Printed on FSC approved paper
Printed and bound in Great Britain by Marston Book Services Ltd, Oxfordshire

Contents

Figures

Tables

Contributors

Vic Adamowicz is a professor in the Department of Rural Economy, University of Alberta and an Adjunct Professor in the Department of Economics, University of Alberta. He is also currently the Program Leader of the Sustainable Forest Management Network of Centres of Excellence, a research network with an annual budget of over $5 million and one of Canada's 18 Networks of Centres of Excellence. He received his PhD from the University of Minnesota and MSc and BSc degrees from the University of Alberta. His main research areas include environmental benefits estimation, economic assessment of environmental changes and consumer choice modelling.

Melissa Ruby Banzhaf received her BA in economics from Duke University and currently is a PhD student in economics at the University of North Carolina at Chapel Hill. Previously, she was on the staff of Triangle Economic Research in Durham, North Carolina, where she conducted research in environmental and health economics.

Jeff Bennett is Professor of Environmental Management in the National Centre for Development Studies at the Australian National University and is a Visiting Fellow at the University of New South Wales. He holds an honours degree in agricultural economics from the University of New England and a PhD from the Australian National University. He has published widely in environmental and resource economics and has been at the forefront of the development of non-market valuation techniques in Australia. Jeff is also a director of Wetland Care Australia, a not-for-profit company that carries out wetland protection and rehabilitation works.

Russell Blamey is a Senior Research Officer with the Australian Health Insurance Commission in Canberra. Previously, he was a Research Fellow in the Research School of Social Sciences at the Australian National University, where he researched stated preference methods such as choice modelling and contingent valuation. He also recently lead a major research project examining the potential use in environmental management of discursive processes such as the citizens' jury. He has also worked as a Research Fellow at the University of New South Wales, and as a Research Officer for the Bureau of Tourism Research and the Queensland Department of Primary Industries. He received his PhD from the Australian National University.

Ross Chapman is Manager of the Sydney office of the Centre for International Economics (CIE). He was formerly Dean of the Economic Department at the University of New South Wales. During much of the 1990s, he participated in several projects undertaken by the CIE including reviews of the regulation of firms in Indonesia, financial sector regulation in Zimbabwe and the regulation and pricing of water in the Sydney region. Ross has also served as an Associate Commissioner with the Industry Commission on inquiries into waste recycling and water policy. He has completed a large number of projects in the area of contracting out and the private supply of infrastructure services, especially water.

Jenny Gordon has been with the Centre for International Economics since February 1995. She was formerly an Assistant Professor in the United States, having completed her PhD at Harvard University in 1993. Jenny has conducted extensive work in the areas of electricity markets, agroforestry, environment, health care and social analysis such as the role of women in agriculture and factors influencing sustainable management in the rangelands. International economics and development is her other main area of expertise. Since joining the CIE Jenny has built on her previous research work in the areas of international financial markets and trade, including developing agendas for improved economic governance, long term growth modelling and exchange rate forecasting.

F. Reed Johnson is Vice-President for Research and Development at Triangle Economic Research in Durham, North Carolina. He has been a member of the economic faculties at the US Naval Academy, Illinois State University, Simon Fraser University, and the Stockholm School of Economics. He also worked as a staff economist in the Offices of Policy Analysis at both the US Department of the Interior and the US Environmental Protection Agency.

Jordan J. Louviere received his PhD from the University of Iowa in 1973. Since then he has taught at Florida State University, the University of Wyoming, the University of Iowa, the University of Utah, the University of Alberta, the Australian Graduate School of Management and the University of Sydney. Since 1993 Jordan has been involved in a variety of research activities in environmental and resource economics and health economics; he currently is Senior Research Officer in the Centre for Health Economics

Research and Evaluation (CHERE) and Chief Scientist at Memetrics, Proprietary, Limited in Sydney, Australia. Jordan has published more than 100 papers in leading academic journals, chapters in books and proceedings. His research has largely been concerned with design, analysis and modelling of human judgement, decision making and choice behaviour, including theory, methods, experimental design and the external validity of such methods and models. Jordan's work has been published and applied in human geography, transportation planning and research, marketing, environmental and resource economics and health economics.

Kristy E. Mathews is a Senior Economist at Triangle Economic Research in Durham, North Carolina, where she conducts non-market valuation studies. Previously, she was a research economist in the Natural Resource Valuation and Assessment program at Research Triangle Institute. She received her BA from Alma College and her MA in economics from the George Washington University.

Mark Morrison is a lecturer at Charles Sturt University where he teaches both economics and marketing. He has worked as an economist for the State Government as well as for several economic consulting firms. He has completed a Bachelor of Economics (Honours) at Macquarie University and a PhD at the University of New South Wales. His principal research interests are environmental economics, economic evaluation, market research and health economics.

John Rolfe is a resource economist who is Research Coordinator for the Central Queensland University at Emerald. He has a commerce degree and an economics degree with first class honours, both from the University of Queensland, and a doctorate in economics from the University of New South Wales. John has a number of research interests in natural resource management, agriculture and regional development. He has a background on the land and, with his family, operates a large cattle property in the Central Highlands region of Queensland.

Acknowledgments

A primary driver for the preparation of this volume was a research project aimed at the development of Choice Modelling as a tool for the estimation of non-market, environmental values. The project, which stretched over the period from 1996 to 2000, was funded by the Land and Water Resources Research and Development Corporation, Environment Australia, New South Wales Environment Protection Authority, New South Wales National Parks and Wildlife Service, Queensland Department of Primary Industries and Queensland Department of Natural Resources. The Australian Centre for International Agricultural Research is also acknowledged for funding precursory work on stated preference techniques.

Particular thanks must go to Jill Kenna for her diligence and good natured patience in preparing this manuscript.

The continued love and support of our respective spouses Ngaire and Karen has made this endeavour possible.

JB and RB

1. Introduction

Jeff Bennett and Russell Blamey

1.1 ENVIRONMENTAL CHOICES AND VALUES

The emergence of the environment as a major issue facing society in recent decades has had profound implications for the decisions made by consumers, industry, government and non-government organisations. Consumers, for example, now commonly choose 'environmentally friendly' or 'green' products in preference to other products serving the same basic functions but not considered to be environmentally friendly. Many consumers also seek to escape the stresses of urban life and directly experience the natural environment during their leisure time. In both cases, consumers are demanding products with environmental attributes and the public and private sector is seeking to supply products that meet these needs. To achieve this, producers need to understand in quantitative terms the attributes and 'brands' demanded by consumers and their relative importance. They need to know how the market share for a product will vary when the environmental and other characteristics of the product are varied, and how much extra money green consumers will pay for green products.

Increasingly, decision makers have also sought the quantification, in dollar terms, of the effects their choices will have on the environment. In the private sector, more and more companies are producing annual reports not only on their financial performance but also on their environmental performance (Rio Tinto 2000). Whilst most of these 'environmental report cards' rely on biophysical indicators of performance, valuation of the various types of impacts is a logical next step. There is also some movement on the part of resource development companies to embed environmental values in their internal investment appraisal processes (PPK 1998).

In the public sector, the appraisal process for capital investments which impact on the environment is now more frequently required to incorporate non-market as well as market benefits and costs (Gillespie and Bennett 1999). Similarly, policy decisions regarding the allocation of natural resources between conservation and development options are now more likely to be informed by estimates of environmental values (Snowy Water Inquiry 1998). Governments concerned with the sustainability of their nation's economic and environmental systems have increasingly looked to enhancing their national accounts to take into account the values of environmental assets (National Land and Water Resources Audit 2000). The demand for value estimates for environmental impacts extends through to requirements for research funding and community project applications to include them as part of formal justification processes (Natural Heritage Trust 2000).

The growing interest in environmental choices and values has arisen largely in response to a growing relative scarcity of environmental goods and services. In turn this has been caused by a pincer movement being executed on environmental resources. Increasing consumption levels during the postwar years was associated with heavy demands for products of the natural environment. Simultaneously, the ability of the environment to supply these products has been shrinking due to its use to satisfy competing, consumptive demands. The conflict between conservation and development uses of the environment has thus become more starkly apparent. The complexity of that conflict and the trade-offs it implies have also become more apparent to decision makers and their advisers. In the face of that complexity (from both a technical perspective and a political one), the benefits of seeking out more information about the choices available and their impacts on the community have been enhanced.

A key component of that information relates to the values of the environmental outcomes at stake. For example, if the environmental values associated with conservation options for resource use could be estimated in dollar terms, then comparisons with the values derived from alternative resource development options would be greatly facilitated. Similarly, if consumers are willing to pay a price premium to obtain products that do not harm the natural environment but are otherwise equivalent, producers who can identify this premium can then compare it with any additional costs involved in supplying such products. Finally, recreation planners who understand the values that actual and potential recreationists assign to particular sites and site attributes will be better positioned to make informed and socially and economically beneficial planning decisions. Pressure has therefore been exerted on economists and market researchers to develop cost effective techniques that can meet the demand for environmental value estimates.

1.2 SUPPLY PROSPECTS

Estimating environmental values in dollar terms is a challenging task because environmental benefits and costs are usually not traded in markets. This means that the standard market based estimation techniques – which rely on gaining insights into people's preferences for goods and services by reference to patterns of buying and selling – cannot be applied.

Two fundamental pathways have been taken by economists in their development of non-market, environmental valuation techniques. The first involves the exploration of people's preferences as revealed through their actions in markets which are specifically related to the value of interest. This group of techniques has become known as the revealed preference techniques and includes the travel cost method (Bennett 1996; Mendelsohn and Brown 1985) and the hedonic pricing technique (Fraser and Spencer 1998; Smith 1985). Whilst these techniques have been extensively applied and have established their theoretical and practical credentials, they have not been able to satisfy all the demands for non-market valuation. This is largely because of the limited array of situations in which they can be applied. First they are limited to the provision of information regarding values that have been experienced. Where new circumstances are expected to emerge from a proposed change in resource allocation, preferences revealed in the past may be of little interest. Furthermore, there is only a limited number of cases where non-market values exhibit a quantifiable relationship with a marketed good.

These and other limitations of revealed preference techniques have become increasingly apparent as attention has become focused on the estimation of the 'total economic value' (Randall and Stoll 1983) of environmental impacts. This value includes changes not only in the use values of environmental resources – such as recreational and aesthetic values – which are often well suited to the application of revealed preference techniques, but also non-use values. These values arise without any direct contact with the environment. For instance, a person may experience an 'existence value' simply from knowing that a species or an ecosystem remains protected without ever having been exposed to it. Clearly such non-use values are unrelated to marketed goods and services and so are unlikely candidates for estimation through the application of revealed preference methods.

The only other pathway available to understand environmental behaviour and estimate environmental values involves asking people to state their preferences for alternative circumstances. The methods that follow this strategy are collectively known as the stated preference techniques. The best known of these techniques, the contingent valuation method (CVM), provides a good illustration of how they operate. A CVM application entails a sample of people likely to be affected by an environmental impact being asked if they would be willing to pay a specified amount to secure the change (if it is advantageous to them) or to avoid it (if it is disadvantageous). Different sub-samples of respondents are given differing dollar costs. The relationship between the probability of a respondent agreeing to pay is then modelled against these differing dollar amounts. Hence, it would be expected that the higher the amount of payment required, the lower would be the probability of a respondent agreeing to commit to the payment. From this relationship, the mean and median values (willingness to pay) can be estimated.

Hence, the people responding to a CVM questionnaire are given details about a proposed change in resource allocation and asked to state their preferences for or against that change via an option to pay. The hypothetical trade-off they make between the environmental impact and the monetary cost enables inferences of value to be drawn. By varying the description of the proposed change presented to different sub-samples, limited information regarding the sensitivity of choices and values to variations in the scope of the environmental change can also be obtained.

1.3 THE LIMITATIONS OF CONTINGENT VALUATION

The use of stated preference techniques provides sufficient flexibility to enable the estimation of total economic values associated with environmental impacts. However, their use has been the subject of considerable criticism. That criticism has been centred on the techniques' reliance on people's statements of preference (their intentions). This is in contrast to the revealed preference techniques where values are estimated on the basis of people's actions. Hence, numerous biases have been hypothesised to inflict stated preference technique results.

For instance, in CVM applications, concerns regarding the validity of results have been expressed as a result of (amongst others):

- strategic bias (respondents deliberately misrepresent their preferences in order to influence the decision making process);
- yea-saying (respondents agree to pay not because of the strength of their preferences for the environmental impact but because of a desire to make themselves look good);
- insensitivity to scope variations (respondents' values are invariant to the extent of the environmental impacts involved); and
- framing (respondents' values do not reflect the availability of substitute goods).

The CVM validity issue came to a head during the litigation that followed the Exxon Valdez oil spill. Under US legislation, the results of CVM applications were admissible evidence in claims for compensation for damage caused to the natural environment. The parties contesting those claims disputed the validity of CVM-generated estimates of the damage and, in an effort to resolve that dispute, an independent panel of economists was commissioned to report on the method's use (Portney 1994). Whilst the panel expressed guarded optimism, scepticism remained.

The same picture was concurrently emerging in Australia, where a highly publicised application of the CVM aimed at estimating the environmental damage associated with mining adjacent to Kakadu National Park was similarly criticised (Imber *et al.* 1991).

Those contemplating initiating a CVM application were confronted with the unpleasant prospect of a highly contentious result. So rather than producing a situation in which policy making would be better informed and less contentious, the use of CVM was likely to yield another dimension to a resource allocation dispute.

1.4 CONJOINT ALTERNATIVES

With the CVM being viewed by many policy makers and their advisers in a less than positive light, some economists have contemplated alternative stated preference techniques that could be used to fill the resultant supply gap. A small number of studies had developed the contingent ranking and contingent rating methods. These involved survey respondents rating or ranking a number of possible resource allocation options, each of which featured a different environmental impact (see, for example, Mackenzie 1992 and 1993).

However, the use of ranking and rating techniques suffered from several theoretical and practical obstacles. These concerns include the difficulty involved in making interpersonal comparisons of ranking or rating data, the difficulty for respondents of ranking large numbers of alternatives, and the fact that ratings tasks in particular involve a departure from the contexts of choice actually faced by consumers (Morrison *et al.* 1996).

The contingent ranking and rating methods are variants of techniques widely used in marketing known as conjoint analysis. A common feature of this type of approach is the requirement that survey respondents consider alternatives which are described in terms of their component characteristics or 'attributes'. The alternatives are constructed by combining attributes at different 'levels'. For instance, a conjoint analysis of a car purchase may involve respondents being asked to compare alternative cars described in terms of 'attributes' like colour, fuel consumption, number of seats and so on, where the attributes are variable across several 'levels', say green, white and yellow; 8,10 and 12 litres per 100 kms and so on. The conjoint techniques have as a conceptual foundation the work of Lancaster (1966), who developed his characteristics approach to the analysis of product demand.

1.5 CHOICE MODELLING

The concerns of economists regarding the use of ranking and rating studies were mirrored by their marketing colleagues. A consequence of this was the evolution of a type of conjoint analysis in which respondents are asked to choose between a selection of different alternatives. As with other conjoint variants, these alternatives were defined in terms of product 'attributes' and the different alternatives between which respondents were asked to choose were constructed by systematically varying the attribute 'levels'. However, whilst other conjoint techniques required respondents to rank or rate the alternatives, under the new technique respondents were asked to choose between alternatives.

The resultant sequence of choice outcomes enables the probability of an alternative being chosen to be modelled in terms of the attributes used to describe the alternatives. Hence, it would be expected that the higher the level of a desirable attribute in an alternative, other factors held constant, the greater the satisfaction or utility associated with that option and the more likely it would be for a respondent to choose it. Conversely, the more of an undesirable attribute in an alternative, the lower the utility and the less likely would be its selection. Such models provide a wealth of information on the willingness of respondents to make trade-offs between the individual attributes and their likely responses to different product circumstances.

The technique became known as choice modelling, also known as the choice experiment. It was found by those developing and applying it to be useful in predicting market shares where a new product or a variation of an established product was being contemplated (Louviere *et al.* 1983). This was particularly the case where the stated preference choices were used in conjunction with data on revealed preference data collected by surveying actual choices. Economists working in the transportation sector found it to be an attractive tool for forecasting the market shares enjoyed by alternative modes of transport when some change was under consideration (Hensher, *et al.* 1989).

The marketing and transport economics applications shared a specific characteristic. They both involved the generation of data in circumstances where no existing market was available to generate the type of information required to make a resource allocation decision. They were, in essence, going beyond the bounds of revealed preferences and so shared some of the difficulties confronting non-market environmental valuation. This similarity of circumstances was not lost on economists seeking to estimate non-market environmental values, who have subsequently developed choice modelling in this context.

1.6 THIS BOOK

This book is focused on the development of choice modelling as a tool for estimating environmental values in particular, but also the level of community support for given environmental policies and the market share for green products. Its goals are fourfold:

- to introduce the technique by providing an appreciation of its theoretical underpinnings and a step by step guide to its application;
- to demonstrate its application through the documentation of several case studies;
- to provide some insights into a range of methodological issues that confront choice modelling practitioners; and
- to draw out some conclusions regarding the prospects for the technique.

These four goals form the basis of the structure of the book.

In Part One, the Choice Modelling technique is detailed. This is achieved in two chapters. The first (Chapter 2) is written by Jordan Louviere, who has played a leading role in the development of the technique. In that chapter, the theoretical foundations of choice modelling are laid down along with a description of its evolution. The second (Chapter 3) is written by Jeff Bennett and Vic Adamowitz, who have been associated with a number of applications of the technique across a variety of circumstances. This chapter sets out a step by step guide to the implementation of choice modelling and so takes the theory into practice.

Part Two of the book consists of three chapters in which a number of case studies are presented. Each chapter presents a different type of case study and is intended to demonstrate the versatility of the technique. In the first (Chapter 4), choice modelling is applied to provide policy makers with information regarding the community's ranking of alternative water supply options. The authors, Jenny Gordon, Ross Chapman and Russell Blamey, performed this application for Australian Capital Territory Electricity and Water, the authority responsible for deciding the most appropriate way to supply Canberra's growing demands for water. Different alternatives would involve different environmental impacts so information on the environmental values held by the community was an important ingredient in the decision making process.

In Chapter 5, two case studies in which Jeff Bennett, John Rolfe and Mark Morrison used choice modelling to estimate environmental values are reported. The studies presented in this chapter were amongst the first in the world to investigate non-use values using the technique. The contexts for these studies were typical resource conservation versus development dilemmas. One involves the issue of tree clearing for agricultural development in Central Queensland. There the value of conserving remnant vegetation is estimated so that proposals to restrict tree clearing for cattle grazing can be better assessed. The other is concerned with proposals to reallocate water away from irrigation areas so that it could be used for wetland rehabilitation. Environmental values associated with wetland rehabilitation are estimated in that application.

Finally in Part Two, a case study in which choice modelling is used to predict market shares is detailed. The setting involves consumer choice of a marketed product – toilet paper – that embodies some environmental attributes: the use of unbleached and recycled paper. Hence, the application is designed to investigate consumers' values for these individual attributes and the market shares for green products as a whole. The authors of this chapter, Russell Blamey, Jeff Bennett, Jordan Louviere and Mark Morrison, straddle the boundary between standard marketing applications of choice modelling and environmental valuation applications.

In the development of choice modelling, numerous methodological issues have been encountered. In Part Three, a selection of these are reported. Like CVM results, choice modelling estimates of environmental values are contingent on the scenario established by the questionnaire. It is therefore important for practitioners to have a thorough understanding of the potential impacts of questionnaire design features. A number of the chapters in Part Three address this requirement.

In Chapter 7, the impacts of alternative ways of structuring the choices respondents are asked to make in a choice modelling questionnaire are examined by Blamey, Louviere and Bennett. A key step in any CM application is the selection of the attributes to be used to describe the choice alternatives. In many cases this will not be straightforward; for example, because of links existing between potential attributes and because of apparent contradictions between what policy makers regard as the key factors and what respondents think really matters. The way in which the available alternatives are presented to questionnaire respondents is also a factor that may impact on value estimates. Following a general overview of choice set design issues, two issues are singled out for more detailed analysis in this chapter. These concern practices regarding the labelling of alternatives and the handling of causally related attributes.

A critical component of most choice sets that is only briefly considered in Chapter 7 is the inclusion of an opt-out option. The opt-out option allows respondents to indicate that they would not choose any of the experimentally designed alternatives presented to them. Depending on how the opt-out option is defined, they would rather choose the status quo, do nothing, or choose their usual option. In Chapter 8, Melissa Banzhaf, Reed Johnson and Kristy Mathews provide a detailed review and analysis of the role of the opt-out option in CM studies. Their case study involving anglers' site choices also provides an excellent example of how CM studies can be applied in the recreational context.

One of the primary criticisms levelled at CVM results is that they are influenced by the presence of 'yea-saying' behaviour amongst respondents. It is hypothesised that respondents take the opportunity afforded by a CVM questionnaire to demonstrate their concern for the environment by agreeing to pay the required amount of money, no matter how much that sum is. Choice modelling results may be vulnerable to the same type of behaviour. To test for this effect, the study of Blamey and Bennett reported in Chapter 9 involved two samples of respondents being given choice modelling questionnaires. The only difference between the questionnaires was that one included a prompt identifying the survey as being concerned with environmental issues. It was hypothesised that such a prompt would be more likely to trigger yea-saying behaviour. A unique contribution of this chapter is a validation exercise in which the market share and model predictions associated with the stated preference data are compared with those corresponding to revealed preference, scanner, data. A number of the issues involved in combining stated and revealed preference data are also considered.

Another criticism of CVM results that can also be applied to CM studies is that estimates are not appropriately 'framed' in terms, especially of available substitute goods. In other words, respondents indicate their preferences for one environmental good that is given special prominence because it is the focus of the survey without adequate consideration being given to the array of other (substitute) goods that they value. One potential advantage that CM has over CVM is its ability to embed a range of potential substitute goods within the array of alternatives from which respondents are asked to choose. This approach would explicitly require respondents to consider substitute goods when formulating their responses. The potential of the framing opportunities offered by choice modelling is explored by John Rolfe and Jeff Bennett in Chapter 10.

Choice modelling is still a comparatively novel technique for estimating environmental values. What the chapters of this book are able to show is that the technique shows some real promise as a way forward. But it also demonstrates some weaknesses. For more progress to be made, the strengths offered by CM must be considered in the light of the weaknesses. In the final chapter of the book, a strengths and weaknesses analysis is performed. Conclusions are drawn as to the future CM is likely to face and the directions research into the technique should be taking in order to enhance that future.

PART ONE

The Technique

2. Choice Experiments: an Overview of Concepts and Issues

Jordan J. Louviere

2.1 INTRODUCTION

2.1.1 Choice Experiments: an Introduction to Concepts

It is now almost 20 years since the idea of designed choice experiments arose out of limitations encountered in using conjoint analysis techniques to model transport and telecommunications choices in Australia (Louviere 1981a; Louviere *et al.* 1982). Some options that competed had different attributes and different ranges of attribute levels, and there was a need to estimate true demand by separating choosers from non-choosers. Much has been learned about choice experiments since that time, there have been several recent reviews of this literature and a fairly comprehensive book on the topic is forthcoming (see, for example, Louviere 1994; Adamowicz, Boxall, Louviere, Swait and Williams 1998; Adamowicz, Louviere and Swait 1998a; Louviere, Hensher and Swait 1999; Louviere, Hensher and Swait 2000). Thus, rather than attempt an encyclopedic review, I briefly outline the theory and experimental methods, and use the outline as a way to explain points raised in the discussion that follows. Thus, the purpose of this chapter is to review briefly basic concepts that underlie choice experiments, clarify several issues that remain muddled in the literature, address a variety of unsubstantiated and incorrect opinions and beliefs that persist and discuss new trends and unresolved issues in applying choice experiments in environmental and resource economics.

Choice experiments are samples of choice sets or choice scenarios drawn from the universe of all possible choice sets. The samples are drawn a priori according to statistical design principles in such a way that the overall choice experiment consists of a set of choice set that satisfy certain estimation requirements of certain forms of choice models. In general, a choice experiment consists of the following elements:

- a set of fixed choice options (= 1, ..., A) or subsets of the A total options that may have explicit names or labels, such as brands, types of habitat (for example, rainforest, dry upland plain) and so on, or may simply be generic monikers, identified by uninformative labels such as option A, option B;
- a set of attributes (= 1, ..., K) that describe potential differences in the A choice options, and typically are included in a research project because it is known or hypothesised that they play a major role in the choice behaviour of interest;
- a set of levels or values assigned to each attribute of each choice option to represent a range of variation in that attribute appropriate to the research objectives of a particular study; different attributes may have different numbers of levels assigned to them depending on the research objectives and/or because some attributes are binary (pertain/don't) while others are discrete or numerical; and
- a sample of subjects evaluates all or a subset of the choice sets in the total experiment and chooses one of the possible options available to be chosen in each set. The choices supplied by the sample of subjects are used to estimate various members of the family of random utility theory based choice models.

Thus, choice experiments elicit preferences from consumers, but there are many ways to elicit preferences, including the well-known method of revealed preference (RP) by which actual decisions made by consumers are observed and preferences inferred from what was chosen and rejected. Choice experiments belong to the family of stated preference (SP) methods, and, more particularly, classes of SP methods consistent with random utility theory (RUT) in economics and psychology (for example, Manski 1977). In general, any preference elicitation method that provides information about preference orderings for all or a subset of choice options should be consistent with RUT (see, for example, Luce and Suppes 1965). For instance, the following types of response tasks used to elicit preferences generally are consistent with RUT:

- a single discrete choice from a set of M options – the one chosen option is deemed to be preferred to all unchosen options;
- multiple choices of $j <$ to those not chosen (sometimes called 'pick any' choices);
- partial or complete ranking of M options – higher ranked options are deemed to be preferred to lower ranked options;
- rating of M options of some numerical or quasi-numerical scale of preference, such as a category rating scale – higher rated options are

deemed to be preferred to lower rated options; and
* many more.

These response tasks include many, if not most, previously considered by environmental and resource economists. For example, closed-ended contingent valuation method (CVM) tasks essentially are 'yes/no' or 'accept/reject' response tasks, such that all options that receive a 'yes' are preferred to those that receive a 'no' RUT allows data from all these response tasks to be modelled and compared on a level playing field, including RP data. This general property of RUT remains under-appreciated by many academics and practitioners, especially in marketing and disciplines that borrow techniques from marketing; however, comparisons of SP and RP data are now well-established in transport and environmental and resource economics. A key takeaway of this discussion is that RUT makes it possible to compare and test whether preferences are invariant and/or in what ways preferences differ among sources of preference data *regardless of whether the sources are RP, SP, RP and SP, SP and SP, and so on.*

To understand the above conclusion, I briefly review RUT and deductions from it relevant to the discussion. RUT postulates that utility is a latent construct that exists (if at all) in the mind of the consumer, but cannot be observed directly by the researcher. However, if a researcher designs and implements a valid preference elicitation procedure, it is possible to understand (that is, explain) a significant proportion of the unobservable consumer utility, but some proportion of the utility always will remain unexplained (that is, is random or stochastic from the researcher's viewpoint). That is:

$$U_{an} = V_{an} + \varepsilon_{an} \tag{2.1}$$

where U_{an} is the latent, unobserved utility for choice alternative a held by consumer n, V_{an} is the systematic, observable or 'explainable' component of the latent utility that consumer n has for option a, and ε_{an} is the random or 'unexplainable' component of the latent utility associated with option a and consumer n. Because of the random component, a researcher can never hope to understand perfectly and predict preferences; hence, the problem is inherently stochastic from the researcher's view, which naturally leads to formulating expressions for the probability of choice:

$$P(a|C_n) = P[(V_{an} + \varepsilon_{an}) > (V_{jn} + \varepsilon_{jn})], \tag{2.2}$$

for all j options in choice set C_n.

All terms are as previously defined, except P(•), the probability expression. Equation (2.2) states that the probability of consumer n choosing option a from choice set C_n is equal to the probability that the systematic and random components of option a for consumer n are greater than the systematic and random components of option j for consumer n in choice set C_n. In order to calculate the choice probabilities, the researcher must make assumptions about the distribution of the random component. Typical assumptions are that the εs are (a) independently and identically distributed Gumbel random variables, which assumption leads to the familiar binary or multinomial logit (MNL) models or (b) not independent nor identically distributed normal random variates, which assumption leads to reasonably complex binary or multinomial probit (MNP) models.

In practice it is difficult to distinguish normal and Gumbel models that otherwise are derived from the same assumptions about dependence, variance and covariance of random components because many observations in the far tails are required to distinguish them. Thus, at the present time, choice of one or the other distribution is a matter of logic or computational preference: for example, normals might be preferred as a limiting distributions, whereas Gumbels might be preferred on computational or tractability grounds. Those who favour Bayesian estimation methods typically prefer normals because Markov chain Monte Carlo (MCMC) methods can be used to reduce the problem to simulating from Gaussian distributions (see, for example, Allenby and Rossi 1999; Wedel *et al.* 1999). For those who prefer maximum likelihood, software packages like Limdep (Greene 1999) support a wide array of assumptions about random components as well as distribution(s) of parameters.

A variety of parameters can be estimated from choice data depending on the distributional and associated assumptions that are made to derive a particular model form. For example, the systematic or explainable component can be parameterised as follows:

$$V_{an} = \beta_a + \sum_k \beta_k X_{kn} + \sum_p \theta_p Z_{pn} + \sum_{kp} \phi_{kp} X_{kn} Z_{pn} + \sum_{pa} \varphi_{pa} \beta_a Z_{pn}, \qquad (2.3)$$

where β_a, β_k, θ_p, ϕ_{kp} and φ_{pa} are parameter vectors conditional on, respectively,

(a)   a vector of intercept terms for A−1 of the a = 1, ..., A choice options;
(b)   a matrix of k = 1, ..., K attributes or measures that pertain to choice options, X_{kn};
(c)   a matrix of p = 1, ..., P characteristics or measures that pertain to individual choosers, Z_{pn};
(d)   a matrix of possible interactions of choice option attributes with

individual characteristics, $X_{kn}Z_{pn}$; and

(e) a vector of possible interactions of individual characteristics with choice option intercepts.

This formulation allows a very general representation of the mean of the systematic component, although more general forms are possible, such as assuming that the elements of the parameter vectors are sampled from a joint multivariate distribution (for example, normal) and estimating the moments of that distribution. Similarly, random components can have unequal variances and non-zero covariances, which adds form and parameter complexity to choice models.

Choice experiments typically are designed to elicit preferences such that as wide an array of possible choice model forms can be estimated from the resulting choice data. In contrast, many forms of preference elicitation, of which RP choice data are an excellent example, do not design the data collection in advance to ensure satisfaction of particular model forms, but instead data come as choices observed. In the latter case, choice sets, attributes of choice options and individual characteristics are not controlled or designed a priori but rather occur and co-occur (that is, are observed) as a consequence of a particular sampling plan. Thus, without a priori design and control of data collection exemplified by typical RP data collection efforts, it generally is not possible to know a priori whether any particular model form and parameters will be identified given the data, much less how well-conditioned the data will be or how reliable the estimates will be. For example, Adamowicz *et al.* (1994) provide an example of RP data that exhibit extreme levels of non-identifiability and multicollinearity. Thus, choice experiments are systematically *designed* a priori to ensure that sets of model parameters can be identified given a maintained hypothesis about the form of the choice model. In practice, choice experiments typically can be designed to ensure independent estimation of a fairly wide array of model specifications and parameters conditional on those specifications.

Choices made in real markets can reveal consumer preferences if the data satisfy certain sets of assumptions (such as identifiability of model parameters), and designed SP choice experiments also reveal consumer preferences from the choices that they make in choice scenarios (choice sets) in much the same way(s). Thus, choice experiments constitute ideal vehicles for studying choice behaviour under controlled conditions, because unlike the observations in a typical RP data source, choice experiments are designed to ensure independent estimation of parameters given a maintained hypothesis about model form. On the other hand, RP data ensure that external validity is maximised because the choices observed are real market choices in which consumers have committed money, time or other resources. Thus, the real issue is whether choices observed in choice experiments reveal the same information about preferences as choices observed in parallel RP data sources because consumers in SP experiments typically commit neither money, time nor other real resources other than effort expended to answer questions. Fortunately, this question has been addressed in a fairly large number of studies since 1990, and perhaps surprisingly to many economists and psychologists, the answer seems to be that SP choice experiments and RP data sources provide similar information about preferences. We return to the latter issue later in this chapter, but now the design and analysis of choice experiments are briefly reviewed.

2.2 CHOICE EXPERIMENTS: AN INTRODUCTION TO THEIR DESIGN AND ANALYSIS

Choice experiments are samples of choice sets or choice scenarios systematically designed a priori to satisfy certain estimation requirements of forms of choice models. The objective of a choice experiment is to design the choice sets in such a way that model identification is assured and one can obtain the best possible estimates of the parameters of the model forms of research interest ('best' defined to be consistent with a statistical objective like 'most efficient'). Note that at one extreme, one could simply create choice sets or scenarios by randomly selecting a subset of choice options and a set of attribute levels for each, repeating this process until some desired number of choice sets or scenarios is created. Alternatively, the number of choice options might be fixed at say, exactly A, and the attribute levels of each of the K attributes could be chosen at random to create some desired number of choice sets. Yet another option would be to select the attribute levels randomly but draw them from a joint multivariate distribution that reflects current or projected inter-attribute correlations. Although somewhat easy and straightforward to implement, these approaches generally cannot ensure identification or the quality of parameter estimates a priori. None the less, given a sufficiently large sample of choice sets, identification and reasonable estimation quality should result.

Yet it is unclear why one would want to leave identification and estimation quality to chance, especially when design alternatives are available that avoid this. Indeed, much has been learned about how to design choice experiments to ensure identification and reasonable estimation quality. For example, Louviere and Woodworth (1983) discussed a variety of ways to design choice experiments depending on the particular type of choice model one wants to estimate. In general, however, we know much more about model identification, but far less about the quality of model parameter estimates, particularly their statistical efficiency. Louviere and Street (2000) recently reviewed the available literature for paired and multiple comparison designs and concluded that there were a few results for relative statistical efficiency for binary choice experiments, but virtually no such results for multiple choices. Street *et al.* (1999) also reviewed this literature, and extended existing results for paired comparisons to include relative statistical efficiency results for classes of paired choice designs that can be used to estimate main effects, main effects plus two-way interactions, and so on. However, despite this progress, it is fair to say that the science of optimal design for choice experiments is in early infancy, and much more research is needed to guide design selection for particular practical problems.

Although relative design efficiency remains an unresolved issue in most cases, Louviere and Woodworth (1983) and subsequent work (for example, Louviere 1988a and b, 1994; Kuhfeld *et al.* 1994; Huber and Zwerina 1996) continues to suggest that so-called 'Mother Logit' (ML) design strategies ensure that many forms of choice model can be identified. 'Mother Logit' refers to the most general logistic regression specification possible (McFadden *et al.* 1977). ML involves specifying the utility for each choice option to include the effects of the attributes of that particular choice option as well as the so-called 'cross-effects' of all other attributes of all other choice options on the choice of that particular option (see, for example, Louviere 1988a, b, 1994; Batsell and Louviere 1991). This design strategy has been extended to include designs in which the presence/absence of choice options is systematically varied to create subsets of choice options that are 'present' (also called 'availability' designs; see Anderson *et al.* 1995). Such designs ensure identification of all random' component variance and covariance terms. In general, ML designs 'over-design' choice experiments in the sense that significantly more choice sets are generated than a minimal optimal design (if it is possible to identify such designs a priori as discussed later). However, this may not be 'bad' in the sense that it ensures considerably more observations than parameters. The latter should improve statistical efficiency, although there are no results that demonstrate this formally.

In simple terms, ML designs treat all $K \times A$ attributes that describe choice options as a collective factorial, and are based on orthogonal main effects plans constructed from the collective factorial. For example, let there be three geographical regions that contain endangered rainforests, say Vanuatu, Far North Queensland and Amazonia; and let each option be described by the degree of improvement or decline in a set of three attributes that would be realised for a particular level of a payment vehicle. Three attributes plus a payment vehicle comprise four variables, and suppose we assign each variable four levels to represent the range of variation possible in the three locations. ML designs treat the four variables that describe the three locations as a collective factorial: for example, each location can be described by a 4^4; hence, collectively there are $(4^4)^3$ or 4^{12} possible combinations. ML designs are orthogonal main effects designs selected from the full 4^{12}. Each variable or attribute has three degrees of freedom (df) because it is represented by four levels, hence in this example there are 12×3 total df for main effects, or 36 df. Thus, any orthogonal main effects design with more than 36 total attribute level combinations (that is, 'treatment combinations') will suffice to estimate all effects of interest orthogonally. For example, orthogonal designs exist for 48 or 64 combinations (that is, choice sets or scenarios – each 'row' in such a design is a choice set), but one might want to select a larger design, such as 128 choice sets, because this provides more power to test effects of interest and should improve efficiency.

Many more design options have been discussed in the literature and used to create choice experiments of various types. Details of many of these can be found in Louviere *et al.* (2000), but suffice it to say that choice experiments are very flexible. Typically it is possible to create choice experiments that come as closely as one needs to simulating the essential details of a real market choice of interest. In fact, in the limit, if there are sufficient resources available, one can design choice experiments that exactly mimic real markets (see, for example, Chapter 6 for a description of a study that simulates real supermarket choices). In spite of the design literature, academics and practitioners often adopt questionable design 'strategies', including using main effects plans instead of designs that permit interactions to be estimated (for example, Elrod and Chrzan 1999), using minimal designs with few degrees of freedom for estimation when much larger designs could have been used (for example, Kuhfeld *et al.* 1994), and using ad hoc designs that provide poor statistical information (for example, Shively, Allenby and Kohn 2000).

Finally, it is worth noting that designed choice experiments are simply (large) incomplete and often sparse contingency tables. Although many sophisticated statistical models have been proposed, derived and applied to choice experiment data, at the end of the day significant insights into the results of choice experiments can be obtained from simple analyses applied to contingency tables. That is, tabulations and cross-tabulations of choice data can be informative and are 'model-free' in the sense that the results are what they are, and do not depend on a maintained model hypothesis for interpretation. For example, tabulations of choice outcomes provide the overall choice shares from which model intercepts are estimated; 'cross-tabs' of choice outcomes by each attribute provide main effects of each attribute; cross-tabs of choice outcomes by any two attributes provide two-way interactions of the attributes (if identified and estimable); cross-tabs of choice outcomes by each individual characteristic provide an unconditional estimate of the effects of each individual measure on model intercepts; and so on. This list can be expanded to other analyses, but in the interests of brevity we stop here, and pick up the theme of effects in the next section.

2.3 TYPES OF EFFECTS THAT ARISE IN CHOICE EXPERIMENTS

As discussed above, potentially there are many possible effects that arise in choice experiments depending on the nature and complexity of the experiments and the resulting models that one can estimate. To illustrate some of these effects, consider a simple binary experiment in the closed-ended CVM response style (that is, yes/no) that offers samples of people who fish for trout, scenarios that describe degrees of change in a popular trout stream. Let there be two attributes: number of trout over 12 inches long per quarter mile of stream and the cost of a licence to fish for trout in that stream or region. Let each attribute have two levels that describe improvements, as shown in Table 2.1. One can design much more complex and realistic experiments, but this simple example illustrates the issues in this section rather than being an example of good design practice.

Table 2.1 shows 16 different possible responses (R1–R16) to the design. Indeed, in any binary choice experiment, if there are C total scenarios (choice sets), there will be 2^C possible response patterns. In general, if there are M choice outcomes and C scenarios, there will be M^C possible response patterns. As M or C increase, the number of possible patterns increases exponentially, quickly reaching levels that exceed realistic sample sizes or even available populations of humans who might be studied. If the pattern in the above table were to be realised in a choice experiment, it would result in retention of the null for all effects in a sample aggregate analysis because subjects totally differ. However, some subjects exhibit systematic response effects; for example, R11 responds 'yes' (=1) whenever per cent more licence fee = 25 per cent and 'no' whenever it = 100 per cent, but does not respond to increases in fish. In contrast R4 says 'yes' when fish = 50 per cent and 'no' when fish = 25 per cent, but shows no fee sensitivity.

The example illustrates the problem of trying to infer patterns of heterogeneity in choice experiment data. At one extreme, if all subjects respond exactly alike except for sampling fluctuations, there will be a single segment, and a choice model that estimates the mean effects of interest (main plus interaction effects) should closely approximate the choices. At the other extreme is the pattern illustrated in the table in which all choice sequences are equally likely, and each individual is a unique segment of one. Choice experiment data typically fall between these extremes, and the ability of researchers to model preference heterogeneity will depend on the empirical pattern exhibited in a particular study. If one relies on models that describe heterogeneity as distributions or individual-level estimates of effects, there is an obvious problem: the observed response distribution is an outcome of the experiment that was designed and administered and the sample that was drawn. If one changes the experiment in a material way, such as altering the level of a particular attribute outside the experimental range and/or one uses the results of the experiment to formulate and implement successful policy, one potentially can change the distribution of responses (altering the level) or the distribution of respondents (policy implementation). In either case, the estimated model may not be useful for future forecasting because it was merely a statistical description of what happened and not a true model of the choice process and/or changes in the population of interest.

Table 2.1 Responses of 16 experimental subjects (R1–R16)

Subject	Attributes levels							
	20% more fish	25% more licence	20% more fish	100% more licence	50% more fish	25% more licence	50% more fish	100% more licence
R1	0		0		0		0	
R2	0		0		0		1	
R3	0		0		1		0	
R4	0		0		1		1	
R5	0		1		0		0	
R6	0		1		0		1	
R7	0		1		1		0	
R8	0		1		1		1	
R9	1		0		0		0	
R10	1		0		0		1	
R11	1		0		1		0	
R12	1		0		1		1	
R13	1		1		0		0	
R14	1		1		0		1	
R15	1		1		1		0	
R16	1		1		1		1	

Thus, the example nicely illustrates why it pays to 'engage brain' and/or make use of theory or logic before estimating complex statistical models. That is, one must be able to predict how a population will change in response to a policy as well as how they will respond to a change in the experiment. Complex statistical models that merely capture the joint multivariate distribution of the parameters and/or the variance-covariance matrix of the random components are not theories, and without links to observable measures that can be forecast into future time periods, complex models may not be very useful unless they can be constantly updated. Thus, complex models can be estimated: there are now a number of examples in the literature (for example, Allenby and Rossi 1999; Revelt and Train 1999), but their usefulness beyond mere description deserves to be questioned. Simply put, scientific quests for parsimony, insights and understanding have not been overturned by the ability to formulate and estimate complex statistical models.

It also should be noted that the responses in the table illustrate how different subjects can exhibit different propensities to say 'yes' (or 'no'). These propensities are captured in model intercepts, and can be parameterised as a function of observable measures that describe individuals as previously indicated. However, the responses also exhibit degrees of serial correlation, which can be estimated and may capture some of the propensity of individuals to say 'yes' or 'no.' For example, Gerard *et al.* (1999) recently compared models that interacted sociodemographic measures and intercepts with models that took serial correlation into account. Surprisingly, despite several highly significant sociodemographic effects in the non-serial correlation models, sociodemographic measures no longer were significant in the models that took serial correlation into account. A model with a single serial correlation term fitted the data significantly better than a model with a dozen extra sociodemographic effects without serial correlation.

Thus, a variety of issues remain unresolved in the choice modelling literature, particularly regarding choice experiments. However, one issue that can be resolved to some extent is confusion about the relationship between conjoint analysis (CA) and choice experiments (CEs), to which we now turn our attention.

2.4 WHAT IS CONJOINT ANALYSIS AND HOW DOES IT DIFFER FROM CHOICE EXPERIMENTS?

Let me begin by bluntly asserting that RUT-based CEs are not CA, and while some CEs resemble CA applications, the resemblance is superficial. So as not to belabour the point, CA is a generic title given to a broad family of methods for measuring consumer preferences and tradeoffs that share the following in common with CEs:

- Key variables or *attributes* that underlie preferences for goods are identified and assigned values or *levels* to represent a range of variation relevant for a particular research purpose.
- Experimental design or other techniques are used to combine the attribute levels into profiles or scenarios to be evaluated in some way by a sample of respondents.
- Respondents' evaluations are analysed using statistical models to *decompose* the valuations or preferences into components due to each attribute level.
- A simulation method is used to forecast preferences or choices or value options.

Despite common characteristics, CA methods differ widely in task characteristics, especially the nature of the observed responses and the statistical models used to analyse them and derive preference models (Louviere 1988a, 1994). Moreover, most CA methods are based on statistical and mathematical considerations, not behavioural theory. This is nowhere better illustrated than in marketing, where techniques and methods (especially statistical) tend to dominate academic and commercial practice even when they lack behavioural or theoretical support; and practical prediction typically is favoured over scientific understanding of process (which, indeed, often seems to be confused with true understanding of process). CA arose out of attempts to place preference orderings across multi-attribute options on a firm mathematical basis. It was originally termed 'conjoint measurement' (for example, Krantz and Tversky 1971; Krantz *et al.* 1971).

Conjoint measurement provided an axiomatic basis to represent preference orderings (or indeed, any ordering) of multi-attribute options, such that the observed orders can be described as if they were generated by additive, multiplicative (more generally, multi-linear) and so on, rules for combining (integrating) the separate attribute values. Conjoint measurement is axiomatic and not behavioural; that is, it is a theory of the behaviour of numbers (ranks) assigned to multi-attribute combinations (options) created by factorial enumeration of all possible combinations of attribute levels. However, if ranks assigned by consumers to express preferences satisfy the axioms, the assigned numbers can be represented as if they were generated by various forms of multi-linear models.

Subsequently, other more behavioural paradigms emerged, such as information integration theory (IIT) and its associated method of functional measurement (Anderson 1970). IIT not only is more behavioural, but also has an error theory to test if responses violate the underlying axioms. Despite attributions to Lancaster's (1966) characteristics of goods theory, little attention has been paid in marketing, transport and environmental and resource economics to the consistency of CA techniques with economic theory in general or economic valuation in particular. We return to the latter issue later in this chapter, but for now note that, in general, virtually no flavours of traditional CA used in marketing or other fields are consistent with economic theory. Thus, traditional CA should not be used for valuation purposes.

In contrast to the non-behavioural, predominantly statistical and methods-driven CA methods common in marketing, CEs are based on sound, well-tested, long-standing behavioural theory that evolved out of Thurstone's (1927) theory of paired choices (that is, RUT). The empirical applications of CEs follow directly from RUT and permit tests of assumptions underlying RUT as well as tests of model forms that are similar to axiomatic conjoint measurement and its successors (such as IIT). Unlike CA, CEs can be designed to resemble real market choice situations as closely as is desired, including at the limit designing actual market choice situations. While CA also can do this in principle, CA remains largely an 'evaluate one multi-attribute option at a time' way to model preferences and tradeoffs. However, real markets typically involve multiple, competing choice options, including the choice to choose none or select multiple quantities of each option. RUT provides a comprehensive behavioural theory of these processes, from which a wide range of statistical models can be derived and used to approximate choice processes.

It is also worth noting that conjoint measurement and its CA successors are individual-level measurement and modelling methods, and an individual-level modelling focus dominates traditional CA applications. In part this stems from the psychological origins of these techniques, but also pays homage to Arrow's (1963) impossibility theorem by avoiding aggregation of incommensurable utilities. In contrast, environmental and resource economists tend to be more interested in estimating group instead of individual-level values, but it can be argued that the former can be derived from properly understanding the latter.

Thus, despite more than three decades of CA research and application, it is unclear what can be inferred about human behaviour from such techniques. Taken literally, traditional CA techniques simulate a behaviour that is rarely observed in a real market, namely a consumer systematically and deliberately evaluating every option available – one at a time. For example, CA simulates evaluation of every brand-size combination of ready-to-eat cereals on a supermarket shelf, such that a consumer rates each option on a scale, ranks them all in preference order, considers or not each for purchase, and so on. Modern supermarkets frequently stock many dozens of such goods (for instance, Australia has more than 80 brand–size combinations), so it is not difficult to see that CA tasks lack face validity in many cases and simulates behaviour rarely observed in real consumers.

Thus, a key advantage of CEs is that they can simulate real behaviour as closely as one's resources allow, including choice of cereal(s) from modern supermarket shelves (see, for example, Chapter 6). Moreover, such simulations are based on sound, behavioural theory, not merely statistical techniques, and the theory is sufficiently general to cover a very wide array of associated behaviours. For example, some choices are indeed discrete, like travel mode decisions (one cannot travel in two modes simultaneously), but others involve choices of multiple options from sets of options, and even multiple quantities of options (one can choose three different brand–size combinations of cereal, including four boxes of one, two of another and none of a third). As well, choice experiments can be designed to handle ancillary or related choices consequential to antecedent choices such as changes in mode of travel and residential location following choice of a new job. I'm unaware of any other comprehensive theory similar to RUT, and no such theory underlies CA. Thus, 'tradition', 'software availability', and 'applications experience' are not substitutes for theory and logic, and environmental and resource economists would be well advised to learn and understand the differences between valuation methods which are based on sound behavioural theory that is consistent with economic theory and methods which are not.

Specifically, CA rating and ranking tasks pose serious theoretical and empirical questions about exactly what behaviour is being simulated or modelled. For example, if subjects cannot indicate that they would not support, vote, pay for, or otherwise prefer *any*, each, or all options, how does one interpret the outcome of a CA experiment? The answer to this question is not obvious empirically, but it is true to say that not incorporating the choice 'not to choose' renders tasks and resulting models inconsistent with demand theory. Thus, if the basic data from which CA models are derived are inconsistent with economic theory, it is unclear how to interpret resulting welfare measures such as willingness to pay (WTP) and willingness to accept compensation (WTA). Indeed, the only logical interpretation is that results are conditional on making a choice (as opposed to not choosing), which begs the question of how to identify choosers in the first place. Clearly, a random sample of consumers from a particular population *must* include non-choosers, except by chance. Thus, traditional rating and ranking CA or other related tasks (for example, rating pairs of options) inherently risks sample selection bias in its outcomes if non-choosers are included in the sample. If choosers cannot be distinguished from non-choosers (that is, choices from non-choices), the extent of the bias is unknown but is likely to be serious. Yet, if one knows choosers and non-choosers a priori, it begs the question of why one would conduct a choice experiment in the first place.

Thus, a great advantage of RUT-based preference elicitation methods is not only an economic and behavioural basis, but the fact that RUT provides an error theory and associated mechanisms with which to compare and test models. Over the past decade numerous papers have been focused on how RUT allows one to compare and contrast models, including pooling data from various sources, such as stated and revealed preference data (for example, Ben-Akiva and Morikawa 1990; Swait and Louviere 1993; Adamowicz *et al.* 1994). In brief, RUT predicts an inverse relationship between the scale (magnitude) of the estimated utilities and the amount of error or choice variability (more generally, 'response' variability). Model comparisons must take these differences into account to test if model parameters differ; error variability differs; error variability is equal, but model parameters differ; or both differ. RUT is indifferent to the source of preference data so long as data are consistent with or can be transformed to be consistent with RUT. Few CA researchers and practitioners seem to have recognised that RUT provides a sound theoretical and statistical way to determine if data satisfy underlying assumptions and/or if different tasks, experiments and so on yield the same information about preferences. Indeed, we have been able to make such comparisons and perform rigorous tests for some time, as noted by (inter alia) Swait and Louviere (1993), Louviere *et al.* (1999, 2000) and Hensher, Louviere and Swait (1999).

For example, one can test if rating scales satisfy the equal interval assumptions required to use traditional CA statistical models such as ordinary least squares regression. That is, RUT allows one to formulate ordered logit or probit models for rating data and to test if category interval cut-points are equally spaced for individuals or groups. Rating and ranking response data can be transformed to implied orders and equivalence of preference parameters can be tested after taking differences in error variability in the ranking depths and/or data sets into account (see, for example, Louviere *et al.* 2000).

Surprisingly, there have been few comparisons of traditional CA methods with CEs based on RUT (for example, Ben-Akiva *et al.* 1991), and I'm aware of no comparisons of CA results with real behaviour. In contrast, there are many comparisons of CEs with real behaviour (see, for example, Louviere *et al.* 2000), some of which are discussed in more detail later in this chapter. However, in the interest of completeness we note that comparisons of CA model predictions against hold out judgements or choices are not external validity tests. Environmental and resource economists should require those who wish to promote or apply such methods to compare their results with real market behaviour, as the CE paradigm has done repeatedly since the late 1980s. We have more to say about this important issue later in this chapter.

Perhaps more serious, however, is the issue of preference aggregation illustrated earlier. That is, choice experiments traditionally have relied on sample or segment aggregate models, and CA traditionally has relied on individual-level models. CA adherents argue that maintaining individuals as the unit of modelling analysis avoids aggregation fallacies inherent in Arrow's (1963) work. Naturally, there is some validity to this argument, but it begs the question as to whether assumptions required to estimate individual-level models and obtain reliable and unbiased estimates are satisfied. Not surprisingly, this can be questioned on several grounds, including failure of human subjects to satisfy assumptions inherent in the use of rating and ranking responses and/or interpretation of empirical outcomes even if response assumptions are satisfied (that is, not allowing non-choice responses). Discrete choice response tasks avoid many assumptions inherent in ordinal or metric responses, but beg the question as to how to compare subjects properly.

The latter issue of inter-individual utility comparisons is non-trivial. Recently, there has been much interest in Bayesian estimation procedures, primarily applied to traditional CA tasks (see, for example, Wedel *et al.* 1999). Indeed, it seems fair to say that the 'hype' at academic and practitioner conferences and some of the claims made in marketing seem to suggests that, whatever the question, Bayesian estimation is the answer. For example, hierarchical Bayes techniques have been used recently to estimate individual-level choice model parameters from samples of subjects (for example, Allenby and Rossi 1999; Revelt and Train 1999; Sawtooth Software 1999). Moreover, it has been suggested that accurate estimates of individual choice model parameters can be estimated from relatively small numbers of observations (for example, 10–20). Leaving aside the fact that I am unaware of any comparisons of Bayesian methods with more traditional maximum likelihood methods in terms of the ability of models estimated from CEs or traditional CA experiments to predict actual behaviour in real markets, estimation of individual-level effects in choice models raises serious issues about model complexity and the usual scientific search for parsimony. To wit, why would one need or want to estimate the thousands of individual-level parameters possible in typical applications, and why would one expect temporal stability in such models? In fact, this is unnecessary, as McFadden (1986) explained, when he discussed some of the same issues more than a decade ago.

Indeed, one can argue that these statistical exercises constitute little more than complex statistical descriptions of the recent past behaviour of a sample and beg the question as to how one might forecast either the trajectories of the subjects over time or the model parameters or both. As previously discussed, statistics, however complex and elegant, are no substitute for behavioural theory and/or understanding how real markets work. Thus, despite the hype and attention currently devoted to all things Bayesian, these estimation procedures are just another way to estimate statistical models; and given any particular maintained model form, parameters estimated with maximum likelihood or Bayesian estimation must be the same if the estimation is unbiased. Thus, the real issue is which methods are better (in some sense) for which estimation and application purposes.

For example, Revelt and Train (1999) recently showed that a new simulation estimation approach applied to random parameter mixed logit (RPML) models does at least as well as hierarchical Bayes on CE data, and they discuss advantages provided by RPML which are not provided by hierachical Bayes. Thus, parsimony and the ability to forecast observables and changes over time are real issues; and estimation of overly complex statistical models should be given less priority by researchers than development of behavioural theory that can lead to more parsimonious models. The fact that one can estimate individual-level choice model parameters does not mean that one should do so, especially in the absence of behavioural theory (see also Louviere *et al.* 1999). Moreover, it is worth noting that each individual's mean preference parameters are perfectly inversely correlated with their choice (error) variability; thus, it is unclear how to interpret a *distribution* of choice model parameters estimated for a sample of individuals. Which distribution is it? Is it the distribution of mean preference parameters, or the distribution of choice variability, or perhaps a mixture of both?

2.5 CHOICE VARIABILITY AS A BEHAVIOURAL PHENOMENON

The foregoing leads naturally to a discussion of the behavioural outcomes of CEs. As mentioned earlier, the efficiency of the model estimates from any particular CE, given a maintained model, is not well understood. There are several reasons why this is so, but for the sake of brevity let me consider only two:

(a) choice models are non-linear and the efficiency of any particular CE depends on knowing the true parameters (or equivalently, the true choice probabilities), but if these were known a priori, there would be no need to run a CE to estimate them; and

(b) humans interact with choice experiments in ways not considered by the choice modelling community, such that one must take into account not only *design efficiency* but also *respondent efficiency* to determine the total efficiency of a CE (Severin 2000; Louviere and Hensher 2000).

The former is self-explanatory, but the latter deserves elaboration. As alluded to above with respect to individual-level model parameters, in RUT-based choice models, the magnitude of the estimated model parameters – the so-called 'scale' of the parameters – is inversely proportional to the variance of the random component of utility. Thus, when analysts estimates a k-element parameter vector, β_k, conditional on a k-column design matrix X_k, they actually estimate $\lambda\beta_k$, where λ is the scale of the parameter vector. In the widely used multinomial logit (MNL) model, $\lambda^2 = \pi^2/6\sigma^2$, where π is the natural constant and σ is the standard deviation of the random component. In the classical formulation of RUT-based choice models, the latent utility of option a, U_a, is expressed as equation (2.1). There has been little critical examination of the role played by ε_a except in the case of differences in the variances of random components in two or more sources of preference or choice data (for example, Ben-Akiva and Morikawa 1990; Swait and Louviere 1993). Indeed, it is fair to say that many academics and practitioners seem to view the random component as a single-error component.

Yet, a unidimensional error component view is not only simplistic, but recent research suggests that it is quite incorrect. Specifically, recent theoretical reasoning and empirical research suggest that the random component is multidimensional, and in the case of CEs it contains sub-components representing within-individual variation, between-individual variation, task variation, and variation due to (potentially, many) other sources. That is, other sub-components can be recognised, but most are constant in any one CE. Thus, when one designs a CE, the CE design itself can impact the sub-components that comprise the total random component, and different CEs may impact sub-components differently. For example, if the range of a payment vehicle is sufficiently large, many subjects should agree that certain values are 'low' and certain other values are 'high'. In turn, they should respond more consistently to the low and high values, hence decreasing variability at the extremes and increasing it in middle ranges. Alternatively, if subjects differ a lot in sensitivity to the payment vehicle, they may respond more extremely to extreme values, increasing between-subject variability (that is, preference heterogeneity). Thus, all CEs trade-off statistical or design efficiency for sub-components of respondent efficiency. For example, Huber and Zwerina (1996) proposed 'utility-balanced' CEs in which subjects choose among options that are close in utility. However, such CEs may increase task difficulty substantially because the closer the utility of options, the harder the choices. Thus, respondent efficiency is likely to decrease in such CEs, offsetting gains from statistical efficiency.

Some results are beginning to emerge on the latter issue. Swait and Adamowicz (1997a) and Deshazo and Fermo (1999) studied task complexity effects on response variability and parameterised the random component variance as a function of task complexity measures. They found that models that took task complexity into account were significantly superior statistically to those that did not. Thus, recognition of these issues is recent, and research has just begun into their ramifications (for example, Louviere and Street 1999; Louviere and Hensher 2000), so more work is needed.

A related area of recent research attention is pooling and comparison of sources of preference and choice data. Following the pioneering effort of Ben-Akiva and Morikawa (1990), there have been several comparisons of models estimated from real market choices with models estimated from so-called 'stated' choices, including several in environmental and resource economics (for example, Adamowicz *et al.* 1994, and the study reported in Chapter 9 of this volume). The theory to undertake such comparisons is based on the inverse relationship between scale and random component variability discussed above (see Ben-Akiva and Morikawa 1990). That is, if subjects exhibit the same preference patterns in an experiment as they do in a real market, RUT suggests that random component variances may differ but mean parameters will be the same; and if preference parameters are the same but random component variances differ, the two vectors of preference parameters (real and stated) will be proportional.

The latter deduction leads to a general way to compare and test models based on RUT that can be applied to any sources of preference or choice data that are consistent with or can be transformed to be consistent with RUT (see, for example, Louviere *et al.* 1999). In fact, it is fair to say that this paradigm consistently has found underlying preference parameters to be remarkably similar, but random component variances often differ (for example, Louviere *et al.* 1999a; Louviere *et al.* 1999, 2000). Louviere *et al.* (1999a) note that failure to take random component variance differences into account in empirical analyses of choice data may account for many published reports of differences in mean outcomes associated with various types of choice data. Moreover, this paradigm suggests that many previously reported differences in mean actually may be differences in response variability not taken into account.

The latter issue has a number of significant implications for research in environmental and resource economics. For example, many previously published comparisons of WTP and WTA were based on closed-ended CVM experiments in which subjects received an elaborate resource description and a random draw from a payment vehicle distribution. Depending on the task frame, subjects had to decide whether to pay a cost for a resource improvement or accept compensation for a resource deterioration. In both cases, there is a single payment vehicle parameter to be estimated in a binary choice model. The Ben-Akiva and Morikawa (1990) deduction requires comparisons of WTP and WTA to take differences in their respective random components into account. As previously noted, this amounts to a restriction on a model estimated from a data set that pools WTP and WTA response data. The restriction requires the parameter vectors to be proportional, and the constant of proportionality will be the ratio of the scales of the parameter vectors (or equivalently, the ratios of the random component variances). Unfortunately, with only a single model parameter (that is, the payment vehicle) an infinite number of ratios will satisfy the restriction, hence variance ratios cannot be separately identified in this case.

This suggests that some comparisons of WTP and WTA may have confounded model parameter (means) differences with random component variance differences, which also suggests that one may wish to question the empirical basis for reported differences in mean welfare estimates. That is, some previously published empirical differences may have been due to random component differences, and there may be reason to suspect them. For example, most subjects in such CMV experiments should be familiar with WTP judgements, but less familiar with WTA judgements. Thus, one might expect the response variability for WTP tasks to be significantly lower than for WTA tasks, all else equal. If underlying preferences are the same in both tasks, but variances differ, model parameters estimated from WTA tasks should be significantly smaller than those estimated from WTP tasks, all else equal.

However, the empirical record suggests otherwise, namely WTA estimates consistently are larger than WTP estimates. Yet, this also may be the result of a variance and not a mean effect. For example, if WTA experiment subjects are unfamiliar with either the concept or the task and/or find the idea itself objectionable (that is, asking them to accept money to be made worse off), they might simply say no to anything except very large amounts of money (which they can use to do other things – perhaps even move away from the problem!). If they respond in that way, the variance in WTA responses would be significantly smaller than in WTP, and the welfare estimates would be higher.

The key takeaway message is that a proper test of differences in WTP and WTA *requires at least two model parameters* (attribute effects); the strength of the test should increase with more attributes, but no research yet suggests the optimum number.

2.6 TASK COMPLEXITY

The next issues I want to discuss have to do with CE tasks and the way in which they are administered. There seems to be no shortage of academics and practitioners who hold strong opinions and beliefs about CEs, but few empirical results bear on how CE task complexity or length affects empirical outcomes. For example, Louviere *et al.* (1993b) reviewed results in a number of disciplines, including marketing, transport, psychology, sociology and other fields with respect to task lengths, numbers of attributes, numbers of attribute levels and numbers of choice options. Virtually no empirical studies dealing with CEs were found, and most empirical evidence available directly contradicts popular opinions and beliefs. Unfortunately, this literature is rarely cited by the CA or choice modelling community, and seems to have been ignored or is unknown to most academics and practitioners outside narrow sub-areas.

Moreover, since the Louviere *et al.* (1993b) review, several empirical studies directly bear on these issues in choice experiments that are reviewed in Louviere and Hensher (2000) and Louviere *et al.* (2000). The results of these studies consistently support the idea that task complexity and length primarily impact on random component variances and not mean parameters. In turn, this suggests that widely held opinions and beliefs in environmental and resource economics derived from empirical applications experience with the CVM may not transfer directly to CEs. Of particular concern is the finding noted by Louviere *et al.* (1993) that virtually no studies reviewed were conducted in a double-blind manner. Without double-blind controls, experimenters, field managers, interviewers and others can influence the outcomes of empirical research in directions that favour their preconceived views of the world. Thus, it is surprising how few studies in environmental and resource economics seem to have used double-blind techniques, holding many open to questions of systematic bias. Even more surprising is the fact that I find little evidence that the survey research community associated with the CVM understands the need for double-blindness. Thus, many empirical results generated by CVM survey research can be questioned on the grounds that they were not conducted in a double-blind manner.

The latter is not a trivial issue; for example, Louviere *et al.* (1993) noted that they personally experienced many incidents since 1979 in which results were biased when individuals influenced subjects to behave in ways consistent with their preconceptions about choice experiments – typically reporting that subjects couldn't or wouldn't do CEs because they were too complex. In every instance in which CEs were repeated using double-blind procedures there were no reports of subject difficulties. In light of opinions I've heard expressed at several major environmental and resource economics related conferences since 1994, particularly by survey researchers with CVM experience, it would behove the field to consider making double-blindness a condition for publication.

It bears repeating that there is *no* empirical evidence to suggest that increasing numbers of attributes, numbers of choice options or numbers of choice sets (scenarios) impact mean preference parameters, but there is evidence that increases in these factors impact random component variability. However, optimal levels of these variables remain unknown for particular applications, although Brazell and Louviere (1996) reported that subjects in two different survey conditions completed 96 and 120 choice sets with little impact on response rates and no systematic impacts on response means or random component variability. Results consistent with these observations also have been reported by Orme and Johnson (1995), Deshazo and Fermo (1999) and Swait and Adamowicz (1997a). That is not to say that researchers will not find that these factors impact response means; instead, it is fair to say that currently there is no evidence of same. Thus, much more open-mindedness and scientific objectivity would be welcome on these issues than this author has observed.

2.7 WITHIN-SUBJECT VERSUS BETWEEN-SUBJECT EXPERIMENTS

The final issue I want to address is within- versus between-subject experiments. For reasons that remain unclear to me as a newcomer to environmental valuation, there appears to be a widespread belief on the part of the CVM community that between-subject experiments are greatly preferred to within-subject experiments. There is no theoretical or logical rationale for such a view, especially as this would be tantamount to suggesting that longitudinal panels also should be avoided. In fact, if I had a panel of observations on the same subjects regarding their fishing destination choices over a period of, say, three years, there is little structural difference between that panel of observations and a 'compressed-time' panel of 16 or more CE fishing scenarios to which subjects respond sequentially. Thus, there is no logical reason to avoid within-subject designs; hence, the argument must be that valuation estimates from within-subjects designs are biased. I know of no empirical evidence that supports such a view as far as CEs are concerned; and, in fact, the empirical record in psychology, especially in judgment and decision-making, contains many examples of within-subject experiments that contradict this.

Brazell and Louviere (1998) addressed the issue of bias in two survey length experiments that embedded latin square designs within smaller choice set conditions to control for order. This allowed models to be estimated from order one versus all other orders, which is the same as having only one choice set per respondent. Both studies showed that order impacted random component variances, but order and random component variance were not systematically related. This supports the fact that within-subject CEs are not biased, or at least are no more or less biased than between-subject CEs. Having said that, I can see that there could be difficulties in conducting traditional closed-ended CVM experiments that manipulate only a single payment vehicle as within-subjects experiments, and this difficulty would generalise to any CE that manipulates only one variable because of dominance/domination problems. However, to suggest that such difficulties carry over to more general CEs not only is illogical, but flies in the face of years of empirical research and evidence to the contrary. Again, much more scientific objectivity and understanding of diverse research literatures would be welcome.

2.8 CONCLUSIONS

Over the past 20 years there has been considerable progress in understanding how to design, analyse and model choice experiments and their behavioural outcomes. Despite progress, much remains unknown and unresolved, particularly regarding optimally efficient designs for particular purposes and the degree of model complexity that is desirable and/or necessary to understand adequately, explain and predict choice behaviour. On the positive side, there has been considerable progress in understanding how to pool sources of preference and choice data and compare models of preference estimated from these sources on the level playing field provided by random utility theory. However, it is surprising how few academic researchers outside transport seem to be aware of these developments, especially in light of a decade of research in this emerging paradigm. The consistent empirical successes of this paradigm suggest that often there are few differences in preferences expressed in real markets and experimental markets. In turn, this suggests that much more research is now needed to understand the best ways to design experiments and elicit preferences to obtain consistently reliable choices, given that several methods appear to be approximately equally valid elicitors of preferences.

We also argued that traditional conjoint analysis is not the same as RUT-based choice experiments, and that for environmental and resource economics, considerable caution should be exercised in using traditional CA techniques for valuation. Similarly, we reviewed and discussed a variety of issues related to choice experiments that can best be described as 'academic urban myths' in so far as they have little if any empirical basis, but rather considerable empirical evidence exists to the contrary. Our review also suggests that with respect to the issues discussed, it is likely to be less than useful to try to extrapolate practices and findings from the CVM to choice experiments because many do not apply in scale or scope, or they apply only to a very narrow range of issues and problems that the CVM addresses. Finally, it is worth noting that closed-ended CVM tasks are simply subsets of much more general RUT-based choice experiments, but these subsets are at one end of a continuum of design and modelling complexity. In particular, the CVM is on the simple and not very demanding end of this spectrum, which is why many issues that apply to extended concept tests like the CVM do not extrapolate to the more general choice experiment case.

3.   Some Fundamentals of Environmental Choice Modelling

Jeff Bennett and Vic Adamowicz

3.1 BACKGROUND

The demand for dollar estimates of non-market values, especially those associated with environmental impacts, has grown steadily over the past two decades. In the public sector, decision makers assessing capital works proposals and alternative natural resource management policies have sought quantitative assessments of environmental costs and benefits. In the private sector, an increasing number of firms find it useful to incorporate environmental value estimates in their project appraisals and environmental reporting processes.

To meet this demand, economists have developed an array of techniques that go beyond traditional market-based means of estimating benefits and costs. The techniques can be classified as either 'revealed preference' or 'stated preference' methods. The revealed preference pathway involves the use of information from markets that are specifically related to the non-marketed value under consideration to infer value estimates. Examples of such methods include the travel cost method for estimating use values of recreation areas and the hedonic pricing technique which has been used extensively to estimate pollution costs. The stated preference pathway uses people's responses to questions regarding their willingness to pay for hypothetical situations.

Interest in stated preference methods has been kindled by their capacity to yield estimates of the full array of use and non-use environmental benefits and costs.[1] However, the most commonly applied method in this type, the contingent valuation method (CVM) has been widely criticised because of a range of potential estimation biases that it may generate. Most notably, CVM studies have been criticised because of the potential for 'strategic bias' whereby respondents deliberately misrepresent their preferences in order to influence the decision making process in their favour.[2] In the face of such criticism, the CVM has been steadily evolving.[3] In addition, other stated preference methods have been developing. One such method is choice modelling (CM) or choice experiments.[4]

Because CM has only recently emerged as a non-market environmental valuation technique, there are few resources available to those seeking a greater understanding of its operation. It is the goal of this chapter to provide some insights into the fundamentals of conducting a CM application. It is intended to give those contemplating using CM some foundations upon which to base their work. It is also intended to give those who are using the results of CM applications in decision making an understanding of how those results are obtained.

It is not intended that the reader of this chapter should be immediately able to undertake a CM application. That would trivialise the many difficulties involved in applying the technique. Rather it should be seen by potential practitioners as a first base from which they can go on to a deeper consideration of the theoretical issues and practicalities that are embedded throughout a CM application.

In the next section of the chapter, a brief outline of the principles underpinning CM is provided. This includes a description of the structure of a typical CM questionnaire used to estimate non-marketed environmental values. Subsequent sections of the chapter present the stages of a CM application. In each section, a CM stage is described including an outline of the practicalities involved with potential pitfalls identified. The chapter finishes with some conclusions regarding the strengths and weaknesses of CM. In this way, some future directions for research endeavours are identified.

3.2 WHAT IS CHOICE MODELLING?

The basic idea behind any stated preference technique for estimating non-market environmental values is to quantify a person's willingness to bear a financial impost in order to achieve some potential (non-financial) environmental improvement or to avoid some potential environmental harm. Different stated preference techniques approach this task in different ways. In order to elicit passive use values, or values not associated with behaviour or participation in an activity related to the environmental good, CM and CVM techniques would ask respondents about their choices of environmental quality settings (with and without an environmental improvement for example) along with a value or cost to their household of the options. Such a case is outlined below. For cases of use values (values for changes in environmental quality that can be inferred through examination of behaviour – hiking, fishing and so on) CM can be used to expand the range of existing environmental quality levels, and to reduce confounding of the environmental effects and other effects so as to isolate the value of the specific change.

3.2.1 An Example of Passive Use Valuation

The most widely used stated preference technique, the CVM, involves survey respondents being asked if they are willing to pay some amount of money to achieve a hypothetical environmental goal, or if they would choose an alternative, in a referendum perhaps, that involves payment for an increase in environmental quality. This amounts to people being asked to choose between the 'status quo' situation (that involves them paying nothing extra to secure the environmental conditions that prevail under current policy) and a 'proposed' situation (that involves them paying an extra amount of money to achieve an environmental outcome that is superior to that which the current policy would provide). An example of a typical CVM question is provided in Figure 3.1. The method requires different sub-samples of the population being asked the same question except that the amount of the financial payment required is varied across the sub-samples (say from the $20 in the example in Figure 3.1 to $10, $50, $100 and $200). The different proportions of respondents agreeing to pay the different amounts of money are used to infer the amount overall that people are willing to pay for the environmental improvement.

Question X: Do you support the proposal to protect the environment that will ensure:

- an increase in the number of endangered species present from 5 to 10
- an increase in the area of healthy native vegetation from 1500 ha to 1800 ha
- an increase in the number of visitors from 2000 pa to 3000 pa

to be funded by a one-off levy of $20 on your income tax, or do you oppose it?

Please circle the option that most closely represents your view:

I support the proposal with a $20 levy 1
I oppose the proposal and the $20 levy 2

Figure 3.1 Typical contingent valuation method question

A CM application involves asking survey respondents a very similar type of question. However, instead of being asked only one question regarding one 'proposed' situation as occurs in a CVM questionnaire, CM respondents are often asked to make a sequence of six to eight choices involving a constant 'status quo' situation (often referred to as the *constant base*) and a number of different 'proposed' situations. Each choice question involves the 'status quo' option and several (perhaps two or three) 'proposed' alternatives. The groupings of 'status quo' and 'proposed' alternatives are known as *choice sets*.

The 'proposed' alternatives in each choice are all different in terms of the condition of the environment described to respondents and the financial burden they impose. The descriptors of the environment and the financial impost involved are known as the *attributes* of the alternatives. They may be characteristics such as 'the number of endangered species present', 'the area of healthy vegetation remaining' or 'the number of visitors per annum'.

The variations across the 'proposed' alternatives in the choice sets are achieved by assigning different *levels* to the attributes. Hence, the attribute 'number of endangered species' could be allowed to vary across the 'levels' of 5, 10 and 15. The financial burden attribute could vary between the levels $10, $20 and $50. Different levels are assigned to attributes to create the proposed alternatives for inclusion in the choice sets according to a systematic process known as *experimental design*.

A sample choice set is displayed in Figure 3.2. In a CM questionnaire, six to eight of these choice sets would be presented to respondents as separate questions.

By observing and modelling how people change their preferred option in response to the changes in the levels of the attributes, it is possible to determine how they trade-off between the attributes. In other words, it is possible to infer people's willingness to give up some amount of an attribute in order to achieve more of another.[5]

Hence, from a CM exercise it would be possible to estimate (in the context of the example in Figure 3.2) the amount of visitor access people would be willing to forgo in order to have more endangered species present at the site.

Given that one of the attributes involved is a dollar cost, it is possible to estimate how much people are willing to pay to achieve more of an environmental attribute. This is called a *part worth* or *implicit price* estimate and can be estimated for each of the non-monetary attributes used in the choice sets.

Furthermore, it is possible to use CM results to infer the amounts people are willing to pay to move from the 'status quo' bundle of attribute levels to specifically defined bundles of attribute levels that correspond with policy outcomes that are of interest. In other words, the willingness to pay to change from the status quo to a specific alternative can be derived. These estimates of *compensating surpluses* are consistent with the principles of welfare economics and are therefore suited for inclusion as value estimates in benefit cost analyses of policy alternatives.

Question Y: Consider carefully each of the following three options. Suppose these options were the only ones available, which one would you choose?

Alternative Attribute	'Status Quo' alternative	Proposed alternative 1	Proposed alternative 2
Number of endangered species	5	15	15
Hectares of healthy native vegetation	1500	1800	2100
Visitor days per annum	2000	3000	2000
Cost to you ($)	0	20	10

Please circle your preferred option.

I would choose the status quo at no cost to me................ 1

I would choose alternative 1 at a $20 cost to me............. 2

I would choose alternative 2 at a $10 cost to me............. 3

Figure 3.2 Choice modelling choice set

Monetary estimates of the values ascribed to particular resource use alternatives (described by specific bundles of attribute levels) may not be considered applicable in some circumstances. Choice modelling results can provide another type of information to policy makers. The relative support that various alternatives could be expected to receive from the public can be estimated from CM data. Where there are a number of competing alternatives (status quo included) between which policy makers must choose, the percentage of the public that would choose each can be estimated.[6]

3.2.2 Choice Modelling, Behaviour and Valuation

Most practitioners in the field outline the advantages of CM in *behavioural analysis* thus:

1.   the control of the stimuli is in the experimenter's hand, as opposed to

the low level of control generally afforded by observing the real market place;

2.   the control of the design matrix yields greater statistical efficiency and eliminates collinearity (unless explicitly built into the design);
3.   the development of more robust models because wider attribute ranges can be applied than are found in real markets; and
4.   the introduction and/or removal of products and services is straightforwardly accomplished, as is the introduction of new attributes. (Adamowicz *et al.* 1988a, p. 7)

CM is used to provide behavioural predictions (models) or is used to augment revealed preference models (Adamowicz *et al.* 1994). Once the behavioural model is developed, the trade-offs implied, for example between the cost of travel and the quality of a recreation site, can be examined.

In the example presented in Figure 3.3, individuals are asked to choose between three alternatives two recreational hunting sites and an option of staying at home. Their choice provides information on the trade-offs they are willing to make between attributes of the alternatives. By varying the attributes of the alternatives presented to the respondents, information is gathered on the trade-offs between all of the attributes.

This information could also be collected in a type of contingent valuation task. Presented in Figure 3.4 is a contingent valuation or contingent behaviour question eliciting information on whether the hunters would be willing to travel additional distances (incur increased costs) for a hunting site quality improvement. The question focuses on two attributes (travel distance and moose populations) rather than all of the attributes that are presented in the choice task.

In developing choice models of behavioural activities, it is very important to attempt to construct the choice task with as much realism as possible. The questions should try to *mimic* the decision that the respondent normally makes in the activity in question. Thus, in the examples presented above the questions focused on which site (alternative) the individual would choose. In other cases the decision facing the respondent may be the quantity of an item that they would choose (perhaps the number of units of a particular product that they would purchase). The most important aspect of choice modelling efforts in the analysis of behaviour is that the task reflects the decision process of the respondent and that the attributes be constructed in a fashion that is consistent with the actual behavioural process being examined.

A further application of choice modelling is to combine CM data with revealed preference or actual choice data. This provides the flexibility of CM data (free from correlations and a broader range than the current market) as well as the anchoring of actual choices from actual markets. This topic will be discussed in more detail later in this chapter.

Assuming that the following areas were the ONLY areas available, which one would you choose on your next hunting trip, if either?

Features of hunting area	Site A	Site B	Neither Site A nor Site B
Distance from home to hunting area	50 kilometres	50 kilometres	I will NOT go moose hunting
Quality of road from home to hunting area	Mostly gravel or dirt, some paved	Mostly paved, some gravel or dirt	
Access within hunting area	Newer trails, cutlines or seismic lines, passable with a 2WD vehicle	Newer trails, cutlines or seismic lines passable with a 4WD truck	
Encounters with other hunters	No hunters, other than those in my hunting party, are encountered	Other hunters, on ATVs, are encountered	
Forestry activity	Some evidence of recent logging found in the area	No evidence of logging	
Moose population	Evidence of less than 1 moose per day	Evidence of less than 1 moose per day	
CHECK ONE AND ONLY ONE BOX	☐	☐	☐

Please complete all 16 of the scenarios that follow. Missing any of these questions will not allow us to properly analyse your choices!

Source: Boxall *et al.* (1996)

Figure 3.3 Example of one of sixteen choice sets in choice experiment task

---

The instrument used to gather contingent valuation estimates of the environmental quality change.

Currently, the average moose hunter hunting in Wildlife Management Unit 344 sees or finds evidence of (sounds, tracks, browse, droppings) **One moose every 2 to 3 hunting days**. The proposed habitat improvement program and access limitation would increase moose populations, and the average hunter could expect to see or find evidence of 1–2 moose per hunting day.

Would you be willing to travel an extra X kilometres to hunt in this WMU given the increase in the moose population? Please check YES or NO below.

☐ YES   ☐ NO

If you answered NO to the question above is it because (please check one or more of the statements below):

☐ The proposed changes are not good enough to justify the extra distance
☐ There are many other sites in which I could hunt instead
☐ This distance is too far to travel

Source: Boxall *et al.* (1996)

Figure 3.4 Value of moose hunting improvements

3.3 IMPLEMENTATION OF CHOICE MODELLING

Choice modelling provides opportunity to assess preferences and estimate benefits and costs of environmental quality changes. However, to achieve these results requires the careful implementation of a number of stages that combine to form a CM application.

Applications of CMs generally follow the seven steps outlined below (see Adamowicz *et al.* 1998a):

1. *Characterisation of the decision problem* This involves the identification of the problem at hand (change in environmental quality affecting recreation behaviour, change in provision of public goods that requires a social choice mechanism to be specified for this issue, and so on).

2. *Attribute and level selection* The number of attributes and value of the levels for each attribute is defined in this stage, as appropriate for the decision problem at hand.
3. *Questionnaire development* The questionnaire can vary from chapter and pencil tasks to computer aided surveys. As in any survey-based research, pre-testing of the questionnaire is a necessary component of the research programme.
4. *Experimental design development* Once attributes and levels have been determined, experimental design procedures are used to construct the choice tasks, alternatives or profiles that will be presented to the respondents.
5. *Sample sizing and data collection* The usual considerations of desired accuracy levels versus data collection costs must guide definition of sample sizes.
6. *Model estimation* The most common approach has been the use of multinomial logit (MNL), and the most common estimation method has been maximum likelihood, although the most appropriate method will depend on the issues being examined.
7. *Policy analysis* Most CM applications are targeted to generating welfare measures, or predictions of behaviour, or both. Thus, the models are used to simulate outcomes that can be used in policy analysis or as components of decision support tools.

In the following sections of this chapter, these stages are outlined.

3.4 ESTABLISHING THE ISSUE: CHARACTERISING THE DECISION PROBLEM

For CM results to be useful as inputs into a benefit-cost analysis, the framework of the CM application must be consistent with the principles of benefit-cost analysis. It is of particular importance therefore that the issue to be examined using CM is established in accordance with the concept of change at the margin.

Because policy making regarding the environment is inevitably concerned with assessing the relative merits of making a change (or of avoiding a change), the tools of analysis which are aimed at assisting decision makers are primarily concerned with marginal analysis. This is certainly true of benefit-cost analysis whereby the extent of the net benefit resulting from a change in resource allocation is estimated. Hence, estimates of values to be used in benefit-cost analyses must also be 'at the margin'. Therefore, the values of interest are the additional benefits and costs resulting from the implementation of alternative policy options relative to some pre-defined status quo alternative.

If CM results are to be consistent with this marginal value framework, the issue under consideration must be defined in terms of change from a 'status quo' reference point or a base situation. In passive use value applications, the constant base alternative used in each choice set must reflect this status quo. Respondents to a CM questionnaire are therefore always asked to compare alternatives against the status quo. In behavioural models, the status quo may be to stay with the existing choices, or to choose 'none' of the good, where the other alternatives are choices of some quantity or alternative to the current choice. The choice set questions are thus focused on an assessment of proposed change. Inherent in this process is the definition of the environmental impacts under consideration. That is, what is the marginal benefit or marginal cost that is being estimated. A 'boundary' must be established around the value to be considered. The CM analyst must be able to define the value – be it a use value, a non-use value or the total economic value[7] – in order to approach the task of describing the status quo and the proposed alternatives.

In defining the alternatives, the value under consideration must be defined. As an example, consider a situation where policy makers are contemplating the introduction of a regulation to restrict the use of a pesticide. The CM analyst must clarify whether, for instance, it is the non-use values associated with environmental damage caused by pesticides that are to be estimated or if use values are also to be estimated. The status quo – used as the constant base in the choice sets – would involve a listing of attribute levels describing the outcome of a continuation of the current pesticide use regime. Note that this may be defined at some point in the future when the effects of the pesticide use had reached their most environmentally damaging extent. The alternatives in each choice set would then involve levels of the descriptor attributes – at the same point of time in the future – which demonstrated the environmental improvements and financial cost penalties associated with changes from the status quo. Of course, the scenarios presented and the choice context must be understandable and the respondents must have a degree of confidence that the alternatives are reflected of actual possibilities.

In modelling choice behaviour the decision problem must be understood by the researcher and the choice questions constructed with this process in mind. For example, in order to evaluate the recreational benefits of improved water quality, the recreational choice decision, and the linkage between recreation and water quality, must be examined. Recreationists may choose sites that have better water quality. However, this is only one aspect of site choice. Other attributes (distance to the site, facilities at the site and so on) will affect the site that individuals choose. The choice task must be constructed based on the main elements that influence choice. Water quality may affect site choice as well as the frequency of recreational visits. In this case, a choice modelling task may be required to examine how the frequency of visits changes in response to change in various attributes.

Once the basic valuation issue has been defined consistent with the principles of benefit-cost analysis, any other features of the resource allocation choice should be considered. This must be done at an early stage in the application process so that the structure of the research process can be designed.

It must be determined if there are any methodological sensitivities that require specific investigation. If there are, it may be necessary to set up parallel CM surveys which differ only in terms of the factor causing the hypothesised sensitivity. For instance, the inclusion/exclusion of an attribute may be hypothesised to have an impact on the value estimates obtained from a CM application. The two parallel surveys would thus differ only in that one survey's choice sets would include the attribute whilst the other would not.

There may also be concerns regarding the geographic extent of the values under consideration. That is, the question of whether the effects on people living proximate to the environmental impacts of concern are greater than those living further away. To test this hypothesis, two CM applications may be required – one carried out using a survey of local residents and the other using a sample of people living further from the site – but with both surveys using exactly the same questionnaire. An alternative to this approach would be for a single questionnaire to be distributed across a wide geographic area, given that the questionnaire included a question regarding the respondents' place of residence. This would afford an analysis of how value estimates are influenced by respondents' distance from the site of the environmental effects.

In applications to behavioural modelling there may be specific sub-samples of the population of interest that require different treatment. Local residents and their preferences for a recreation site may base choices/behaviour on very different attributes than individuals who travel long distances for long term holidays at that same site.

With the research issues defined, the structure of questionnaire versions, the 'splitting' of the overall sample of respondents into sub-samples and the extent of sampling required can in turn be defined. Next, attention can be turned to issues involved in questionnaire design. The first of these issues is the definition of attributes to be used to define the environmental impacts.

3.5 DEFINING THE ATTRIBUTES AND LEVELS

Once the value to be estimated has been determined, the attributes to be used to describe the outcomes yielding that value can be defined. The attributes are used to describe the outcome of a continuation of the status quo and what would happen if an alternative were to be introduced. Two perspectives of these outcomes need to be taken into account when determining which attributes should be used.

First, it is important for the CM analyst to be cognisant of the requirements of policy makers. The attributes used to describe the alternatives in each choice set should be relevant to the policy making process. They should therefore be consistent with the policy instruments that are being used to form the outcomes depicted in the alternatives.

Second, the attributes used must have meaning to the people who will answer the questionnaire. If the attributes used are irrelevant to respondents, the likelihood of valid responses being received is reduced and response rates could be diminished.

To take into account these perspectives, the attributes must first be defined. Discussions with policy makers can be used to determine their perspectives. A more formal approach could involve the surveying of policy makers – and their advisers – using a structured questionnaire. In such a questionnaire, respondents could be asked to nominate the attributes that are believed to be most relevant to the decision making process. A Delphi process[8] could be used to allow respondents to refine their selection of attributes, given knowledge regarding other respondents' views.

The perspective of those who will be faced with answering the final CM questionnaire can be determined through a number of vehicles. A simple telephone survey of prospective respondents can be used to ask people what matters to them in the process of selecting between alternatives (for example, 'What do you need to know before making a choice?' or 'What are some good things and some bad things about possible alternatives?'). Further refinement of the list of attributes so obtained could take place in focus groups.[9] These groups of around eight people – selected from the population of potential CM questionnaire respondents – involve the structured discussion of points relevant to the design of the CM questionnaire. One of the points of discussion should be the determination of attributes. It is preferable for the policy-relevant attributes to have already been established at this stage so that their relevance to potential respondents can be determined. What is required is a reconciliation of the two perspectives, if they do not already coincide. This may involve some give and take from both perspectives.

A specific problem that is common in the definition of attributes is the existence of some attributes that are 'causally prior' to other attributes. For instance, the amount of pollution in a waterway may be regarded as a relevant attribute, as may the number of fish present in that waterway. However, before more fish can live in the waterway, the level of pollution would need to be reduced. The issue is whether the pollution is an attribute in itself, or whether it is merely a stepping stone to achieving what is valued by people, and that is the number of fish. Such issues need to be determined in focus group discussions but, by and large, the omission of causally prior attributes is the preferred strategy.

Care must be taken not to exclude important attributes. For instance, if individuals are presented with a series of improvements to environmental quality, without an indication of how these are being paid for, they will make assumptions about the cost considerations. The researcher will have no knowledge of what the respondents have assumed about the missing cost information, and thus the responses will provide biased information about preferences. Respondents will make assumptions about attributes and their levels and the research must be as careful as possible in making sure that the attributes are described accurately and consistently.

With the attributes defined, the range over which they vary must be set. This involves establishing the levels that the attributes will take in the alternatives presented to respondents in the choice sets.

First, the way in which the levels are to be presented needs to be determined. Levels can be expressed either qualitatively or quantitatively. For instance, a water quality attribute may be expressed quantitatively in terms of the level of dissolved oxygen. Alternatively, the water's suitability for different purposes may be used to establish qualitative levels such as 'suitable for boating', 'suitable for fishing' and 'suitable for drinking'. The quantitative expression of levels has distinct advantages in terms of the modelling and valuation potential afforded and should be a goal in most circumstances.

Quantitative levels may be presented in absolute terms. For instance, the number of endangered species attribute may take on the level 10, thus informing the respondent that the alternative will result in ten endangered species being protected. Alternatively, the levels may be presented as changes from what is currently present. This form of presentation may be particularly suited to cases where all alternatives, including the 'status quo', involve levels which are different from the current situation. Hence, if there are currently ten endangered species present and the status quo policy (that is, no change in policy) would mean that only four species would remain in ten years time, the status quo level for the endangered species attribute could be −6, with other alternatives providing smaller or zero declines. Percentage changes can also be used where it is important to demonstrate some relativities. The most appropriate presentation will need to be established through focus group testing.

The attributes must be allowed to vary across levels that are realistic. The range must however be sufficiently large to reflect the possible future values the attributes could take under all the policy options being considered. The selection of the range of levels to be taken by the financial attribute is of particular importance. It is necessary, most appropriately in focus groups, to establish the upper bound for the financial attribute's level. This is an issue that also arises in contingent valuation cases – the design of the bid range. The lower bound for the financial attribute is set at zero largely because of the practicalities of establishing an attribute that can take on negative as well as positive values (that is, that can accommodate both willingness to pay and willingness to accept compensation).

In choice tasks corresponding to behavioural decisions, it is usually less difficult to develop the range for the financial variables since they have actual market analogues, and ranges around the current market prices (or travel costs in recreation cases) can be developed. In these cases, however, many individuals have experience with the attributes being presented, and may perceive them differently from how they are being presented by the researcher. Care must be taken when presenting the levels to make them relate to the respondent's perception of the attribute. In the recreational site choice example presented in Figures 3.3 and 3.4, the levels of moose populations are presented in terms of 'evidence of moose' which is described carefully in a glossary. The attribute and levels are not presented in terms of moose actually seen as this is not the way that abundance of moose populations are perceived by the individuals.

With the range set for the levels of each attribute, the increments between each level must be set. This implicitly determines the number of levels each attribute can take. For example, if it is determined that the number of endangered species could vary between 10 and 30 depending on the policy adopted, a choice of interval of 10 endangered species would imply a three level attribute (10, 20 and 30).

Introducing risk into the specification of levels has received little attention; however, it is possible to define levels in terms of expected values and some associated variance or as a range of values. Alternatively, some overarching measure of risk could be introduced as a separate attribute.

3.6 QUESTIONNAIRE DEVELOPMENT

With attributes and levels determined, the issue and research design must be embedded into the structure of a questionnaire or sequence of questionnaire versions.

The questionnaire structure will in part be determined by the method that will be used to survey the population identified as being affected by the environmental impact under investigation. For instance, visual aids cannot be used in a telephone survey. Not withstanding such differences, a CM questionnaire follows a fairly standard pattern. This pattern is explained under the following sub-headings.

3.6.1 An Introduction

Respondents must first be introduced to the issue under investigation and the people who are undertaking the investigation. Hence, in the first part of a questionnaire, be it in the form of an introductory letter or as a preface, the purpose of the exercise must be explained. In particular, the importance of the information being gathered needs to be stressed so as to encourage participation. The credentials of the study team must also be displayed to induce respondent confidence and to allay any fears of unscrupulous behaviour. Respondents also have a right to know how they were selected to participate, given an opportunity to raise queries, be assured of the confidentiality of their responses and told of the time commitment they are being asked to make in answering the questionnaire. Some guidance as to how the questionnaire should be completed and returned may also be desirable.

3.6.2 Framing

Respondents to any stated preference questionnaire must be made aware that the environmental good under consideration is embedded in an array of substitute and complementary goods. It is important that the questionnaire does not lead to respondents giving untoward weight to the issue in question because they have put the context or *frame* of the issue to the backs of their minds. The questionnaire must strive to establish the frame in respondents' minds which is appropriate to the circumstances of the policy decision being made.

For instance, estimating the values of a single river's environmental attributes would not yield appropriate results if the policy being informed by those estimates involved the restoration of numerous rivers.[10] The overestimation of the 'stand-alone' estimates would be more exaggerated, if as well as considering river environments, policy makers were also contemplating forestry policy. The appropriate frame must make respondents aware of these competing demands for public funds but it must also remind them of their own budget constraint and other ways in which they may wish to use their money.

Hence, the decision as to just what makes an 'appropriate' frame will need to take account of the policy environment of the decision to be made and the frame of reference that exists in respondents' minds prior to being informed of the specific issue at hand. The latter can be identified during focus group sessions through questioning participants regarding their priorities for spending their personal funds and how taxation revenue ought to be allocated amongst competing public goods.

On the basis of these findings, the CM questioning can begin by asking respondents to rank competing spending claims, with one of those claims relating to the issue at hand. This places the specific in the context of the wider picture and so establishes a frame of reference for the respondents. Such a question also provides a good 'warm-up' exercise for respondents, so that they get into the process of answering the questionnaire. Notice that a ranking exercise is recommended as it requires respondents to make comparisons between competing interests. This begins to generate the concept of the trade-off that features so strongly in the choice set questions forming the heart of the questionnaire.

3.6.3 Statement of the Issue

With the frame established, the issue under consideration can be introduced. This is achieved through a statement of the dilemma that is being addressed. This may be the decision to correct an environmental decline or to create an environmental improvement. Some details of the relevant environment will usually be appropriate: What are the current conditions and what will happen if the status quo prevails? The description can be based around the attributes to be used in the choice sets. A separate information pamphlet complete with some photographic evidence can be a useful means of presenting this information.

3.6.4 Statement of a Potential Solution

After some questions have been asked regarding respondents' experience of the environment at issue and their general sentiment regarding the severity of the problem at hand, a potential solution to the problem can be provided in the questionnaire. Respondents must find the solution offered believable despite its inherently hypothetical nature.

Visual aids may again prove useful in demonstrating differences in attributes between the status quo and the alternatives. Careful focus grouping of such materials is important to ensure that the message carried is appropriate to the context of the questioning.

An important component of the proposed solution must be a *payment vehicle*. The solution must be available only if funds can be generated to pay for it and those funds must come from respondents indicating a willingness to pay. Hence a key component of the plausibility of the proposed solution must be a plausible payment vehicle. Focus group testing of alternatives is a key part of ensuring plausibility. Focus group participants can be asked what they would deem to be an appropriate payment vehicle or to suggest the vehicle they believe would be most likely used to generate the revenue required.

To help ensure that respondents answer the choice sets truthfully (that is, that they don't engage in strategic behaviour) it must be stressed that the payment made to effect the solution would be compulsory. The potential financial effect of the solution on the individual must be made very clear.

Following the explanation of the potential solution, some questions regarding the plausibility of the setting, the solution and the payment vehicle especially can be asked.

There must be some expectation that the information provided by the respondents will be used, in some fashion, in making decisions. If the respondents view the process as entirely hypothetical then their responses will not be meaningful in any economic sense (Carson *et al.* 2000). Furthermore, the framing of the task and how it affects individuals' perceptions of their payment obligations, and the impact of their choices on the potential for supplying the public good (providing improved environmental quality) must be examined. If, for example, individuals feel that they would never be charged the fee or tax increase listed in the choice scenario, then they may behave strategically when responding to the choice questions (ibid.).

In behavioural choice modelling, there is less concern regarding payment vehicles and the statements of potential solutions. The choice task is often set out as a 'game' that asks respondents to describe how they would choose if faced with this 'experimental' choice set. Since the attributes are usually items that the respondent would normally consider when making choices of this type (if the researchers have done their homework regarding the construction of the attributes and levels) questions about the believability of the payment vehicle are reduced. Furthermore, the alternatives are not presented as 'solutions' they are simply alternatives that may or may not be representations of existing alternatives. The point of the behavioural choice task is not to assess what people are willing to pay for alternatives, but how they make trade-off decisions when faced with actual choices – albeit described by experimentally designed attribute levels.

3.6.5 Choosing Not to Choose

A very important element in behavioural choice tasks is providing the option for respondents to not choose any of the available alternatives. As Adamowicz *et al.* (1998a) point out 'one should design stated choice experiments to allow one to observe and model non-choice because it's such an obvious element of real market behaviour'. In other words, individuals making actual choices have the option not to choose any of the alternatives offered (not go on a recreation trip for example) or they may choose an alternative that is not presented. It is important for the creator of the choice task to identify the 'other' alternatives and describe them as clearly as possible. In the hunting choice task presented above, individuals were offered the option of 'not going hunting'. This is a very important option because it indicates what the quality attributes must be to move a person into not participating in the activity. Thus, one could model the choice as well as the participation decision. If environmental quality declined enough, or if prices rose enough, we would expect people to stop participating in the activity. Choice sets with an 'other' choice structure can identify such participation rates.

3.6.6 Introducing the Choice Sets

Respondents will need some help to comprehend the choice set questions that follow. Hence a section needs to be devoted to an explanation of the task they will be asked to perform and some ground rules for their answers. Usually this will involve stating that there are many variants to the solution just outlined and that people's opinions as to which variant is best for them is a useful input to policy determination. In other words, respondents are being asked to have a say in what future policy should look like. An example of what a choice set looks like can be provided and a sample answer given.

A final reminder to respondents to keep in mind the frame of the exercise – all the other goods that they may wish to buy and the constraint their income imposes – should immediately precede the choice sets.

3.6.7 The Choice Sets

The presentation of choice sets is a matter both of clarity for respondents and technicality for the analyst. Presentational clarity is vital for respondents to be able to understand the nature of the question that is embedded in the choice sets. Again, focus group testing is vital here as there is no predetermined 'appropriate' format.

Some technicalities do interpose. First, the alternatives that are presented to respondents can be either labelled or unlabelled. A 'labelled' or 'alternative specific' choice set includes descriptors of each alternative that go beyond the attributes. The labels may relate, say, to the policy that gives rise to the alternative. For instance, the status quo may be labelled 'current policy' whilst the alternatives may be labelled '10 per cent more water' and

'20 per cent more water' to indicate the broad policies that underpin those alternatives. Where no labels are used – apart, say, from the headings Options 1, 2 and 3 – the choice sets are said to be 'generic'. In behavioural models the alternatives may be 'real' alternatives (labelled as such) or they may be generic.

The choice between the labelled and generic choice set formats is important. Where the means of achieving environmental change is considered important (that is, where the policy mechanism is a factor in determining choice) the labelled format is more appropriate. It is also better suited to situations where differing policy options give rise to widely differing levels of the attributes. With the labelled format, different level ranges can be specified for the attributes in the different alternatives. However, labels can prompt respondents to select their preferred alternative on the basis of the label alone and the impact of the varying levels of the attributes on respondent choice could be trivialised. Whilst this may be a true reflection of people's choices in some cases, in others it may simply be a reflection of the difficulties respondents are having in dealing with the choices presented in the format of a questionnaire. A case-by-case assessment of these matters during focus group testing is required to determine which format is more appropriate.

Further technicalities are involved in determining the number of alternatives to present to each respondent in each choice set and the number of choice sets to present in each questionnaire. This issue revolves around a trade-off between the cognitive ability of respondents, that is; their ability to comprehend the volume of information presented in a single choice set, their tenacity/patience in answering the multiple choice sets, and the number of variations in the attribute levels that is required to support an empirical model of the impact of attributes on choices made. Evidence is emerging which suggests that the number of alternatives affects the variance of choices and that respondents may even change their decision strategies depending on the complexity of the choice set (Swait and Adamowicz 2001a and 2001b).

The choice sets presented to respondents carry a wealth of information that must be assimilated by respondents and acted upon. If the amount of information exceeds a respondent's ability to deal with it, the questionnaire as a whole may be rejected or the answers given may not reflect true preferences either because random answers are given or decision making short cuts or 'heuristics' are used.

On the other hand, sufficient variations to the alternatives presented to respondents must be provided in order to establish statistically the impact of attribute levels on choices made.

To assess this trade-off, the capacity of respondents to answer bigger choice sets and longer strings of choice set questions must be established. Focus groups again provide a vehicle for this process. The selection of appropriate experimental designs to ensure an appropriate variation in attribute levels is presented to respondents is also critical. This issue is discussed in the next section.

3.6.8 Follow-up Questions

Immediately after the choice set questions comes a series of questions designed to explore the motivations behind respondents' choices. In particular, these 'follow-up' questions should be targeted at picking up any response aberrations such as:

- payment vehicle protests (a respondent always chooses the status quo option or 'other' option because of an objection to the way in which their cost is to be imposed);
- lexicographic preferences (respondents always choose the alternative with the highest level of one attribute, or the lowest cost, or appear always to choose on the basis of a single characteristics of the task); and
- perfect embedding (respondents agree to pay in order to experience the 'warm glow' of supporting a good cause rather than as a reflection of their value for the environmental benefits available).

In addition, follow-up questions can check to see if there were any specific problems faced by respondents in answering the choice set questions. Specifically these problems may relate to:

- ability to understand the questions;
- the amount of information provided;
- the presence of bias in the questionnaire;
- perceived plausibility of the setting; and
- confusion created.

3.6.9 Socio-economic and Attitudinal Data Collection

The final section of the questionnaire must be devoted to questions seeking socio-economic data (age, sex, educational status, occupation, income and so on) and information regarding attitudes (especially general sentiments regarding the environment). Beyond the general data of interest, specific cases may call for the collection of specific respondent information. For instance, if distance of the respondent's place of residence from the site at issue is hypothesised as a factor that impacts on values then distance data would need to be collected.

These data are required as inputs into the modelling phase of the application, for verifying data and for checking how well the sample represents the population of interest.

A final expression of thanks to the respondent and an opportunity to provide any additional comments on the questionnaire and survey process is appropriate.

3.7 EXPERIMENTAL DESIGN

Choice modelling relies on the estimation of a relationship between the probability of a choice being made and the relative levels of the attributes in the alternative chosen. The model is driven by differing attribute levels in the attributes available to respondents giving rise to differing probabilities of alternatives being chosen. With multiple attributes and with each attribute varying across multiple levels, it is apparent that for a model to be able to separate out the effects on choice of individual attributes, a lot of choices between alternatives which incorporate a lot of different combinations of attribute levels will need to be observed. In fact to identify completely the relationship, all the possible combinations of attribute levels should be presented to respondents.

The array of all possible combinations is called the 'full factorial'. For example, if there were two attributes, each allowed to vary over three levels, a total of nine possible combinations would make up the full factorial. If the three levels for attribute 1 were A, B and C and the attribute 2 levels were X, Y and Z, the full factorial would be: AX, AY, AZ, BX, BY, BZ, CX, CY, and CZ. Hence the first alternative put to respondents for comparison against a status quo, constant base option would be described by attribute 1 at level A and attribute 2 at level X. Other alternatives making up the choice set would then be selected in a systematic fashion from the pool created from the full factorial. The way the alternatives' levels are set and structured into the choice sets is known as the 'experimental design'.

As the number of attributes and number of levels increase, the size of the full factorial grows rapidly to the extent that the total number of choice sets required to present them all to respondents soon exceeds the ability of respondents to cope. Two strategies are used to overcome this problem: the use of a 'fractional factorial' and the 'blocking' of the experimental design.

A 'fractional factorial' is a selection of the available attribute level combinations that go to make up the full factorial. The process of selecting a fractional factorial requires the maintenance of the orthogonality property of the full factorial (that is there is no correlation between the attributes). However, the smaller the part of the full factorial that makes up the fractional factorial, the less able is the experimental design to drive a model that can identify all the possible interactions which may occur between the attributes.

So whilst a smaller fractional factorial may be preferred because it gives fewer choice sets for respondents to evaluate, it may not be capable of driving a model that accurately represents the relationships existing between choice probabilities and attribute levels. Alternative fractional factorial designs are available in design catalogues such as Hahn and Shapiro (1966) and an increasing number of computer packages that are used for statistical analysis.

The second strategy used to cope with the large number of choice sets created even with the use of a fractional factorial is to segment the fractional factorial into blocks. Each respondent, therefore, is only exposed to the alternatives that comprise one block of the fractional factorial. If the fractional factorial is divided into three blocks, it takes three respondents to provide choices that cover all the alternatives that are created under the fractional factorial. The blocking strategy has obvious implications for the size of the sample of respondents needed to generate enough data to estimate a model, but it also requires an assumption of identical preferences across respondents.

The creation of the alternatives to be used in the choice sets is only the first phase of the creation of an experimental design. The second phase involves the combining of alternatives together to form the complete choice set. Commonly, choice sets comprise a constant base or status quo option that stays the same across all choice sets and two or more alternatives that involve varying attribute levels. The experimental design must be used to provide the combinations of alternatives.

Two approaches are available. The first, known as the sequential approach, involves taking the alternatives created in the fractional factorial and assigning them to choice sets using a particular strategy. For instance, a separate experimental design can be used as the assignment instrument.

The second approach, the simultaneous method, uses an expanded version of a fractional factorial that determines the levels of the attributes for all the alternatives in the choice sets. L^{MN} designs (where L is the number of levels, M is the number of alternatives in each choice set and N is the number of attributes) perform this function.

Once the choice sets have been created using the experimental design, it is important to review each choice set for the presence of implausible or dominated alternatives. Implausible alternatives are those in which the experimental design has dictated that the levels of the attributes move in directions that would be counter-intuitive to most respondents. Dominated alternatives are those that are combined with other alternatives that are universally superior in their experimental design driven attribute levels. Dropping choice sets with implausible or dominated alternatives is one strategy to remove the problem but this can cause departures from the orthogonal character of the fractional factorial used. There is a trade-off associated with dropping implausible or dominated alternatives because, without an orthogonal design, the attributes may be confounded and the resulting parameter estimates will not isolate the effects of each attribute.

The problem of implausibility can be avoided by adequately explaining why alternatives can appear counter-intuitive at the beginning of the choice set questions. Furthermore, the issue of what is a dominated alternative is usually far from clear cut. What appears to be dominated to one person can be a logical choice for another, especially when the attributes are qualitative in nature. Some researchers leave 'dominated' alternatives in choice sets to confirm that respondents are carefully assessing the tasks.

3.8 SURVEYING THE RESPONDENTS: SAMPLE SIZE AND DATA COLLECTION

The sampling frame to be used to generate potential respondents will be dependent on the nature of the particular application. The sample drawn will need to be split into a number of sub-samples. First, sub-samples will need to be drawn to reflect the number of blocks used in the experimental design process. Hence if the blocking strategy used has created four lots of choice sets then there will be four versions of the same questionnaire and four sub-samples will be needed to answer each of these versions. The size of the sub-samples drawn will depend on the size of the population and the statistical power that is required of the model derived. However, the minimum size of the sub-sample should be in the order of 50 respondents depending on the statistical power that is required for the estimation process. (See Louviere *et al.* 2000 for details on sampling.)

If the research design calls for the testing of a specific hypothesis which involves changing some element of the questionnaire, then the block sub-samples will need to be replicated for the two versions of the questionnaire. Hence, for a four block experimental design and one hypothesis test, a set of eight sub-samples will need to be drawn.

The delivery of the questionnaires to respondents can be via:

- mail-out/mail-back;
- personal drop-off with a later personal pick-up;
- telephone;
- telephone with mail-out/mail-back;
- email and internet delivery;
- personal interview.

In addition, surveys can be administered in 'central facilities' where individuals are asked to gather in a central place (town hall, meeting room and so on) and the surveys are explained and administered as a group.

Each delivery mode involves both benefits and costs. For instance, whilst telephone surveys are relatively low cost, they do not allow the provision of visual material to respondents and it is difficult for the interviewer to control the 'environment' of the interview from a remote location. Personal interviews are relatively expensive but do generate higher response rates. They are however subject to possible 'interviewer bias'. Postal delivery is relatively low cost but can be prone to low response rates and consequential sampling bias. Using the post does however allow respondents the time to contemplate their answers more completely and removes the prospect of interviewer bias. The drop-off/pick-up option is almost a hybrid of the mail-out and personal interview approaches. It is a compromise on cost, interviewer bias, giving respondent adequate time for consideration and response rates. The decision regarding the most appropriate form of delivery will depend on the case at hand and budget availability.[11]

3.9 PREPARING AND ANALYSING THE DATA: MODEL ESTIMATION

With the survey work complete, the data must be coded. It is important to recognise that the data generated from the survey are only the tip of the iceberg of the data used to determine the models of choice. For each choice set, the respondents indicate their preferred alternative. That is, each provides one piece of data. For the modelling work, that data element must be combined with information about the levels of the attributes of the alternative chosen and the levels of the attributes not chosen and the socio-economic/attitudinal data relating to the person who made the choice. Hence for a choice set that involves three alternatives, including the constant base, three lines of data emerge. Each data line depicts one of the alternatives: its attribute levels,[12] the characteristics of the respondent, and whether or not (0 or 1) the alternative was chosen.

As well as the levels of the attributes, modelling constants must be included in the rows of data. These constants are known as the 'alternative specific constants' (ASCs). If there are three alternatives in a choice set, two of the alternatives must be associated with an ASC. Hence, new 'attributes' must be created for two of the three alternatives, which take on the value of 1 in the lines of data relating to their alternative and zero otherwise. It is the role of the ASCs to take up any variation in choices that cannot be explained by either the attributes or the socio-economic variables.

The choice models of the data are generated by statistical routines in software packages such as LIMDEP. The most straightforward of the model estimation procedures is known as multi-nomial logit (MNL).[13] Under the MNL procedure, the probability of choosing an alternative is modelled as a function of the attributes and the socio-economic characteristics of the respondents. That is, the probability of a respondent choosing an alternative increases as the levels of desirable attributes in that alternative rise and the levels of undesirable attributes falls – relative to the levels of the attributes in the other alternatives that are available. The probability is therefore an indication of the relative *utility* (defined by economists as well-being or satisfaction) provided by the alternatives, given that an individual will choose the alternative that provides the greatest utility.[14]

What the modelling of respondents' choices is able to provide is a sequence of equations each of which describes the probability that alternatives will be chosen. These equations can thus be interpreted as the conditional indirect utility (V) derived from the alternatives.

For a three alternative choice set with three quantitatively[15] described attributes (A_1, A_2 and A_3) the estimated (linear in parameters without any attribute interactions) model (without socio-economic factors) would be:

Status quo: $V_1 = \beta_1 A_1 + \beta_2 A_2 + \beta_3 A_3$
Alternative 2: $V_2 = ASC_2 + \beta_1 A_1 + \beta_2 A_2 + \beta_3 A_3$
Alternative 3: $V_3 = ASC_3 + \beta_1 A_1 + \beta_2 A_2 + \beta_3 A_3$

The β values are the coefficients associated with each of the attributes.[16]

Note that the ASC used for Alternatives 2 and 3 could be equivalent ($ASC_2 = ASC_3$) if the model formulated is generic. If the choice sets used are labelled, then an alternative specific form of the model is required.

To introduce respondent heterogeneity (that is, differences between the individual respondents) into the model, socio-economic variables can be used as independent variables in each of the equations estimated. This can be an important part of the model estimation process as the socio-economic variables may help to overcome problems associated with violations of important assumptions that underpin the MNL model.[17]. However, they cannot be introduced alone into the modelling. Because respondent characteristics do not vary across alternatives, 'Hessian singularities' arise in the model estimation process unless the socio-economic characteristics are introduced as interactions with either the attributes or the ASCs. The basic MNL model examines the relative attractiveness of each alternative and if characteristics do not vary across alternatives then they cannot be estimated.

More complex models involving non-linear forms and interactions between attributes can be estimated but care must be exercised in ensuring that the experimental design used as the foundation for the data collected is sufficient to the exercise. Two forms of models that introduce heterogeneity across individuals are *latent class models*, in which the data help determine groups of individuals with similar preferences, and *random parameter models*, in which the taste parameters are assumed to have statistical distributions arising from the (potentially) different parameters for each individual. (See Swait 1994 or Boxall and Adamowicz 1999 for examples of latent class models and Layton 1996 for examples of random parameter models.)

The validity of the model estimated can be assessed using a number of tools. First, the logic of the relationships estimated must be considered: do the equations estimated accord with any priors established in theory? Second, the model's statistical properties can be assessed. The significance of the individual β coefficients can be assessed with reference to their t-statistics (a t statistic greater than 1.96 indicates that the attribute coefficient is statistically significantly different from zero at the 5 per cent level). The overall explanatory power of the model can be assessed using the log-likelihood statistics and the McFadden's (or pseudo) R^2 statistic (values between 0.2 and 0.4 are considered adequate).

3.9.1 Combining Choice Modelling Data and Revealed Preference Data: Data Fusion

As discussed above, a major advantage of CM is that models estimated from the CM data can be combined with actual choices. Both revealed preference and stated preference choices can be modelled using random utility theory and are thus both consistent with the same theoretical base. For example Ben-Akiva and Morikawa (1991), Swait and Louviere (1993), Adamowicz *et al.* (1994), and Adamowicz *et al.* (1997) jointly estimate choice models from CM experiments and market place choices. The CM data and the RP data are essentially 'stacked' to appear as if they are one data set. However, one element that has arisen in empirical analysis of data fusion is that the CM and RP data often have different error variances. That is, the CM data may be less 'noisy' than the RP data because of the more focused nature of the CM task. Econometric procedures are used to take into account the difference in error variance between the two data sets. The result is often a model that shows that preferences (tastes) are undistinguishable between the two data types. (See Hensher *et al.* 1999 for a detailed analysis of data fusion.)

The log likelihood function has a unique maximum at that value of the scalar multiplier (which will be the relative scale of the two error terms) which best estimates the scale ratio. The resulting model utilities for the joint model will be scaled relative to the units of the reference data set (for example, SC rescaled to market as reference).[18] While this procedure is convenient for those who have access only to MNL estimation software it should be noted that this method will generate underestimates of the standard errors.

3.10 ANALYSING THE RESULTS: POLICY ANALYSIS

3.10.1 Part-worths

In a *linear* statistical model,[19] the β coefficients estimated under the MNL model can be used to estimate the rate at which respondents are willing to trade-off one attribute for another. For instance, the amount of recreational days a person is willing to give up in order to ensure the survival of an additional endangered species can be estimated by dividing the β co-efficients of the endangered species attribute by the β coefficient of the recreation days attribute and multiplying through by -1. Where the attribute being sacrificed is a monetary attribute, the trade-off estimated is known as a 'part-worth' or an 'implicit price'. They demonstrate the amount of money respondents are willing to pay in order to receive more of the non-marketed environmental attribute:

$$\text{Part-worth} = - \left(\beta_{\text{non-marketed attribute}} / \beta_{\text{monetary attribute}} \right)$$

Hence, if the β coefficient estimated for the monetary attribute was -0.012 and the β coefficient for an attribute describing the number of endangered species present was 0.05, then the implicit price for an additional endangered species would be \$4.16.

Estimates of implicit prices are made on a 'ceteris paribus' basis – that is, they are estimates of the willingness to pay of respondents for an increase in the attribute of concern, given that everything else is held constant.

Note that the principles applying to the determination of part-worths can also be applied to derive the willingness to trade-off between any pairs of attributes. Hence by the division of β coefficients, the marginal rates of substitution across all the attributes, monetary and non-monetary, can be estimated. Such estimates may be useful when policy calls for environmental remediation efforts to be put into place that restore community well-being, not necessarily by the payment of financial compensation for environmental losses. Thus, a CM application that uses different ecosystems as the attributes may be capable of determining how much additional rainforest protection would compensate people for the loss of a wetland.

The implicit prices are useful in that they demonstrate the trade-off between individual attributes. They allow an analysis of the composition of potential alternative allocations of resources. A comparison of the implicit prices of attributes affords some understanding of the relative importance that respondents hold for them. On the basis of such comparisons, policy makers are better placed to design resource use alternatives so as to favour those attributes which have higher (relative) implicit prices. For instance, if it is found that the recreational use of a natural area delivers relatively little value when compared to the protection of biodiversity, then management regimes that limit recreation and foster species protection can be recommended.

The comparison of relative values afforded by the calculation of implicit prices is not possible simply through the comparison of the coefficients associated with each of the attributes. It can be tempting for analysts to observe the indirect utility functions estimated using CM and conclude that the coefficients represent the contributions to that utility of each of the attributes. This is an incorrect approach because the coefficients by themselves are confounded by what is known as a 'scaling parameter' that is dependent on the variance of the error involved in the estimation process. In other words, the extent of the variance of the statistical error involved in the estimation process has an impact on the absolute magnitude of the β coefficients. It is only through the division of the β coefficients that is integral to the process of part-worth calculation that the scaling parameter is cancelled out and the confounding effect of the error variance is eliminated.

In addition, it is important to note that the comparison of implicit prices across attributes should be undertaken in full recognition of the differing units used to define the attributes. Hence, care should be taken when comparing the implicit prices of 'days of recreation' and 'numbers of endangered species present'. Similarly, the costs of achieving the mix of attributes that is indicated by the relativities of attribute implicit prices are not a component of this analysis. The relative merits of alternative management packages of attributes would need to be further assessed in a cost-benefit framework. This type of assessment requires the estimation of economic benefits created by different alternatives under consideration.

Finally, it is important to note that part-worths are generally not welfare measures that can be used in benefit-cost analysis. Part-worths express the marginal rates of substitution within an alternative (or conditional indirect utility function). In random utility models each alternative has some probability of being realised, thus welfare measures must take into account the probability of being realised, plus the change in all the attributes being examined, not just a single attribute.

3.10.2 Economic Surplus

A particular strength of CM is its ability to generate estimates of the values of many different alternatives from the one application. Hence, from one set of choice data, the values of an array of alternative ways of re-allocating resources can be estimated. This feature of CM arises because it specifically investigates trade-offs between attributes. Thus, different combination of the attributes that are used to describe alternatives can be evaluated.

In theory, economic welfare measures are (a) the amount of money (given or taken away) that make a person as well off as they would be before a change, or (b) the amount of money (given or taken away) that make a person as well off as they would be after a change. Algebraically, welfare measure (a) – compensating surplus or CS – can be expressed as:

$$V(M, 0) = V(M - CS, 1) \qquad (3.1)$$

where V is utility, M is income, CS is compensating surplus, and the second argument in the utility function is 0 for the base situation and 1 for the 'changed' situation. Suppose the change is an environmental improvement relative to the base situation. CS is the amount of money that is taken away from the person to make the utility with the environmental improvement equal to the utility before the change. While there are other forms of welfare measure employed in economic analysis, we will only outline the use of the CS measure for simplicity.

There are two main categories of welfare measures that arise from the two approaches to using CM in applied studies. The first is the so-called 'State of the World' approach in which one compares the utility in the base case with the utility in a 'changed' case. In these State of the World models there is only one alternative in each case (multiple alternatives do not exist in each case). In contrast, in behavioural studies, the improvement may be a quality change at one recreation site – but there are still multiple sites to choose from. The base case contains multiple alternatives and so also does the improved case, thus the welfare measure must examine the utilities with and without the improvements, as well as the probabilities of choosing each alternative. If there is an improvement at a site that has little chance of being chosen, then the welfare impact will be small.

3.10.3 Welfare Measures in 'State of the World' Models

Assessment of economic welfare involves an investigation of the difference between the well-being (or utility) achieved by the individual under the status quo (or constant base) alternative and some other alternative. It is therefore a matter of considering the marginal value of a change away from the status quo.

First, the values of the attributes that are associated with the status quo are substituted into the equation that estimates the indirect utility associated with that option. If socio-economic variables are included in that equation, the values to be substituted are the sample means (or individual specific welfare measures can be computed). Note that the monetary attribute is assigned a value of zero for this stage.

Next, the values of the attributes that are associated with an alternative allocation of resources are substituted into the equation that relates to the relevant change alternative. The value of the relevant ASC should be included in this calculation. Socio-economic variables are treated the same as for the status quo option and again the monetary attribute is set at zero.

The value associated with the change alternative is then subtracted from the value associated with the status quo option. If the model is linear (in the monetary attribute) this 'indirect utility difference' is then divided by the negative of the coefficient associated with the monetary attribute:

$$\text{Economic surplus} = -\left(1/\beta_{\text{monetary}}\right)\ (V_1 - V_2) \tag{3.2}$$

A negative value for this surplus estimate would indicate that respondents are willing to pay the amount of the surplus in order to experience an improvement in their well-being caused by a re-allocation of resources from the status quo to the change alternative.

Again, the complexities caused by the existence of the scale parameter within each β coefficient are avoided through the division throughout by the β coefficient associated with the monetary attribute.

By setting up multiple scenarios of alternative resource allocations (by varying the values the attributes can take on) and repeating this arithmetic exercise, an array of values associated with the array of scenarios can be estimated.

Having access to this potential to estimate any combination of attribute levels (within the ranges initially established in the choice set design process) provides the decision maker with the flexibility to consider numerous options without the need to commission separate valuation exercises.

3.10.4 Models with Multiple Alternatives

If there are multiple alternatives available, as in the case of recreation sites or product choice, the welfare measure involves the expected value (or utility for each alternative times the probability of choosing each alternative) of utility arising from the multiple alternatives. The expected value of the base case is compared to the expected value of the 'changed' case and again, in the case of *linear* models the difference is multiplied by 1 over the marginal utility of income to convert the utility difference into monetary values. For MNL models, the expected value across the alternatives can be expressed as the 'log-sum' or $\ln\Sigma\exp(V_i)$ where 'ln' indicates natural logarithm, 'exp' is the mathematical constant 'e', the summation is over all of the alternatives and V_i is the conditional indirect utility associated with alternative i. The expression for welfare in these cases is:

$$\text{Economic surplus} = -(1/\beta_{\text{monetary}})\ (\ln\Sigma\exp(V^1_i) - \ln\Sigma\exp(V^2_i)) \qquad (3.3)$$

where the superscript 1 indicates the base situation and the superscript 2 indicates the 'changed' situation.

3.10.5 Market Shares

The relative values of each of the utilities (V) when different levels of the attributes are included gives an estimate of the 'support' that each alternative would generate. If, for instance, each alternative related to a different forest protection strategy and the status quo, then the percentage of the total of the Vs that was contributed by each of the individual Vs would represent the percentage support that alternative would generate. In a political context, policy makers could therefore use these market share results to predict the voter support that would be generated by alternatives.

In behavioural models market share predicts the number of people who will choose each alternative under different conditions (attribute levels). These market share models can be used to predict visitation at sites or market demand under different conditions, and simulation programmes designed to forecast market share are of great use to managers.

3.11 CONCLUSIONS

Choice modelling is a stated preference technique for the estimation of non-market values. It has some distinct advantages over other techniques – such as the CVM – that have been more widely applied. Its ability to provide a disaggregated view of values is a key feature. With respondents' preferences broken down into components associated with the attributes that go to make up a good, it is possible to use CM results to investigate the relative importance of attributes and estimate the values associated with various combinations of attribute levels (see Adamowicz *et al.* 1998 or Hanley *et al.* 1998 for a discussion of the CVM and CM as well as some formal analysis of the two methods).

However, CM should not be regarded as the 'holy grail' of non-market valuation techniques. Many of the problems facing other stated preference techniques also serve as challenges to CM users. And CM provides additional challenges, especially in the design of the questionnaire which is inherently more difficult, from the perspective of respondent cognition, than a contingent valuation questionnaire.

The process of applying CM is complex. Those intending to use CM need to be skilled in questionnaire design as well as experimental design and statistical modelling. What has been set out in this chapter should be regarded as an introductory guide only. Many of the complexities associated with the technique have been treated only briefly. Other chapters in this volume take up a variety of these challenges.

NOTES

1. Use values generated by environmental assets involve direct contact with the resource. They include direct contact uses such as recreation and indirect uses such as the provision of good quality water from a protected catchment. Non-use values are generated without direct contact. For instance, people may value the biodiversity supplied by an environment without wanting to experience it directly. See Wills (1997) for details of this categorisation of benefits and costs.
2. See Mitchell and Carson (1989).
3. For an example of a contingent valuation method application which was designed specifically in an attempt to avoid specific biases, see Bennett *et al.* (1997).
4. There is considerable confusion regarding the names of these various techniques. For example, choice modelling could also be applied to CVM since most modern applications of CVM employ discrete choice econometric models applied to referendum choices. For a discussion of the stated preference family of techniques, see Adamowicz *et al.* 1998a.
5. In the jargon of economists, these are estimates of marginal rates of substitution between the attributes.
6. This is often referred to as the 'market share' of each alternative.
7. Total economic value incorporates both use and non-use values of the environment
8. The Delphi process involves an iterative sequence of interactions with respondents. Once the responses to a first round questionnaire are collected and analysed, the results obtained are provided to the respondents. An opportunity to revisit their response to the initial questionnaire is then provided. The process can then be repeated until some convergence of results is achieved.
9. See Krueger (1988) for details on focus groups.
10. The observation that values estimated for goods as separate entities will be larger than when estimated as a component of a more inclusive whole is referred to as the 'regular embedding effect' and is entirely consistent with the principles of economics. See Bennett *et al.* (1998).
11. See Dillman (1978) for details of survey processes.
12. Note that if qualitative attribute levels are used, the individual levels of the attributes can be introduced as *effects codes*. These are alternatives to dummy variables. When using dummy variables, one level of variable is left out of the analysis to avoid the 'dummy variable trap'. When using effects codes, instead of leaving one level of attribute out, that attribute is coded as -1 for all dummy variable categories. For example, if there are three levels in an attribute, level 1 would be coded $(1,0)$, level 2 would be $(0,1)$ and level 3 would be $(-1, -1)$.

13. Others included nested logit and the heteroscedastic extreme value model.
14. This is the essence of the random utility model that underpins choice modelling. For more details, see Carson *et al.* (1994) or Ben-Akiva and Lerman (1985).
15. For qualitative attributes, the equations will produce coefficients relating to all but one of the levels of the attribute. So for a three level attribute, two coefficients will be estimated. The coefficient relating to the third level (using effects codes) would be equal to −1 times the sum of the other two levels' coefficients.
16. The β coefficients cannot be interpreted as the contribution made to utility by each attribute in any absolute sense as they are each confounded by a scale parameter (λ). Each CM data set will be characterised by a different value of λ because it is determined by the variance of the statistical error inherent in the modelling. Furthermore, it is not possible to estimate the value of λ in any one model. It is however possible to estimate λ by merging a related revealed preference data set with the CM data set (Swait and Louviere 1993).
17. Most importantly, the MNL model uses an assumption that the error terms are 'independently and identically distributed'. This assumption gives rise to the independence of irrelevant alternatives (IIA) characteristic.
18 Parameter equivalence after accounting for scale differences can be tested using a likelihood ratio test.
19. Note that these results apply only when all attributes enter in a linear fashion. If the conditional indirect utility function is non-linear, part-worths can still be calculated but the expressions will be more complex.

PART TWO

Case Studies

4. Assessing the Options for the Canberra Water Supply: an Application of Choice Modelling

Jenny Gordon, Ross Chapman and Russell Blamey

4.1 INTRODUCTION

4.1.1 The Problem

With a growing population, pressure inevitably arises on existing water supply arrangements. Water supply companies have a variety of options available for meeting demand – including the options of rationing and demand management, as well as engineering solutions such as new dams and recycling. Their problem is which solution to pick. While consumers may dislike the environmental impacts of dams and have concerns about recycled water, they also have an aversion to restrictions. And, with the corporatisation of water supply authorities in Australia, water supply companies have to raise their own capital and pay the shareholders a rate of return. To make long term investment decisions they need to understand all the benefits and costs of the water supply options. While the financial implications of a supply option to consumers are critical, equally important is the willingness to trade-off water costs, environmental costs and amenity values.

In 1996 the Australian Capital Territory Electricity and Water Corporation (ACTEW) contemplated the impact of population growth on long term water supply reliability (ACTEW 1994). The storage capacity of the two dams that service the Canberra area is sufficient for a population of 410 000 at the average per capita usage of 280 kilolitres a year. In 1996 the system supplied around 340 000, but it was projected that population growth of around 2 per cent a year would see this critical population level reached in 2005. Slower growth would see the problem deferred but not averted.

As input into their planning process ACTEW commissioned a study to assess the environmental values associated with water supply options. The Centre for International Economics, with CSIRO, was the successful tenderer to undertake this study.

4.1.2 The Approach

The questions facing ACTEW were:

- what options could satisfy projected demand and at what cost; and
- which did the public prefer given the trade-offs involved?

The study focused on the second issue. Detailed supply information on five options was provided by ACTEW. The other characteristics or attributes of the options – their impact on the natural and urban environments and on household use – were developed by the study team. This chapter provides the results of this work but does not go into detail about how they were derived. Details are available in CIE (1997) and CSIRO (1997). The focus here is to describe the use of choice modelling to identify consumer preferences over the attributes of the options, and hence over the options. We describe:

- the development of the attribute set;
- the questionnaire and survey design; and
- the analysis and results

At the time of the study, choice modelling was just emerging as a technique for use in environmental evaluation. In the last few years the technique has evolved and more sophisticated design and analytical techniques have been developed. Still, there are useful lessons that emerged in the course of the study.

4.2 DEVELOPING THE ATTRIBUTE SET

4.2.1 The Options

The options for meeting the future demand for reticulated water supply were reduced through discussions with the supplier, ACTEW, to five:

1. Tennent Dam on the Gudgenby River;
2. Coree Dam on the Cotter River (between the existing Bendora and Cotter Dams);
3. large scale water recycling for probable reuse, involving construction of a 50 megalitre per day recycling plant with subsequent pumping to Cotter Dam;
4. a demand management – recycling mix resulting in 20 per cent reduction in demand for reticulated water, though water use would be maintained by small scale recycling for public space, voluntary demand management with some incentive schemes and increasing use of greywater recycling, and regulations on new construction to be water efficient; and
5. a demand management agenda with compulsory restrictions resulting in a 20 per cent reduction in demand (education, price increases and restrictions).

All the options supplied sufficient water to meet demand to 2050, under the population forecasts. However, the last option was viewed as a necessary undertaking if no action was taken to increase supply.

4.2.2 The Impact of the Options

The financial and environmental impact of the options was assessed.

Financial impact

A financial analysis of the costs of each of the options was undertaken. For the engineering solutions – dams and recycling – ACTEW provided cost assessments of capital and operating costs. The price of water to the consumers required to cover these costs was modelled, and the results formed the basis of the cost implications of the options.

The demand management options also had financial implications for consumers. Demand management programmes are not costless. Based on the experiences of the demand management scheme adopted in New South Wales and demand management modelling conducted by the Independent Pricing and Regulatory Tribunal of New South Wales (IPART 1996), the cost to the consumer of demand management was estimated. This included the cost of purchasing water saving devices, the cost of administration of the scheme, and sharing the costs imposed on businesses by the scheme. The presumption was that higher water costs to business and government would largely be passed on to the consumer in prices and rates.

Environmental impact

The environmental impact of the dams was a major issue. But focus groups also highlighted the importance of the urban environment – and people's own gardens – to their well-being. The demand management options had strong implications for the ability to maintain a 'green' urban environment. The dam options had very different environmental implications. The Gudgenby River was not dammed, but flowed through an area already disturbed by clearing and grazing activities. The site had been set aside as a potential dam site and no capital improvements had been made to the area for some time. The Cotter River was already dammed but the area was for the most part in pristine natural condition. The major recycling option's main environmental impact was a reduction in the flow of treated water back into the Murrumbidgee River. Currently the treatment works contribute up to 70 per cent of the flow at this point in the river. This has changed the dynamics of the river flow in the area below the outfall with a more consistent and higher flow levels than would otherwise have been the case. The higher nutrient load has also influenced the aquatic life, with platypus communities thriving in the area. The small scale recycling option had no significant implications for the surrounding environment.

The analysis of the environmental impacts had two components. The first focused on the impact of each of the options on the habitat of native animals. The two dam options clearly had the main impact and a landscape capacity assessment was undertaken by CSIRO. This consisted of vegetation mapping and modelling to predict the abundance of various species of flora and fauna. The assessment focused on the impact on habitat of threatened species. An assessment of the relative scarcity of the habitat of threatened species that would be affected by the water supply options was made.

The second environmental impact was the impact on the rivers and aquatic life. Experts at the ACT Parks and Conservation and Canberra University Cooperative Research Centre for Freshwater Ecology provided an assessment of this impact. The main considerations were on the volume and timing of river flows. The impact depended on the current condition of the rivers, the aquatic life and their breeding habits. In focus groups it was found that the main concerns were with the conditions for native fish, although recreational amenity also featured. The two were seen by most people to be positively related.

Other impacts

In addition to the technical studies, focus groups were used to assess the impacts, as perceived by the community, of the different options. In addition to improving understanding of environmental priorities, three clear issues emerged in the discussions.

A third environmental impact that emerged as requiring consideration was the impact on the urban environment. The Canberra region has an average rainfall of around 600 mm a year. However, the rainfall pattern is variable and there can be long periods of little rain, usually in summer, which spell death for most gardens unless watered regularly. Most houses have large gardens and 55 per cent of reticulated water use is on gardens and lawns. The city also maintains extensive areas of parks and gardens. People generally valued these 'public good' characteristics of the city as well as the private benefits of their gardens.

People were also worried about the quality of water. This was an issue with the use of large and small scale recycled water. Regardless of actual quality relative to use, the recycle option was sometimes viewed as having negative impacts. This was due to a perception of health risks and odours associated with the recycling options, and the convenience of being able to have a drink out of any tap.

Convenience turned out to be an issue with restrictions on water use, and in terms of adopting water saving devices. The desire for a 'good' shower was strongly expressed. Voluntary water restrictions also have a poor record in areas where they are used repeatedly as part of demand management.

4.2.3 Desirable Characteristics of the Attributes

In choosing the attributes to be included in the choice modelling experiments there were a number of considerations – apart from ensuring they were feasible and credible:

- The attributes had to describe fully the impact of the options, or at least capture all the elements that were important to people in their decision making.
- The number of attributes that people can think about when asked to make a choice is limited. In focus groups we found that six attributes was about the maximum. Beyond six, people started ignoring what they considered to be less important attributes. While this could theoretically have been accommodated in the analysis, the frustration of trying to consider all attributes reduced willingness to answer the questions and could have affected response rates and quality.
- The attributes needed to be, as far as possible, independent. This was both for ease of analysis (satisfying independence of residuals in the statistical analysis) and to assist in the willingness to answer the

survey questions.
- The attributes would preferably be quantifiable, or at least have some scaling that allowed for relative magnitudes of changes to be assessed. This was the most difficult requirement to satisfy.

4.2.4 Choosing the Attributes and their Values

The significant impacts of the options were seen to be on:

- the cost of water: the price of water, of water saving devices, business costs passed on in prices and costs to government passed on in rates;
- the habitat of native animals;
- the aquatic life, particularly native fish;
- gardens and parks, public and private;
- recreational amenity: access to the surrounding environment and its condition;
- the quality of water – mainly whether all water was potable; and
- convenience: having good showers and not being restricted in use.

It was found, using influence analysis techniques undertaken by CSIRO, that recreational amenity was closely tied to gardens and parks in the urban setting, and to aquatic life and (less so) to habitat of native animals outside urban areas. Including recreational amenity in the list of attributes would have violated the independence criteria, and it was not found to be a dominant influence in preliminary testing. This left six attributes (see Table 4.1).

Several aspects of convenience and quality of water were trialed. Those with the most consistent interpretation were to describe convenience in terms of compulsory reduction in use – leaving it to individuals where they would reduce use – and where – not at all, outdoors, indoors – the household would use recycled water.

The next issue was how best to describe the attributes in an unambiguous way, and how to assign levels to them. Some had relatively obvious quantification, for the others focus groups were used to find descriptors that had a natural interpretation. The range of outcomes under the five possible options set the high and low levels for each of the attributes. Three levels were assigned to each attribute. The only level that was not fixed by the set of feasible options was the upper value for the cost of water. As the recycling option potentially could imply an additional cost of $125, this was used as the high value for additional household water costs. Table 4.1 summarises the six attributes and assigns the levels to each of the policy options.

Table 4.1 Mapping attributes into options

Attribute	Core	Tennent	Large scale recycling	Demand manage: re-cycling	Base option: no increase in supply
Reduction in use (%)	0	0	0	10	20
Use of recycled water	none	none	all pur-poses	outside use	none
Increase in household cost ($)	75	75	50	75	50
Improvement in river flows	some	all	some	all	none
Endangered species losing habitat	10	2	0	0	0
Appearance of urban environment	green	green	green	some brown	brown

4.3 DESIGNING THE QUESTIONNAIRE AND THE CHOICE EXPERIMENT

Having constructed a set of attributes relevant to choice among actual and 'synthetic' options the next task was to design a questionnaire in which to embed the choice experiment.

4.3.1 Questionnaire Design

Information accompanying the survey
From focus group discussions and community forums it was apparent that there was a perception that the solutions to a water shortage were simple and low cost: rainwater tanks and storm water reuse, and reduction in perceived inefficiencies in the supplier ACTEW. These issues were explored with ACTEW and information to refute these perceptions was developed. After piloting to assess the effect of this information, it was

provided with the questionnaire to reduce any bias that might have resulted from this problem.

Use of labels for the options

Dams were, not surprisingly, identified as an emotive issue. While emotive issues do influence the way people vote for an option, the aim of the study was to provide information on the underlying preferences from a policy decision maker's perspective. The decision was made to keep emotive elements out of the attributes and labels were not used for the options.

Inclusion of a constant alternative

Two possible approaches were considered. The first approach was to allow choice between two options, making the current conditions the constant base against which to assess the change in consumer surplus. The other approach was to set out a constant alternative that would be the outcome if the other options were not adopted.

It was decided to take the latter approach: partly to reinforce the idea that the current situation was not a long run feasible alternative. The 'no change in supply scenario' was not a 'no change in use' scenario. It was a heavy demand management regime, with household use of water reduced by 20 per cent compared to current usage, and water charges to increase by $50. The pilot testing indicated that this could be misinterpreted so the distinction was emphasised in the information accompanying the survey and by the interviewers.

Number and format of choice sets

Several pilots of the survey were conducted to test out the presentation and the number of choice sets that could be presented. Nine choice sets was the maximum that people were consistently willing to complete. These were best presented three to a page.

It was found that including the attribute values of the constant alternative cluttered the page and required excessive reading. This option was included as a simple 'no change in supply' alternative in the choice sets.

Experimental design

An orthogonal experimental design was used to ensure that the attribute levels varied independently of one another. This is necessary for their individual effect on respondents' preferences to be isolated. A one-twenty-seventh fraction of the full 3^6 factorial design was used to reduce the number of alternatives to a manageable level. Combinations of the 27 resulting alternatives were assigned to three blocks such that any one respondent would be confronted with no more than nine different options (excluding the constant base option) in nine choice sets.

There was a concern that some of the alternatives would be considered to be implausible by the respondents. For example, in some 'synthetic' options the increase in the household cost of water may be small and yet there is no requirement for any restrictions on use. If few in number, these combinations can be removed from the choice set without significantly disturbing the orthogonality. This turned out not to be an issue as a pre-survey exercise indicated that different individuals have different interpretations of what constitutes an implausible combination of attributes.

The questionnaire

Section 1 of the questionnaire described the water choices for the region in general terms, asking respondents to read an information sheet describing the six main 'features' of the water supply options. The next

Table 4.2 Example choice set

	I prefer option A □	I prefer option B □	I prefer the no change in supply option □
Reduce your household use by:	None	10%	
You would use reclaimed treated water for:	All uses	Not at all	
Your household water cost will increase by:	$50	$75	
Environmental flows improve in:	All rivers	Some rivers	
Some habitat loss for:	No species	10 species	
The urban landscape would be:	Green	Some brown	

section, labelled 'What do *you* think?', asked respondents to rank these six features from most important to least important. This question was included both as a framing exercise for respondents and a means of cross-checking the results of the conditional logit model.

Section 2 then introduced the choice modelling exercise, explaining the task requirements and defining the constant base 'no increase in supply option'. It was emphasised that the 'do nothing' option did not mean 'status quo', as without augmentation in supply (through new dams or recycling or voluntary reduction) restrictions would be necessary. The payment vehicle was defined as an increase in the cost of household water. Although highly plausible given the true policy context, water cost was suspected to bite less with renters than owners as water costs were generally included in the rent and not charged for separately. The nine choice sets followed an example choice set and explanation. Table 4.2 shows a typical choice set.

A series of socioeconomic questions formed the last section of the survey. Respondents were also asked to indicate whether they were currently renting. This permitted the relationship between rental status and other responses to be explored at the data analysis stage.

4.3.2 The Survey

Method
The difficulty of the survey and the need to provide some preliminary information to remove some potential biases led to the decision to conduct a face-to-face survey. This approach adds an element of obligation to encourage people to fill out the questionnaire. It also allows for questions to be answered and the purpose to be explained. A small number of surveys were dropped off in accordance with respondents' wishes, and a time arranged for subsequent survey collection.

A professional survey company was employed and the interviewers briefed on the information and likely questions that had been identified in the focus groups and pilot surveys.

Sample size and selection
The sample size was limited by the decision to use face-to-face methods and the budget. Around 300 usable questionnaires were expected. Stratified random sampling was used to ensure a representative sample. Each choice set was expected to have about 30 observations under this approach.

Interviews were conducted at home at a range of times to ensure a cross section of the population.

4.4 THE RESULTS

4.4.1 Representativeness of the Sample

A degree of bias appears to have occurred in favour of individuals who were better educated, on higher incomes and male. This may be partly because the survey was most likely to be completed by the head of the household.

The main bias in the sample was against lower income households who are also more likely to be renting. As the non-response rate of this segment of the population is generally expected to be higher than for other segments of the population, this problem is not expected to be unique to this survey. However, results clearly need to be interpreted with this bias in mind.

4.4.2 Issues Arising from the Survey Process

The general perception of the survey was that it was quite demanding to complete. A few respondents were frustrated by having to make difficult trade-offs, indicating that they would prefer to simply pick the attributes and values they like most. These survey responses were not included in the analysis.

In some cases respondents were annoyed by the inclusion of what they thought were infeasible options in a particular choice set, a response anticipated through piloting. This problem was to be avoided by having the interviewers explain that some of the options might be thought infeasible, but were included for good reasons. In retrospect, inclusion of a written explanation of why they were included in the choice sets would have been useful.

There is a concern that a small proportion of people would have filled out the questions randomly or by always picking the same choice number. If a comment was made by the respondent that it was *too* hard or they had picked choices not in accord with their actual preferences these surveys were excluded from the analysis.

There was also a small proportion of survey responses where the choice made was always the constant alternative. Unless there was an indication that these were protest votes or the nature of the constant alternative had been misunderstood, these surveys (five in total) were left in the analysis. One risk of including them is that the respondents may have misunderstood the nature of the 'no change in supply' alternative to mean no change in the current situation. However, excluding them could have biased the results against the attributes of the 'no change in supply' alternative.

There was a small proportion of surveys where the 'no change in supply' alternative was never chosen. Again, unless there was some indication that this was a misrepresentation of preferences, these surveys (six in total) were included in the analysis. If people had failed to take the no change alternative into account this would bias the market share and attribute importance information against that corresponding to the 'no change in supply' option.

Of the 321 surveys conducted, a total of 15 were excluded as non-response, 12 were considered unusable, and 30 were only partly usable for the choice set analysis (for example, partially completed). The 294 surveys provided 2544 completed choice sets for analysis.

4.4.3 Results

Approach to the analysis

Several approaches were used to analyse the data. The frequency approach converts individual choices into the frequency with which a particular option is chosen in any given choice set. The main advantage of this approach is that standard goodness of fit analysis is accessible, and the interpretation of the dependent variable is the expected average frequency of a positive response to an option.

Individual choices can be analysed employing a conditional multinomial logit approach. The three qualitative attributes were effect coded rather than dummy coded, the tactical difference with the former being that the control group is assigned a code of -1 instead of 0. The coding is given in Table 4.3, along with a summary of the variable names.

The results of the two approaches were similar, but the second approach provides greater information as individual characteristics can be explored for their influence on choices. The results from examination of the individual choices are presented in this chapter. The analysis was undertaken using LIMDEP, a specialist discrete choice modelling package.

Model results

Table 4.4 presents conditional logit results for three different model specifications.

- Model 1 represents the attribute only specification.
- Model 2 includes the socio-economic variables in an additive form in the indirect utility function.
- Model 3 includes the socio-economic variables in both an additive

form and as interactions with selected attributes.

Table 4.3 Coding of attributes

Attribute	Levels	Variable in regression
Reduction in water use	no reduction in household use 10% reduction in household use 20% reduction in household use	reduce (quantitative) (0, 10, 20)
Use of recycled water	no use of recycled water outdoor use of recycled water outside and inside use of recycled water	recno=1; recout=0 recout=1; recno=0 recout= −1; recno= −1
Increase in water charges	$50 increase in water charges $75 increase in water charges $125 increase in water charges	price (quantitative) (50, 75, 125)
River flows	no improvement in environmental flows improvement in flow of some rivers improvement in flow of all rivers	rivsome= −1; rivall= −1 rivsome=1; rivall=0 rivall=1; rivsome=0
Species habitat loss	some habitat loss for no species some habitat loss for 2 species some habitat loss for 10 species	spec (quantitative) (0, 2, 10)
Urban	brown grass in most public areas brown grass in some public areas green grass in all public areas	sbrown= −1; green= −1 sbrown=1; green=0 green=1; sbrown=0

Model 1

All the coefficients are significantly different from zero at the 95 per cent confidence level, with the exception of 'green', which indicates whether grass can be expected to be green in all rather than some or no public areas. It appears that the residents are satisfied with knowing that only some public areas will be brown. Further reducing this to no brown areas is not a major concern. Most of the variables are also significant at the 99 per cent confidence level. (The signs on the attributes are generally as expected.) The probability that an option would be chosen was reduced:

- the higher compulsory reduction in water use;
- the higher household water cost;
- the lower the flows in rivers;
- the more adverse species effects; and
- the more brown the urban environment would be.

It is interesting to observe that use of recycled water for outside use adds positively to the utility of an option, but the use of recycled water for inside use has a negative effect (the coefficient changes from 0.4624 to −0.1908). From these results the support for grey water recycling for outdoor use is overwhelming, but people are still very wary about the idea of drinking recycled water.

Impact of socio-economic variables
Models 2 and 3 introduce the socio-economic variables. The additive specification requires the socio-economic variables to be interacted with the alternative specific constant because variables taking the same value for all options within a choice set cannot be used to predict option choice.

The following conclusions can be drawn from the results:

- older residents are more likely to choose the no change in supply option than younger residents. This may be because younger residents may be less averse to changes in their living environments;
- income and gender were not significant determinants of option choice. Income has the opposite sign to what might be expected on a priori theoretical grounds, given that the base option is generally the cheapest option. Additional analysis indicated that income did not attain significance when the other socio-economic terms in the model were removed;
- older respondents attach greater importance to reductions in household use of water than other respondents, and are more concerned about price increases. However, older respondents were less concerned about losses in species habitat; and
- renters attached less importance to using recycled water outside than other respondents. The rent*price interaction is not significant, implying that renters are no more or less price responsive than non-renters. This is comforting, given the possibility that renters may discount the payment vehicle if they do not believe landlords would pass increases in water charges on to them. Indeed, the coefficient is

wrong-signed with respect to this hypothesis, which may in part be a reflection of lower renter incomes.

Table 4.4 Estimates of the determinants of choice of option[a, b]

	Model 1	Model 2	Model 3
asc(option1)	0.3673 (0.1407)**	0.8731 (0.2570)**	0.8815 (0.2414)**
reduce	−0.0134 (0.0039)**	−0.0155 (0.0044)**	0.0048 (0.0091)
recout	0.4624 (0.0418)**	0.4753 (0.0473)**	0.5138 (0.0497)**
recno	−0.1908 (0.0431)**	−0.1881 (0.0487)**	−0.2047 (0.0508)**
price	−0.0126 (0.0010)**	−0.0115 (0.0011)**	−0.0067 (0.0028)*
rivsome	0.0915 (0.0422)*	0.0639 (0.0474)	0.0852 (0.0429)*
rivall	0.3831 (0.0423)**	0.3955 (0.0476)**	0.3839 (0.0430)**
spec	−0.0642 (0.0072)**	−0.0692 (0.0081)**	−0.1008 (0.0179**
somebrown	0.0940 (0.0426)*	0.1209 (0.0479)*	0.0811 (0.0433)
green	0.0671 (0.0426)	0.0619 (0.0477)	0.0779 (0.0433)
age*asc		−0.0770 (0.0261)**	−0.0830 (0.0352)*
income*asc		−0.0044 (0.0187)	
sex*asc		−0.0517 (0.1176	
rent*asc		−0.4367 (0.1388)**	−0.1617 (0.1756)
age*reduce			−0.0035 (0.0016)*
age*price			−0.0011 (0.0005)*
age*spec			0.0069 (0.0032)*
rent*recout			−0.2196 (0.0951)*
rent*recno			0.0951 (0.0985)
rent*price			−0.0034 (0.0025)
logL(initial)	−2674.25	−2119.07	−2608.71
logl (final)	−2417.83 (n=2544)	−1908.53 (n=2010)	−2341.34 (n=2481)

Notes:
[a] standard errors are shown in brackets
[b] socio-economic variables were coded as follows: age = age in tens of years; income = household income in units of $10000; sex = 1 if male, 0 female; and rent = 1 if renting, 0 if not. The alternative-specific constant (ASC) is coded 1 for options 1 and 2 in the choice set, and 0 for option 3.
* indicates statistical significance at the 95% confidence level
** indicates significance at the 99% level

Those attribute interactions not included in model 3 were not found to be significant determinants of option choice in preliminary model runs, and were subsequently omitted from the specification reported here.

4.4.4 Ranking the Options

A major purpose of the choice modelling exercise was to provide a
method for ranking the set of feasible options listed in Table 4.1. The
attribute levels in Table 4.1 reflect the values under each water supply
option at a population of 450 000. Because the levels of the price attribute
shown in Table 4.1 reflect the capital, operating and other costs of the
options, the ranking indicates the overall preference ordering of the
options. The highest ranked option provides the greatest net benefit to
consumers, conditional, of course, on some form of action having to be
taken. As long as an option can be described in terms of levels of
attributes represented in the questionnaire (or close to them) it can be
ranked relative to other options.

Table 4.5 Ranking the options and willingness to pay

	Management options				
	Coree (h=1)	Tennent (h=2)	Large scale recycling (h=3)	Demand manage: reuse (h=4)	Do-nothing: restrictions etc. (h=5)
Probability of choosing an option relative to base option	0.619	0.786	0.797	0.874	n/a
Probability of choosing an option out of the five options	0.094	0.214	0.229	0.404	0.058
Market share %	6.4	19.4	18.7	51.5	4.3
Willingness to pay for an option relative to the base option ($)	36.4	98.0	103.1	145.8	n/a

Table 4.5 compares the five feasible options in terms of choice
probabilities and market share. Details of the estimation procedures are in
Blamey *et al.* (1999a). Two different probability estimates are given, the
first indicating the probability of an individual choosing an option when
the only other alternative in the choice set is the 'do nothing about supply'

base option. These binary choice probabilities provide an approximation of the results one might expect to obtain in dichotomous-choice contingent valuation studies. The second set of probabilities correspond to an expanded choice set involving all five management options. Market share estimates provide an indication of the proportion of the region's residents favouring each option.

Results are generally consistent with each other. The demand management recycle option is the preferred option, with the use of recycling for outside water use and the best outcome for the rivers and streams weighing heavily in its favour.

Whilst the Tennent Dam option is the second ranked option according to the probability estimates, its estimated market or voter share comes in slightly behind large scale recycling. This illustrates how allowing for individual differences in choice probabilities when estimating market share can lead to different rankings than probabilities calculated for the average respondent. Although not providing utility through the provision of recycled water for outside use, the Tennent option provides the best outcome for rivers and streams, water restrictions and appearance of the urban environment, outweighing the cost to species.

To illustrate the use of CM in evaluating 'what if' scenarios, assume that under a worst case scenario the Tennent option would result in ten rather than two species affected, with the other attributes remaining unchanged. It is a straightforward exercise to re-estimate market share under this assumption. Results indicate that the Tennent share would fall to 10 per cent, with the share of all other options slightly increasing.

The large scale recycling option is the third most preferred of the five. The lower cost relative to the other 'increase in supply' options accompanied by the medium outcome for flows in rivers and streams are the most important factors. However, it is possible that this option could end up costing say $125 because of problems associated with the disposal of brine rather than the $50 assumed in Table 4.1 (CIE 1997). If this scenario is run through the model, the market share for this option drops from 19 per cent to 12 per cent, with most of the difference being taken up by the demand management recycle option, which increases its share to 55 per cent.

The Coree Dam is second last in the rankings – the loss of flow and additional species affected putting it well below the Tennent Dam option. The 'no change in supply' option is ranked last. The lower price of this option is not sufficient to offset the cost of greater restrictions, lower flows and a brown Canberra.

The rankings shown in Table 4.5 are reasonably consistent with those obtained from the simple attribute ranking question included prior to the choice set questions. Details are given in CIE (1997). The above results can easily be redone under different population or other assumptions. Such an example is given in CIE (1997) where community rankings are estimated for two other population levels, which imply different levels of the attributes of the option, particularly price and compulsory restrictions.

4.4.5 Willingness to Pay

The survey can be used to estimate the amount residents are prepared to pay to obtain one water supply option in preference to another for a population of 450 000. This requires that the no change in supply scenario is a true reflection of the outcome if no provisions are made for an increase in the water supply in the region. The results cannot be used to estimate the willingness to pay for a change from the status quo.

Table 4.6 Attribute valuations

Attribute change	Implicit price (at mean age and rental status) ($)
Prevent 10% reduction in household use	10
Recycled water for all uses, to outdoor use only	55
No use of recycled water to recycled water for outdoor use	47
Environmental flows improve in no rivers, to some rivers	42
Environmental flows improve in some rivers, to all rivers	22
Reduce habitat loss for 5 species	24
Brown urban landscape, to some brown	18
Some brown landscape, to no brown (green)	−0.2

Table 4.6 presents estimates of marginal attribute values, for the average respondent in terms of age and rental status. These are estimated by observing the marginal rate of substitution between the price attribute and the attribute in question.

The results indicate that respondents are willing to trade-off (in today's dollars on an accrual basis) an increase in the household cost of water of:

- $42 for an improvement in river flows from no to some rivers. The equivalent willingness to pay for an increase in improvement from some to all rivers is $22.
- $5 per species, or $24 for five species to prevent losses in habitat for uncommon species.
- $18 to improve the appearance of Canberra from 'brown', the base case outcome, to 'some brown'. Willingness to pay for further improvements (from some brown to green) is insignificant.
- $10 to prevent a 10 per cent reduction in household use of water.
- $47 for the provision of recycled water for outdoor use. Interestingly, WTP for the provision of recycled water for all uses is equally substantial but negative (-$55), a consequence of the desire to avoid drinking recycled water.

Willingness to pay to avoid possible water supply options
Table 4.5 also presents monetary estimates of the differences in utility of the five feasible water supply options listed in Table 4.1. These figures represent how much more people would, on average, be willing to pay to have each specific option rather than the base option.

All estimates are positive in sign as the no change in supply option is considered the worst option of the five.

Results indicate that respondents are on average willing to pay almost $150 to obtain the fourth, demand management, option rather than the base case scenario involving water restrictions of 20 per cent. This $150 is in excess of the $50 increase in charges associated with the base option. In terms of willingness to pay, the next most preferred options are large scale recycling and the Tennent Dam. Respondents are willing to pay substantially less for the outcomes associated with the Coree Dam option than the Tennent option. These results are consistent with the community rankings presented above, with the above-noted exception regarding the second and third ranked options.

4.5 CONCLUSION

The purpose of the study was to provide ACTEW with information to assist them in their long term water supply planning. Several issues that ACTEW will need to consider in planning were revealed by the study. These are:

- the importance of ensuring water supply levels to provide for some green public spaces;
- the willingness to adopt recycling for outside use;
- the resistance to recycled water for potable use; and
- the value of protecting the environment – in particular the rivers in the region.

The study provided ACTEW with a quantitative tool to assess the community acceptability of water supply options. The advantages of the choice modelling study over the contingent valuation study, which was also undertaken as part of the project, were obvious to ACTEW. The choice modelling results have and will continue to be useful in ACTEW's planning process, while the contingent valuation results have already dated as new options for water supply have emerged.

5. Remnant Vegetation and Wetlands Protection: Non-market Valuation

Jeff Bennett, John Rolfe and Mark Morrison

5.1 INTRODUCTION

Benefit cost analysis is an appealing tool for those responsible for the allocation of environmental assets. However, the alternative uses to which environmental assets may be put frequently generate benefits and costs that are not marketed and hence not readily valued in dollar terms. This is especially the case when non-use environmental benefits and costs such as existence values are likely to be pivotal in the selection of the preferred allocation. Hence, for decision makers to be able to apply benefit-cost analysis, these non-market values must be estimated.

Choice modelling has been used to generate estimates of non-marketed, non-use environmental benefits in the two Australian case studies detailed in this chapter. Both case studies involve the allocation of environmental assets where the non-use values of environmental protection are critical in the development of policy.

The first case study is centred on the issue of wetland protection. The Macquarie Marshes in central western New South Wales compete for water with the irrigation industry of the Macquarie River valley. Allocating more water to the wetlands creates primarily non-use environmental values as visitation to the area is relatively minor. It also causes costs in forgone irrigation production. To weigh up these costs and benefits, information regarding the extent of the non-use values generated by allocating more water to the wetlands is useful.

The second case study involves the setting of tree clearing restrictions in the Desert Uplands region of Central Queensland. Conservation interests are keen to restrict tree clearing on cattle properties in the region to maintain non-use values associated with this remnant native vegetation. Cattle growers are keen to clear in order to improve the profitability of their properties and so experience an opportunity cost if clearing is restricted. Again the trade-off involved in setting tree clearing restrictions involves weighing up a monetary cost against the non-use values of the protected remnant native vegetation. Once more, the use values involved are small because so few people visit the area involved.

Both of these case studies are outlined in this chapter. First the Macquarie Marshes case is detailed. Some features of the area and the conflict are set out. The process involved in carrying out the CM application is then described and the results reported. Subsequently, the Desert Uplands case study is detailed in a similar fashion.

5.2 WETLAND CHOICES IN THE MACQUARIE RIVER VALLEY

The Macquarie Marshes is an ephemeral wetland that was once the largest wetlands in New South Wales, with an area of about 5000 km^2. A nature reserve, which is contained in the Marshes, is listed as a wetland of international importance under the Ramsar Convention. The Marshes provide an important habitat for waterbirds and act as a filter that improves downstream water quality. They also provide high quality stock feed for sheep and cattle grazing enterprises.

In 1967 Burrendong Dam on the Macquarie River was opened and a large area of irrigated agriculture was developed. The extensive use of water for irrigation has meant that, compared to pre-irrigation years, much less water reaches the Macquarie Marshes. As a result there has been a significant decline in the size and health of the Marshes. Since 1967 the area of the Marshes has fallen from 5000 km^2 to 1200 km^2 and weeds have affected much of the remaining wetland. The frequency of waterbird breeding events has fallen from every year to every four years, and the number of endangered and protected bird species using the wetlands has fallen from 34 to 12.

The New South Wales Government in conjunction with the local Water Management Committee is responsible for allocating water between the Marshes and irrigators. A reassessment of allocations occurs every two years. One of the objectives in carrying out this case study was to provide information that could be used in this reassessment process.

5.3 THE WETLAND CHOICE MODELLING APPLICATION

The questionnaire used for this case study was developed using the results from eight focus groups and a pretest involving 50 respondents (see Morrison *et al.* 1997). The focus groups were used to determine the attributes that should be included in the choice sets, and to refine a draft questionnaire.

In the questionnaire, respondents were told that there were three broad options available for the management of the Macquarie Marshes: to continue the current situation, to increase water for the wetlands, or to increase water for irrigation. The scenario presented to respondents was that it would be possible to purchase water for the wetlands from farmers on the existing water trading market. This would mean that the sale of water rights would be voluntary and farmers would be compensated for giving up the right to water. Respondents were told that the Government did not have sufficient money to purchase the water from existing revenue and that it would be necessary to charge households in New South Wales a one-off levy on water rates in 1998.

Respondents were then presented with six choice sets showing various options for the Macquarie Marshes, the first of which was an example (see Table 5.1). The options in the choice sets were defined using five different attributes: water rates, irrigation related employment, wetlands area, frequency of waterbird breeding and endangered and protected species present.[1] Respondents were asked for their preferred choice from each of five sets of options. Finally, before answering the choice sets, respondents were requested to keep in mind their available income and other things on which they may need to spend money. They were also reminded that other environmental projects may cost them money in the future.

Over a single weekend 416 drop-off and pick-up questionnaires were distributed in Sydney. Three attempts were made to pick up each completed questionnaire, and after this a mail-back option was provided; 318 usable questionnaires were collected.

The socio-demographics of the respondents and the population average are shown in Table 5.2.

5.4 WETLAND RESULTS

Two different multinomial logit (MNL) models were estimated using the data from the Macquarie Marshes survey. Definitions of the coefficients used in these models are presented in Table 5.3. The first is a basic model which shows the importance of choice set attributes in explaining respondents' choices across the four different options: continue current situation (option 1), increase water to wetlands (options 2 and 3) and less water to the wetlands (option 4). The second model includes both socio-economic and attitudinal variables in addition to the attributes in the choice sets.

Four utility functions (V_{1-4}) were derived from the initial MNL model. Each function represents the utility generated by one of the four options.

Option 1 is the status quo, options 2 and 3 are options whereby more water would be allocated to the Marshes and option 4 involves a reduction in water to the Marshes:

$$V_1 = \beta_1.RATE+\beta_2.JOBS+\beta_3.AREA+\beta_4.BREED+\beta_5.ENDSPECIES$$
$$V_2 = C1+\beta_1.RATE+\beta_2.JOBS+\beta_3.AREA+\beta_4.BREED+\beta_5.ENDSPECIES$$
$$V_3 = C1+\beta_1.RATE+\beta_2.JOBS+\beta_3.AREA+\beta_4.BREED+\beta_5.ENDSPECIES$$
$$V_4 = C2$$

Table 5.1 Example of a choice set from the Macquarie Marshes questionnaire

Outcome	Option 1: Continue current situation	Option 2: Increase water to Macquarie Marshes	Option 3: Increase water to Macquarie Marshes
Your water rates (one-off increase)	no change	$20 increase	$50 increase
Irrigation related employment	4 400 jobs	4 350 jobs	4 350 jobs
Wetlands area	1 000 km^2	1 250 km^2	1 650 km^2
Waterbirds breeding	every 4 years	every 3 years	every year
Endangered and protected species present	12 species	25 species	15 species

☐ I would choose option 1

☐ I would choose option 2

☐ I would choose option 3

☐ I would not choose any of these options because I would prefer more water to be allocated for irrigation

Table 5.2 Socio-demographics of the respondents

Variable	Sample average	Sydney average
Age (>17 years)	44.3	43.9
Sex (% male)	55.8	49.2
Children (%)	72.1	67.0[a]
Own house (%)	71.3	67.4
Education (% > year 12)	74.6	77.4
Income ($)	54,680	46,184 (household)
Employed full or part time (%)	65.7 (> 18 years)	59.3 (>15 years)[a,b]

Notes:
[a]   state average
[b]   the % employed > 18 years was not available
Source: Australian Bureau of Statistics 1996 Census data

There are three alternative specific constants (C1, C1 and C2) in this model for options 1, 2 and 3. The alternative specific constants for options 2 and 3 (the increase water to the Marshes options) were constrained to be equal because a generic format and an experimental design that was close to orthogonal were used to develop the choice sets.

For the first three utility functions, utility is determined by the levels of the five attributes in the choice sets (RATES, JOBS, AREA, BREED, ENDSPECIES). Hence the model provides an estimate of the effect of a change in any of these attributes on the probability that one of these options will be chosen. For the fourth utility function, only an alternative specific constant is included. This is because no attributes were used to define the fourth option in any of the choice sets.

The results for this model are shown in Table 5.4 as 'Model 1'. The coefficients for all of the attributes in the choice sets are significant at the 1 per cent level or better and all have the a priori expected sign. These results indicate that positive non-use values exist for both environmental and social outcomes (that is, respondents valued the environmental attributes of wetland protection and they also valued the non-use benefits of jobs created by irrigation development). The overall model is also significant at the 1 per cent level, as shown by the chi-squared statistic. The explanatory power of the model is relatively high, with an adjusted rho squared of 19.6 per cent.[2]

In order to test the accuracy of the assumption of independently and identically distributed (IID - Gumbell) errors in this basic model, a mother logit model was estimated. A likelihood ratio test was conducted to test whether the multinomial or mother logit is the true model. This test showed

Table 5.3 Definitions of variables

Variable		Mean value
C1, C2	Alternative specific constants for options 2 and 3 and 4 respectively	—
INCOME	Respondent's household income	$54,680
CHILD	Dummy variable showing whether respondents have children	0.72
VISIT	Dummy variable representing whether a respondent is intending to visit the Marshes in the future	0.46
PRODEV	Dummy variable showing that a respondent is pro-development	0.10
PROGRE	Dummy variable showing that a respondent is pro-environment	0.36
RATE	Water rates	—
JOBS	Irrigation related employment	—
AREA	Wetlands area	—
BREED	Frequency of waterbird breeding	—
ENDSPECIES	Number of endangered and protected species present	—

that the initial basic model suffers from violations of the IID assumption at the 5 per cent significance level. There are various reasons why this may have occurred. One possibility is the existence of random taste variations (that is heterogeneous preferences amongst respondents). To test this, a further model that included socio-economic interactions was estimated.

The specification for this model is as follows:

$$V_1 = \beta_1.RATE + \beta_2.RATES*CHILD + \beta_3.RATES*VISIT$$
$$+ \beta_4.JOBS + \beta_5.AREA + \beta_6.BREED + \beta_7.ENDSPECIES$$

$V_2 =$ C1+C1.INCOME+C1.CHILD+C1*PROGRE+C1*VISIT
$+\beta_1$.RATES $+\beta_2$.RATES*CHILD$+\beta_3$.RATES*VISIT$+\beta_4$.JOBS
$+\beta_5$.AREA $+\beta_6$.BREED$+\beta_7$.ENDSPECIES
$V_3 =$ C1+C1.INCOME+C1.CHILD+C1*PROGRE+C1*VISIT
$+\beta_1$.RATES$+\beta_2$.RATES*CHILD$+\beta_3$.RATES*VISIT
$+\beta_4$.JOBS$+\beta_5$.AREA$+\beta_6$.BREED$+\beta_7$.ENDSPECIES
$V_4 =$ C2+ C2*PRODEV

Socio-economic and attitudinal variables can be included in MNL models in two different ways.[3] The first way is by interactions with the attributes in the choice sets. In this model, one socio-economic and one attitudinal variable (CHILD and VISIT) are interacted with RATES. These interactions show how the variables CHILD and VISIT modify the effect of RATES on the probability of choice.

The second method used to include socio-economic and attitudinal variables is through interactions with the alternative specific constants.[4] In this model, four variables are included as interactions with the alternative specific constant for options 2 and 3 (INCOME, CHILD, PROGRE and VISIT) and one variable is interacted with the alternative specific constant for option 4 (PRODEV). These interactions show the effect of various attitudes and socio-economic characteristics on the probability that a respondent will choose either option 2 or 3, or option 4.

Theory provides some guidance in terms of the expected signs of several of the above variables. PROGRE should have a positive sign as respondents with a pro-environmental orientation would be expected to choose options 2 or 3 more frequently. VISIT should have a positive sign as respondents who intend to visit the Marshes in the future may have positive option value (see Bishop 1982). INCOME should have a positive sign as respondents with higher income should have a greater capacity to pay. PRODEV should also have a positive sign as respondents with a pro-development orientation would be expected to favour option 4 with its further development of the Marshes area and the creation of more jobs. The sign for CHILD is, however, ambiguous. Bequest motives would be expected to induce higher willingness to pay, yielding a positive coefficient; however, households with children may have lower disposable income, thereby lowering willinginess to pay.

The results for this model are shown as 'Model 2' in Table 5.4. The four variables (INCOME, CHILD, PROGRE and VISIT) interacted with the alternative specific constant for options 2 and 3 are significant at the 1 per cent level or better. Consistent with expectations, these interactions show that respondents were more likely to support either options 2 or 3 if they (a) had a higher income; (b) had children; (c) had a pro-environmental orientation; and (d) were intending to visit the Macquarie Marshes in the future.

Table 5.4 Multinomial logit models 1 and 2

	Model 1	Model 2
C1	−0.30*	−1.59***
	(0.19)	(0.30)
C1 * INCOME		0.79E−5***
		(0.22E−5)
C1 * CHILD		0.62***
		(0.20)
C1* PROGRE		1.36***
		(0.18)
C1 * VISIT		0.64***
		(0.19)
C2	5.53	5.82*
	(2.91)	(3.46)
C2 * PRODEV		2.42***
		(0.31)
RATES	−0.12E−1***	−0.13E−1***
	(0.81E−3)	(0.21E−2)
RATES*CHILD		−0.35E−2*
		(0.21E−2)
RATES * VISIT		0.42E−2**
		(0.20E−2)
JOBS	0.17E−2***	0.19E−3***
	(0.65E−3)	(0.78E−3)
AREA	0.56E−3***	0.55E−3***
	(0.13E−3)	(0.15E−3)
BREED	−0.31***	−0.29***
	(0.51E−1)	(0.58E−1)
ENDSPECIES	0.50E−1***	0.54E−1***
	(0.97E−2)	(0.11E−1)
Summary statistics		
Log-likelihood	−1756.497	−1184.993
χ^2 (constants only)	362.050	493.480
ρ^2	0.197	0.277
ρ^2 adjusted	0.195	0.275
Iterations completed	6	6

'Model 2' in Table 5.4 contains an interaction between the constant for option 4 and PRODEV. As expected, this interaction indicates that respondents are more likely to choose option 4 (less water to the wetlands) if they have a pro-development orientation.

'Model 2' in Table 5.4 also contains the variables based on the attributes from the choice sets, and two interactions with the RATES variable. Similar to 'Model 1', all of the choice set attributes are significant at the 1 per cent level or better. One of the interactions with RATES (VISIT) is significant at the 5 per cent level and the other interaction (CHILD) is significant at the 10 per cent level. The overall model is significant at the 1 per cent level and the explanatory power is also high. Compared to the initial model, the explanatory power of the model has increased to 28 per cent.

In order to test for the accuracy of the assumption of IID error terms a mother logit model was estimated. The likelihood ratio test indicated that at the 5 per cent significance level the multinomial logit model was the true model. Hence the inclusion of socio-economic and attitudinal variables was sufficient to avoid any violation of the IID assumption. This suggests that the main cause of the IID violation in the first model was the existence of random taste variations.

The estimated models can be used to estimate the willingness to pay for a change in one of the choice attributes. These are the implicit prices or marginal rates of substitution between the attribute of interest and the monetary attribute. The implicit price for wetland area is: $IP_{AREA} = \beta_{AREA}/\beta_{RATES}$. Estimates of implicit prices for each of the non-monetary attributes in the choice sets are reported in Table 5.5. Confidence intervals for the implicit prices have been calculated using the Krinsky and Robb (1986) procedure.

Table 5.5 Estimates of implicit prices ($A1997)[5]

	Model 1		Model 2	
	Mean	95% confidence interval	Mean	95% confidence interval
JOBS	0.13	0.12–0.14	0.14	0.13–0.15
AREA	0.046	0.044–0.048	0.040	0.038–0.042
BREED	24.62	23.80–25.45	21.82	20.98–22.67
ENDSPECIES	4.04	3.86–4.21	4.16	4.00–4.32

These estimates indicate that, for example, respondents were willing to pay 13 cents for an extra irrigation related job preserved and about $4 for an additional endangered species to be present in the wetlands. They are based on a ceteris paribus assumption, that is, all other parameters are held constant except the attribute for which the implicit price is being calculated.

Implicit prices are not estimates of compensating surplus of the type required for use in benefit-cost analysis. Estimating the overall willingness to pay for a change from the current situation requires further calculations. This is because the attributes in the choice sets do not capture all the reasons why respondents might choose to increase water to the wetlands. To estimate overall willingness to pay it is necessary to include the alternative specific constant. The alternative specific constant captures systematic but unobserved information about why respondents chose a particular option (that is, unrelated to the choice set attributes). To illustrate this process, estimates are provided for four alternative scenarios. The current situation and four scenarios are as follows:

Current situation: Wetlands area is equal to 1 000 km^2, waterbird breeding every four years, 12 endangered and protected species present, and irrigation related employment, that is, equal to 4 400 jobs.

Scenario 1: Wetlands area increases to 1 400 km^2, the frequency of waterbird breeding increases to every three years, the number of endangered and protected species present increases to 16, and there are no employment effects.

Scenario 2: Wetlands area increases to 1 400 km^2, the frequency of waterbird breeding increases to every three years, the number of endangered and protected species present increases to 16, and irrigation related employment falls by 100 jobs.

Scenario 3: Wetlands area increases to 1 800 km^2, the frequency of waterbird breeding increases to every two years, the number of endangered and protected species present increases to 20.

Scenario 4: Wetlands area increases to 1 800 km^2, the frequency of waterbird breeding increases to every two years, the number of endangered and protected species present increases to 20, and irrigation related employment falls by 150 jobs.

Estimates of compensating surplus are calculated using the following equation:

$$CS = \frac{-1}{\beta_M}(V_C - V_N) \qquad (5.1)$$

where β_M is the marginal utility of income (assumed to be equal to the coefficient for rates;

V_C represents the utility of the current situation; and

V_N represents the utility of the new option.

To use this equation to estimate compensating surplus it is first necessary to calculate the utility associated with the current option and the option being considered. Using the 'Model 1', this is achieved by substituting the model coefficients and the attribute levels for the current option (that is, V_1):

$$V_C = \beta_{RATES}*RATES + \beta_{JOBS}*JOBS + \beta_{AREA}*AREA$$
$$+ \beta_{BREED}*BREED + \beta_{ENDSPECIES}*ENDSPECIES$$
$$= -0.12E-1*0 + -0.17E-2*4400 + 0.56E-3*1400 + -0.31*3 +$$
$$0.50E-1*16$$
$$= 7.38 \tag{5.2}$$

The value of the utility of the alternative option is estimated in a similar way, except that the coefficient for the alternative specific constant for options 2 and 3 is included and the attribute levels associated with the changed scenario are used. For scenario 1:

$$V_N = C1 + \beta_{RATES}*RATES + \beta_{JOBS}*JOBS + \beta_{AREA}*AREA$$
$$+ \beta_{BREED}*BREED + \beta_{ENDSPECIES}*ENDSPECIES$$
$$= -0.30 + -0.12E-1*0 + -0.17E-2*4400 + 0.56E-3*1400$$
$$+ -0.31*3 + 0.50E-1*16$$
$$= 7.82 \tag{5.3}$$

The compensating surplus for the change from the status quo to the new scenario is then estimated by calculating the difference between these two values, and multiplying this by the negative inverse of the coefficient for rates. For the change to scenario 1:

$$CS = -1/(-0.12E-1) * (7.38 - 7.82) = -\$36.10 \tag{5.4}$$

The negative sign indicates that to maintain utility at level V_c, given an improvement in wetlands quality, income must be reduced by \$36.10. Hence, the willingness to pay per household for an improvement in wetland quality from the status quo to scenario 1 is equal to \$36.10.

Estimates of willingness to pay for the four scenarios are presented in Table 5.6. These are marginal estimates, showing willingness to pay for a change from the current situation. When estimating willingness to pay, all of the attitudinal variables were set to their mean levels, and Sydney averages were used for the socio-economic variables. Note that because Model 1 suffers from violations of the IIA property, Model 2 is the preferred model.

The importance of including employment effects when calculating willingness to pay for an environmental improvement is evident from these willingness to pay results. While the existence values for improved environmental quality outweigh the existence values for rural employment, including employment effects reduces willingness to pay by about 20–30 per cent in the scenarios presented here. Note that Scenarios 1 and 2 and Scenarios 3 and 4 differ only in terms of employment effects.

These per household estimates can be aggregated to determine the willingness to pay of the wider community to achieve the four scenarios for improved environmental quality at the Macquarie Marshes. Similarly, the modelling results described above can also be used to value a range of other scenarios resulting from different water allocations. Water managers could then utilise these value estimates, and estimates of the value of any changes in agricultural production, to determine which scenarios are likely to have the greatest net benefits for the community.

Table 5.6 Estimates of household willingness to pay ($A)

	Model 1	Model 2
Scenario 1	36.10	48.75
Scenario 2	22.36	34.04
Scenario 3	94.73	102.62
Scenario 4	67.25	73.19

5.5 REMNANT VEGETATION CHOICES IN THE DESERT UPLANDS

The Desert Uplands is one of 13 terrestrial biogeographic regions of Queensland. Covering some 6 881 790 hectares (4 per cent of Queensland), it straddles the low tablelands of the Great Dividing Range in central-western Queensland.

The region is essentially a band of scattered woodland country between the open grasslands of the arid western plains and the semi-arid to sub-humid brigalow (*Acacia harpophilla*) country to the east. The region is relatively unproductive for pastoral and agricultural purposes compared to other regions in the south and east of Queensland. This is because of its relatively low rainfall and poor soils and its vegetation, which is reasonably unpalatable to domestic stock (Rolfe *et al.* 1997). One reason why the term 'desert' is attached to the area is because spinifex (*Triodia* spp.), a grass common to the drier areas of Australia, is a major grass species in the region.

The region is used almost exclusively for pastoral purposes. Cattle are bred and fattened for beef production over much of the region, and sheep are also run in some areas. Pastoralists have been attempting to increase the carrying capacity of their land by a variety of methods, including the clearing of trees and the introduction on non-native grass species. Initially these developments were limited to patches of more fertile soils. The region now has one of the highest clearing rates in Australia, with between 4 per cent and 8 per cent of many broad country types being cleared between 1992 and 1995 (McCosker and Cox 1996).

While the region is still relatively undeveloped compared to the brigalow regions to the east, and the integrity of most ecosystems in the region remains high, trends in management and development appear to be impacting on biodiversity (Landsberg *et al.* 1998; McCosker and Cox 1996). Tree clearing is the most visible form of change, but overgrazing, land degradation and weed invasion are also problems.

Approximately 80 per cent of the region is held as leasehold tenure, where the State Government is the legal owner of the natural resources. Leaseholders must gain permission to clear trees through the Department of Natural Resources. In issuing permits for broadscale tree clearing, the State Government policy calls for a balance between the benefits of increased productivity (most of which accrues directly to the landholders) against the environmental costs of diminished vegetation cover (which are more broadly spread across the regional and national communities). It is these environmental costs that the CM application described here is directed at estimating.

The Queensland Government has recently been revising its tree clearing policies, with the result that vegetation communities which are endangered or vulnerable (whether through past clearing activities or limited initial occurrence) are now protected. Other vegetation communities can be cleared to 20 per cent of their original extent on individual properties, with 30 per cent of each vegetation type to be retained across the region.

5.6 THE REMNANT NATIVE VEGETATION CHOICE MODELLING APPLICATION

The project reported here followed a two-stage approach in developing trade-off scenarios for a CM application protection. The focus was on establishing the values that Queenslanders might hold for environmental and social attributes in the Desert Uplands region.

The first stage was a detailed overview of information available about the region relating to environmental attributes and the possible consequences of tree clearing activities. The level of knowledge about environmental systems and relationships is not high, and there is very limited knowledge about the possible long term effects of broadscale tree clearing and the extent to which it might occur (Rolfe *et al.* 1997). This uncertainty results in a very broad spectrum of possible outcomes. These have been reflected in the wide range across which each of the attributes was allowed to vary.

The second stage of the project involved focus groups being held in both Brisbane and Emerald, the latter being a town in the regional area (Blamey *et al.* 1997). The primary purpose of the focus groups was to identify the broad attributes of importance to people in making choices about the impact of tree clearing in the Desert Uplands, as well as to identify levels of knowledge and familiarity with the case study of interest.

A number of possible attributes were identified in the issues and focus group stages of the project. These were subsequently condensed (for logistical and modelling purposes) to six possible attributes:

- levy on income tax;
- income lost to the region ($ million);
- jobs lost to the region;
- number of endangered species lost to the region;
- reduction in population size of the non-threatened species;
- loss in area of unique ecosystems.

The levels across which each attribute could vary reflected the broad possible range of resource use options in the biogeographic region, rather than just the outcomes relating immediately to tree clearing. For example, the number of endangered species that was used in the experiment reflected the total number that might possibly be affected by development and grazing pressure options. Selection of attribute level ranges in this way had the advantage of making the results broadly applicable to resource use options in the region, and avoided the difficulty of disaggregating changes between tree clearing and other development and management impacts. As well, it helped to ensure that choices were framed against the pool of development and preservation outcomes.

To generate a representative sample of the distribution of possible scenarios and to ensure that scenarios were orthogonal, an experimental design process was used. A range of specific modelling issues were tested by offering slightly different versions of the surveys to different samples of the respondents involved. The results of these methodological issues have been reported in Blamey *et al.* (1998a, 1999b).

An example of a choice set presented to respondents is presented in Figure 5.1. Respondents were presented with a status quo option (Option A), which was consistent across the choice sets, and two options for increased preservation (B and C), which varied according to the experimental design. The description for Option A, together with the background material presented, made it clear that some standards of protection were already being met under the current tree clearing guidelines.

The final version of the survey questionnaire included a number of background, attitude and respondent characteristic questions as well as the series of nine choice sets. The questionnaires were administered in a door-knock drop-off/pick-up format to 480 Brisbane households in November 1997.

Implications	Option A Current Guidelines	Option B	Option C
Levy on your income tax ($)	none	60	20
Income lost to the region ($ million)	none	5	10
Jobs lost in region	none	15	40
Number of endangered species lost to region	18	8	4
Reduction in population size of non-threatened species (%)	80	75	45
Loss in area of unique ecosystems (%)	40	15	28

Figure 5.1 A typical choice set

5.7 REMNANT NATIVE VEGETATION RESULTS

Some of the variables that described respondents' attitudes were found to be highly significant in building accurate models of choice. These are described in Table 5.7. The accuracy of the choice models estimated was improved by adopting a nested structure where respondents were assumed to have made an initial choice between 'doing nothing' and 'doing something'. The results of a nested logit model specification are shown in Table 5.8.

If respondents decided they would 'do nothing', they were assumed to have choosen Option A, which was the status quo option in the survey. If respondents made an initial choice to 'do something', they were then assumed to choose between Option B and Option C on the basis of the six attributes and associated levels presented in the choice sets. Three attitudinal variables were found to be significant in determining how respondents made the initial choice between 'doing nothing' and 'doing something'. These are reflected in the branch choice equations, which indicate the relative utility of 'doing something' versus 'doing nothing'.

Table 5.7 Non-attribute variable definitions

Variable	Definition
const	Alternative-specific constant taking on a value of 1 for options 2 and 3 in the choice sets, and 0 for the base option.
const1	Alternative-specific constant taking on a value of 1 for option 2 in the choice sets, and 0 for the base option.
envatt	Dummy variable taking on a value of 1 for respondents indicating that, over the years, when have heard about proposed conflicts between development and the environment, they have tended to 'More frequently favour preservation of the environment'; 0 otherwise.
confuse	Five point Likert scale response indicating extent of disagreement with the statement 'I found questions 3 to 10 [the choice set questions] confusing'.

Respondents with a pro-environment orientation (envatt = 1) were more likely to choose one of the environmental improvement options than respondents with a pro-development perspective (envatt = 0). Those who reported being confused by the choices presented in the questionnaire (confuse = 1) were more likely to choose the status quo, as were those who had problems with the notion of a tree levy (object = 1). The results suggest that despite the best efforts to minimise confusion and protest through questionnaire design, a significant degree of confusion and protest -quo, potentially similar to that reported by Adamowicz *et al.* (1998b).

The choice between Options B and C is modelled as shown under the heading 'Utility functions' in Table 5.8. The attributes in the utility function are all signed as expected and are highly significant. The negative coefficient on *Levy* indicates that respondents are less likely to choose options with increasing payment amounts. The negative signs on the other coefficients means that increasing amounts of the other attributes (for example, more job losses, more endangered species losses) are negatively correlated with choice.[6]

The application enabled the estimation of 'implicit prices' for the different attributes. These are reported in Table 5.9. The implicit prices for all the attributes are positive, implying that Brisbane households have positive values for increases in each attribute.

Table 5.8 Nested logit results

Variables	Coeff.	S. error
Utility functions		
const1	0.1644*	0.0663
levy on income tax	−0.0107**	0.0011
Jobs	−0.0324**	0.0053
Regional income	−0.0597**	0.0138
number of endangered species	−0.1214**	0.0111
Population of non-threatened species	−0.0180**	0.0029
area of unique ecosystems	−0.0392**	0.0065
Branch choice equations		
const	−1.9738**	0.5913
const*envatt	1.1344**	0.1105
const*object	−0.5750**	0.0501
const*confuse	−0.1550**	0.0477
Inclusive value parameters		
do something	0.1904*	0.0795
do nothing	1.0000	0.0000
Model statistics		
n (choice sets)	5769	5784
Log L	−1685.564	−1547.388
adj ρ^2 (%)	20.1	26.7

Notes:
* denotes significance at the 5% level
** denotes significance at the 1% level.

For the environmental attributes, the willingness to pay (WTP) per household to maintain endangered species in the region is $11.39 per species,

the WTP to avoid each 1 per cent loss in non-threatened species is $1.69, and
the WTP to avoid each 1 per cent loss in the area of unique ecosystems is
$3.68. For the social attributes, the WTP for job preservation is $3.04 per
job, while the WTP to maintain each million dollars of regional income is
$5.60.

Table 5.9 Part-worths for the different attributes

Variable	Part-worth $
Jobs	3.04
Regional income	5.60
Endangered species	11.39
Population of non-threatened species	1.69
Unique ecosystems	3.68

A further way of using the CM results is through the comparison of
estimates for changes in community well-being (CS) for different scenarios of
tree clearing restrictions. Because there are some interactions in the way that
people view the attributes together in a scenario, the part-worths cannot
simply be added together to find values for different options. Instead, values
for a particular scenario (X regional income, Y jobs, Z endangered species,
and so on) have to be calculated, and then compared to values for other
scenarios.

The results of such an exercise are reported in Table 5.10. For example,
the value of a policy to restrict tree clearing that would give rise to a scenario
described by option A gives a CS of approximately $87 per household in
Brisbane. This scenario may be unrealistic because of the possibility of losses
in jobs and regional income. When some estimates for these social costs are
added in (as in option B), the CS for the environmental protection falls to $76
per household.

If the exercise is repeated for greater levels of environmental protection,
then similar results occur. Option C involves further protection of the
environment over current measures (for example, ten species will be
protected from being lost to the region, a further 45 per cent of non-
threatened species, for example trees, will be preserved, and an additional 20
per cent of unique ecosystems will be preserved). The willingness to pay for
this scenario is $117 per household. When some offsetting social costs are
added to the scenario (as in Option D), the willingness to pay falls to $88 per
household.

The same type of exercise can be repeated for smaller increases in protection levels. In Queensland there are substantial levels of debate about proposed tree clearing controls over freehold land. These will add some further restrictions to the amount of overall clearing within the region, particularly in ecosystems that are 'Of Concern', 'Vulnerable' or 'Endangered'. There will be little change to clearing rates for 'Not of Concern' vegetation types. Because the controls will affect some remaining pockets of high quality land that remain uncleared, potential production losses may be higher than if only eucalypt woodland were affected.

Table 5.10 Profiles used for welfare estimation

Attribute	Change from current trends OPTION A	Change from current trends OPTION B	Change from current trends OPTION C	Change from current trends OPTION D
Jobs lost in the region	0	10	0	30
Regional income lost	0	$5 million	0	$10 million
Additional species preserved in area	2	2	10	10
Additional % of non-threatened species preserved	30	30	45	45
Additional area of unique ecosystems preserved (%)	10	10	20	20
Compensating surplus ($)	87	76	117	88

In Table 5.11, the values for profiles that involve only a 10 per cent increase in overall clearing restrictions across the region, but relatively greater impacts on preserving unique ecosystems and endangered species than were used in the earlier profiles are presented. These profiles reflect more closely (but not exactly) some of the possible outcomes that might be available if tree clearing controls were extended over freehold land.

It is notable that Option F, which allows some strong social impacts from an increase in protection rates of 10 per cent, still has a substantial compensating surplus of $80. Even if the impact on regional income of increased tree clearing controls is doubled to $10 million (as in Option G), the willingness to pay only falls to $74.50. Job losses would need to rise to 180 (Option H) before the per household willingness to pay of the Brisbane population for the increased protection scenarios falls to zero.

Table 5.11 Additional profiles used for welfare estimation

Attribute	Change from current trends	Change from current trends	Change from current trends
	OPTION F	OPTION G	OPTION H
Jobs lost in the region	50	50	180
Regional income lost ($ million)	5	10	10
Additional species preserved in area	2	2	2
Additional % of non-threatened species preserved	10	10	10
Additional area of unique ecosystems preserved (%)	30	30	30
Compensating surplus ($)	80	74.50	0

The non-use values that can be estimated from these different protection scenarios are suitable for inclusion in a benefit-cost analysis framework. For a study on remnant vegetation in a region such as the Desert Uplands, it would be expected that restrictions on tree clearing will cause subsequent losses of potential production. As well, there may be other indirect impacts of increased restrictions, such as reduced greenhouse gas emissions from lower vegetation loss. Typically, the economic evaluation of whether or not clearing restrictions should be increased will depend on whether the production losses from a protection option are greater or less than the indirect gains as well as the non-use values associated with both the environmental and social changes involved. The CM exercise reported here provides a mechanism for estimating the latter amount.

5.8 CONCLUSIONS

The two case studies reported in this chapter illustrate how non-use values can be estimated for natural resource impacts.   The case studies are representative of two major topics in natural resource conservation in Australia: wetlands protection remnant and native vegetation protection. In each case, non-use values are likely to be an important component of overall value assessment. The results are thus of broad interest and relevance to a large number of other environmental resource issues in the country.

Three outcomes of the case studies reported here are important to note. First, the CM experiments have jointly estimated the non-use values associated with both environmental and social factors. This means that all the major non-use values associated with particular resource use options have been captured in a single exercise, reducing the number of factors that have to be included in other CBA elements. As well, the simultaneous estimation of non-use values for environmental and social factors appears to have significant framing advantages in that scenarios with these (usually) offsetting factors may appear more realistic to respondents than would scenarios that focused on one or the other.

Second, the experiments reported here have generated outcomes where choices can be determined by the attributes used to make up the profiles. As would be expected a priori, the attitudes and socio-economic characteristics of the people responding to the surveys may also be important in predicting how choices are made. In the remnant vegetation study, the attitudinal variables were important in determining the decision path that survey respondents choose when a nested decision tree was modelled. The detail available about preferred choices and trade-offs provides a rich information base for policy makers.

Third, the models of choice that were generated can be used to provide estimates of value in two important ways. Values can estimated for part-worths (value of changes in a single variable with other factors held constant) or for profiles (combinations of variables used to describe different scenarios). This flexibility of value estimates allows policy makers to repeat their assessments of resource allocation for small changes in attributes, thus helping to establish more accurately packages of resource allocation that will maximise overall benefits to society.

In both case studies, the information generated provides policy makers with important inputs to the benefit-cost framework. When the values of the protection profiles reported in this chapter are extrapolated across their relevant populations, substantial estimates of non-use values are gained. While it is unlikely that these will always outweigh the opportunity costs of production/development options in each case, they are likely to allow the identification of some resource use options where protection of natural resources delivers major benefits to Australian society.

NOTES

1. The attribute levels used in the choice sets were: water rates ($0, $20, $50, $150), irrigation related employment (4 400 jobs, 4 350 jobs, 4 250 jobs), wetlands area (1000 km², 1250 km², 1650 km², 2000 km²), frequency of waterbird breeding (every 4 years, every 3 years, every 2 years, every year) and number of endangered and protected species present (12 species, 15 species, 20 species, 25 species).
2. Rho-squared is similar to R^2 in conventional regression analysis. It is equal to one minus the ratio of the unrestricted log-likelihood over the restricted log likelihood. Hensher and Johnson (1981) comment that 'values of rho squared of between 0.2 to 0.4 are considered extremely good fits so that the analyst should not be looking for values in excess of 0.9 as is often the case when using R^2 in ordinary regression'.
3. All variables were initially interacted with both the attribute variables and the alternative specific constants, and were deleted if they were insignificant.
4. Because of the interactions with the alternative specific constants, socio-economic variables can only be included for J−1 alternatives.
5. The means reported in this table differ slightly from the actual implicit prices as they are the means calculated using the Krinsky and Robb (1986) procedure.
6. These results are explained in some detail in Blamey *et al.* (1998a).

6.   Green Product Choice

Russell Blamey, Jeff Bennett, Jordan J. Louviere and Mark Morrison

6.1 INTRODUCTION

The past couple of decades have seen a dramatic increase in the demand for, and supply of, 'environmentally friendly' or 'green' products. Much of the early academic work concerning such products focused on the identification of demographic, attitudinal and personality correlates of the ecologically conscious consumer (Anderson and Cunningham 1972; Kinnear *et al.* 1974; Arbuthnot 1977). Vogel (cited in Simmons 1995, p. 149) observed that as 'environmental concern increases, there is a tendency ... for "ecologically responsible" citizens to express their identification with the public interest by their private purchasing decisions. People can thus influence environmental issues by "voting" with their dollars, as well as with their ballot'. Whilst studies have provided some understanding of the type of individual most likely to engage in pro-environmental acts, explanatory power has typically been only modest (Granzin and Olsen 1991) and results have been mixed (see Schwepker *et al.* 1991 for a review). Recent research appears to be suggesting that correlates and determinants of environmentally responsible behaviour are highly context specific. For example, Pickett *et al.* (1993) found support for Balderjahn's (1998) claim that a 'general picture' of an ecologically consumer does not exist.

Comparatively little academic work has been directed at understanding the behavioural patterns involved in green product choice (Pickett *et al.* 1993). While most of this research has been conducted by market research companies, the results of which are not in the public domain, some findings are scattered throughout publications such as *Marketing News*. For example, two-thirds of respondents to a survey conducted for *Advertising Age* indicated they would switch to a brand of toothpaste in a recyclable tube, with half of these indicating that they would do so regardless of price (Chase 1991).

Results of another survey indicated that 84 per cent of respondents were interested in buying food in environmentally safe packaging and that 78 per cent indicated a willingness to pay a little more for such packaging (Jay 1990).

A growing body of research is now indicating that consumers are only willing to purchase green products within certain constraints. They may have threshold price, quality and/or convenience differences beyond which they are no longer willing to purchase the products. Roberts (1996) found that a measure of environmental concern explained only 6 per cent of the variation in the sample's green behaviour, concluding that 'other factors play a more important role ... It appears that price, convenience and value are the most important buying criteria' (1996, p. 217). Lynn (1991 p. 76) notes that it may 'only be on the fringes, among the deep greens, where people will ... buy something even if it is not really up to scratch'.

Several studies have now shown that consumers are only willing to pay a small percentage extra to obtain products that are 'green'. Miller (1990), for example, found that consumers are willing to pay up to 5 per cent more for a product in an environmentally friendly package. Thomas (1989) reports the results of a study in which half of those interviewed would pay at least 10 per cent more for ozone-friendly aerosols and for products in recycled packaging. According to a study conducted by the Roper Organisation in the US, Americans are only willing to pay a 6.6 per cent price premium for green products (Anonymous 1991). Finally, in an academic study, Simmons found that few green consumers were willing to consider reducing their overall consumption levels, and that, overall, they remained highly price and convenience conscious.[1, 2]

In this chapter, we illustrate the application of choice modelling (CM) to a real market good in the form of environmentally friendly toilet paper purchases. We illustrate how CM can be used to provide estimates of the relative importance of green product attributes and brand names, and the market shares for green products as a whole.

This chapter is structured as follows. Following a brief description of the scope of the study in section 6.2, the questionnaire design phase is described in detail in section 6.3. The sampling strategy is outlined in section 6.4, and results are presented in section 6.5.

6.2 SCOPE OF THE STUDY

After reviewing the different classes of supermarket products with an environmental dimension, a decision was made to focus on toilet paper. Toilet paper was chosen in preference to detergent because an examination of detergent products revealed that the vast majority of products employ a 'green' attribute: biodegradability. Although some detergents go to further lengths to minimise environmental impacts than simple 'biodegradable' claims, it was felt that toilet paper had a less complicated environmental dimension. Specifically, most toilet papers can be classified as using either standard bleached paper or recycled and unbleached paper. A number of products currently sold present variations on this theme.

To simplify sampling requirements and to enhance validity tests, it was decided to focus the whole study on one large supermarket, in an area where there are no other supermarkets of a similar size in close geographic proximity. The supermarket chosen was located in Canberra, Australia. The supermarket management agreed to provide scanner data and promotion and price data for the period during which the questionnaire was in the field. This permitted the results of the stated preference CM study to be compared with revealed preference supermarket scanner data for the same supermarket. Results of this comparison are presented in Chapter 9.

An inventory of toilet paper products on offer at the supermarket indicated a total of 11 brands and 49 different stock keeping units (SKUs). One characteristic of toilet paper is that virtually everyone uses it. Hence, the question the vast majority of consumers face is: Which one or more of these products will I buy?

6.3 QUESTIONNAIRE DESIGN

The questionnaire design phase involved two rounds of focus groups. The first set of two focus groups had the dual objective of identifying key decision parameters in the first half and seeking initial feedback on a draft questionnaire in the second half. A third focus group was run approximately two weeks later with the sole objective of piloting a revised draft questionnaire. Focus group participants were not told that the survey was about green products when they were recruited.

The first two focus groups began with open-ended questions. Participants were asked to write down the toilet paper products they normally purchase and why they purchase those products rather than others. The facilitator then asked each successive participant what they had written down. A laddering style of questioning was employed in order to ascertain why they had focused on certain brands and attributes. Such information not only helps with the design of the experiment, in terms of the selection of brands and attributes, but also provides important information regarding why different features are important to different individuals. This provides insights regarding the appropriate questions to be developed for the purposes of modelling heterogeneity in tastes. The item pool arising from the laddering approach was condensed into a 17 item set of agree–disagree questions. Each question creates a potential independent variable in the choice model.

Based on the focus group discussions, the most important attributes of toilet paper appeared to be softness, price, strength, number of rolls, environmental impact and whether or not the paper was scented. Two segments were most apparent within the focus groups. One segment of individuals appeared primarily concerned with maximising softness and strength, given some notion of a price constraint and household requirements in terms of preferred number of rolls. Ply and number of sheets appeared to operate as indicators of strength (and overall quality). Most individuals appeared to have one, two or three brands in their consideration set. The presence or absence of a special on price appeared to play an important role in choosing from the late consideration set. This is in contrast to whether the paper was scented, which appeared to play an important role in defining the early consideration set, but little role at the late consideration stage. Many individuals ruled out scented toilet paper at an early stage, only considering unscented papers at successive stages.

Focus group discussions also indicated significant habit and inertia in consumer choice processes. The green segment tended to be quite highly involved whilst at the same time exhibiting a high degree of brand loyalty. Some individuals in the green segment appeared to adopt a non-compensatory decision strategy with respect to the environmental attribute.

Unfortunately, it was not possible to include all brands and attributes within the choice sets.[3] Several simplifying assumptions were made to reduce the size of the problem to a manageable level. First, the attributes of three brands with the lowest market share were fixed in each choice set at their true market values. Second, the softness attribute was fixed for all alternatives at the level currently claimed by the manufacturer. The softness of the products was thus deliberately confounded with the brand image and hence the ASCs. This helped maintain a degree of plausibility with respect to brand–benefit associations, as well as eliminating one attribute from the design.

Six attributes were included within the final design. With the exception of the two variable green alternatives, a generic set of attribute levels was employed. Alternative specific attribute levels were employed for the environmental attribute to maintain plausibility and avoid unnecessary adverse reactions to 'green' brands that had been assigned 'non-green' levels of the environmental attributes. Table 6.1 lists the six attributes and their levels. The levels to be assigned to these attributes were chosen such that the resultant attribute-space would encompass the vast majority of the market at the supermarket.[4] All brands available at the store were represented in the choice sets (see Table 6.2). This enabled market share to be estimated. The qualitative variables shown in Table 6.1 were effect-coded so that the base category could be isolated rather than incorporated into the intercept term.

Table 6.1 Attributes, levels and corresponding variables

Attribute	Variable in model	Levels
Price	Price (in $)	16 levels ranging from $0.81–$9.89
Special on price	Special	1=yes (+15% on price) −1=no (−15% on price)
Number of rolls in pack	Rolls	2, 4, 6 or 10
Ply and sheets	Ply250	1= 2 ply and 250 sheets −1=1 ply and 500 sheets
Colour/patterns on paper	White	1=white; −1=prints; 0 if coloured or printed
	Owhite	1=off-white; −1=prints; 0 if coloured or printed
	Coloured	1=coloured; −1=prints; 0 if coloured or printed
Type of paper	Stand	1=standard; −1=recycled but not unbleached; 0 if unbleached but not recycled or both recycled and unbleached
	Ubleach	1=unbleached but not recycled; −1=recycled but not unbleached; 0 if standard or both recycled and unbleached
	Both	1=both recycled and unbleached; −1=recycled but not unbleached, 0 if unbleached but not recycled, or standard

The coefficient for the base level is calculated as the negative of the sum of the parameter values for the other levels.

Table 6.2 Brands included within choice sets

Brand	Fixed attributes or variable?
1. Bouquets	Variable
2. Delsey	Fixed
3. Home Brand	Variable
4. Kleenex	Variable
5. Naturale	Variable
6. Purex	Variable
7. Safe	Variable
8. Tenderly	Fixed
9. Sorbent	Variable
10. Wondersoft	Variable
11. Symphony	Fixed

In focus grouping the draft questionnaires, particular attention was paid to the clarity of the information provided, and whether individuals interpreted the information and questions in the way intended by the researchers. Ways in which the questionnaire could be shortened to reduce cognitive burden and confusion were also explored. Several important issues were identified. One of these involved a form of belief perseverance in which participants were reluctant to let go of the brand–benefit associations they had 'learned' from the market. Research in economic psychology has shown that once individuals have formed strong hypotheses, they are often inattentive to information that contradicts these hypotheses (Rabin 1998). Thus, once respondents have formed a belief, say that the brand 'Sorbent' only uses soft and strong toilet paper, they may either ignore or discount contradictory information presented in choice sets in a CM questionnaire.

Several participants in the first two focus groups always chose the brands they currently purchased, even though they had completely different attributes in some of the choice sets. Further questioning revealed that although some of these participants appeared to be scanning the attributes they perceived to be important, a few individuals completely ignored the attributes. A question that therefore had to be addressed was whether such behaviour might compromise the predictive validity of the experiment. On the one hand, such behaviour may be problematic since individuals are not addressing the CM task in the manner requested. In the market, there are reasons (such as attributes) why individuals have a high degree of brand loyalty to certain brands. Some individuals may not consider these reasons when answering CM questions. On the other hand, brand loyalty may be quite robust to significant product changes in the market place. If in the market respondents were to remain loyal to the same brands even when the attributes of these and other brands change, then replicating this behaviour in the SP context is indeed desirable. However, if the new products were actually introduced, the pre-existing brand loyalty could soon be corrupted and individuals would reconsider their purchases.

A second key issue that had to be identified was whether to include a 'none of these' constant alternative within the choice sets. It was noted above that the vast majority of Canberra residents use toilet paper. Whilst exclusion of a 'none' alternative may introduce a small bias in market share estimates, this problem may be less than the biases potentially arising from how people perceive and use this alternative if included. The focus groups indicated a tendency of participants to tick the 'none' alternative if they did not really like any of the alternatives in a given choice set. Further questioning indicated that participants ticking the 'none' alternative were inclined to think 'I'd buy more next time' or 'I'd shop at another store'. It is likely that such responses may also threaten the validity of the experiment, since such holding strategies are only short term. The goal here is to predict long term purchasing patterns, not temporary strategies for dealing with shock product changes. Given that the scenario had attempted to put people in the position of shopping for toilet paper, it was concluded that even strengthening the scenario may not prevent such behaviour.[5] As a result, it was decided to drop the none alternative altogether.

The final choice scenario read as follows:

Each of the next eight questions shows a hypothetical set of toilet paper products. In each question, you are asked to imagine you are on a **typical** shopping trip for toilet paper, and that the products shown are the only ones available. You will be asked to indicate which one or more of the products you would **actually purchase on that trip**.

Price and special on price	Softness, as claimed by manufacturer
Number of rolls in a pack	Colour and prints/patterns
Number of ply	Type of paper (standard, recycled etc.)
Number of sheets	Whether the paper is scented

Although the brands are real, the products shown mostly have different features from those you currently see at the supermarket. **Some of the features of the products change from one question to the next.** Changing the features in this way allows us to work out how you may respond to changes in existing products.

When answering questions 5–12, treat each question as if you are on a typical shopping trip with toilet paper on your shopping list. Assume that from now on, the products shown will be the only ones available at the supermarkets in Canberra.

There are 11 toilet paper products shown in each question. The features of each product are listed below the brand name. These features are:

The title of the questionnaire was 'Consumer Shopping Survey' and the covering letter stated inter alia that 'By completing this survey, you will assist our understanding of what people do when they go shopping'.

To ensure that the attributes varied independently of one another, such that their individual effects on respondents' preferences could be isolated, a near orthogonal experimental design was used to assign attribute levels to options. A fractional factorial design was used to reduce the number of alternatives to a manageable level. Choice sets were constructed in such a way that a high degree of orthogonality both between and within alternatives was ensured. In order to reduce implausible attribute combinations, two orthogonal attributes in the design were used to create two correlated attributes in the experiment. One hundred and twenty-eight choice sets were allocated to 16 blocks of eight choice sets. A combination of an orthogonal blocking variable and random assignment was used to assign each choice set to one of the 16 blocks.

The final questionnaires were presented in the form of an A4 booklet with a light blue cover containing the covering letter and light yellow internal pages. Brand names were represented in the choice sets as digital images. These images showed the existing brand name as it appears on existing products. Where necessary, the area surrounding the brand names was digitally modified to remove attribute information.

6.4 SAMPLING STRATEGY

Two main sampling strategies were considered. The first would have involved a systematic random sample of residents living in suburbs most likely to shop at the supermarket in question. Whilst this strategy would permit extensive follow-ups with a view to maximising response rates, the population upon which the sampling is based could only be considered a rough approximation of the true shopping catchment. Some individuals recruited at the supermarket for the focus groups lived some distance away, tending to shop on the way home from work. Some means of adjusting for differences in store patronage and purchasing patterns regarding toilet paper would thus also be required. Ideally, individuals would be sampled in proportion to the number of times they purchase toilet paper at the supermarket.

The second sampling strategy, and the one employed in this study, involved random sampling of individuals as they left the store, stratified by hour and time of day. Unfortunately, scan data regarding sales by time of day and day of the week were not available. However, subjective estimates of traffic by time and day were obtained from the store manager, along with an overall indication of when toilet paper sales are most frequent. From this information, an interviewer schedule was set up specifying, among other things, the number of questionnaires to be handed out in a given period. Although this sampling strategy has some weaknesses, independently observing traffic patterns for a two week period was outside the project budget.

Approximately 1100 questionnaires were handed out over a two-week period. Respondents were requested to provide their phone number so that they could be followed up if necessary. Respondents were told that both their phone number and responses would be treated confidentially and not handed over to any other parties. They were told that the research was not being conducted for profit, and was not sponsored by one or more companies. The response rate for the survey was approximately 40%.

6.5 RESULTS

The socio-economic and attitudinal variables that were included in models to account for heterogeneity in preferences are set out in Table 6.3. Not all variables in Table 6.3 were entered into every utility function estimated. The final column of Table 6.3 indicates the utility functions each variable entered. Initial specifications were driven by a priori expectations regarding the brands for which the various attitudinal and demographic variables might be expected to influence choice.

The final discrete choice model estimated for the data is presented in Table 6.4. The vast majority of attributes are highly significant, the exceptions being selected levels of the qualitative, paper type and colour attributes. As one would expect, cheaper products and price specials are preferred when other attributes are held constant. Respondents had a general preference for more toilet rolls per pack and for two ply paper with 250 sheets. The focus groups indicated that ply and sheets were highly correlated with perceived paper strength.

The results displayed in Table 6.4 indicate a significant increase in the utility provided by toilet paper that is both recycled and unbleached among those who are committed to green product choice. The interaction of 'Green' with the ASCs for the three green brand-names, 'Safe', 'Naturale' and 'Delsey', indicates an increase in the unobserved utility component of approximately 1.65 units for each of these brands. This has an equivalent effect on utility to a price reduction of \$3.27. The magnitude of the coefficient for 'Both' is also five times higher for these respondents.

Table 6.3 Socio-economic and attitudinal variables

Variable	Description	Utility functions entered
Green	1 if agree that 'I would only buy toilet paper that is made from recycled or unbleached paper'; 0 otherwise.	Delsey, Naturale, Safe
Irritate	1 if agree that 'Scented toilet paper irritates my eyes or nose'.	Symphony
Cheap	1 if agree that 'There is nothing wrong with cheap toilet paper'.	1. Delsey, Homebrand 2. Kleenex, Sorbent[a]
Decor	1 if agree that 'I like to match toilet paper to the decor of my bathroom'; 0 otherwise.	Delsey, Homebrand, Naturale, Safe
Clean	1 if agree that 'I like to my toilet paper to have a clean, pure look'; 0 otherwise.	Homebrand, Naturale, Safe
AGE	Respondent age in years.	Delsey, Home

Note:

[a]   The notation '1' and '2' indicates that separate coefficients on 'Cheap' were estimated for two different pairs of brands.

6.5.1 Implicit Prices

Now consider the implicit price of specified changes in the 'paper type' attribute. The qualitative nature of this attribute requires that specific changes in paper type be specified in order to calculate marginal rates of substitution with the price attribute, and hence implicit prices. Furthermore, the interaction of green attitudes and the attribute variable 'Both' in the regression implies that implicit prices depend on the level of the variable 'Green'.

Table 6.4 SP results on individual data

	Coeff.	Std. err.	P-value
ASC_BOUQUET	−0.823	0.125	0.000
ASC_DELSEY	−1.682	0.306	0.000
ASC_HOMEBR	−1.348	0.257	0.000
ASC_KLEEN	0.743	0.110	0.000
ASC_NATURE	−0.864	0.151	0.000
ASC_PUREX	−0.497	0.119	0.000
ASC_SAFE	−0.567	0.147	0.000
ASC_TENDERLY	−0.694	0.125	0.000
ASC_SORBENT	0.682	0.110	0.000
ASC_WONDERS	−0.357	0.116	0.002
PRICE	−0.418	0.022	0.000
SPECIAL	0.179	0.024	0.000
ROLL	0.240	0.014	0.000
PLY250	0.290	0.024	0.000
WHITE	0.136	0.038	0.000
OWHITE	−0.046	0.039	0.239
COLOURED	0.045	0.039	0.253
STAND	−0.070	0.049	0.150
UBLEACH	−0.100	0.094	0.290
BOTH	0.094	0.048	0.050
SCENT	−0.166	0.024	0.000
BOTH*GREEN	0.546	0.072	0.000
IRRITATE	−0.594	0.225	0.008
CHEAP1	0.886	0.135	0.000
CHEAP2	−0.675	0.087	0.000
GREEN	1.631	0.104	0.000
DECOR	−0.762	0.130	0.000
AGE	0.014	0.005	0.004
CLEAN	−0.643	0.101	0.000
% correct predict		17.5	
Choice set obs		3143	
LogL (final)		−6331.862	
Adjusted ρ^2		15.9	

Table 6.5 Implicit prices

Change in paper type	Implicit price for average respondent ($)
standard→unbleached only	−0.04
standard→recycled only	0.09
standard→both unbleached and recycled	0.66

The implicit prices associated with obtaining each of the three environmentally friendly types of paper considered in the experiment, rather than standard paper, are presented in Table 6.5. These results are calculated for the average value 'Green'.

The average respondent is willing to pay no more for paper that is unbleached, but not recycled, than standard paper. However, paper that is recycled is valued more highly than standard paper, particularly when it is also unbleached. The average respondent is prepared to pay approximately $0.66 extra to obtain paper that is both recycled and unbleached, other factors held constant. Those respondents with a preference for environmentally friendly toilet paper appear to value paper that is both recycled and unbleached. Indeed, recomputing the estimates in the last row of Table 6.5 for Green=1 increases the implicit price to $1.69. By contrast, the price for Green=0 respondents is $0.39.

Finally, it must be recognised that the implicit prices reported in Table 6.5 require careful interpretation. Whilst these prices indicate willingness to pay for environmentally friendly toilet paper, it is assumed that all other attributes, and brand, are held constant. In reality, some respondents with positive implicit prices for environmentally friendly paper may actually choose products with standard paper, because only these products satisfy their preferences for other attributes or qualities. None the less, implicit prices give an indication of how much people would be willing to pay to obtain a product that is environmentally friendly, but equivalent in all other respects to an existing product that is made of standard paper.

6.5.2 Market Share

The SP model presented in Table 6.4 can be used to predict the market shares for new or existing toilet paper products on offer at the supermarket in question. Products can be added, removed or varied from the set of products on offer at the supermarket at the time data were collected.

Estimates of market share are based on predicted probabilities, which are calculated on the basis of a set of values for the explanatory variables. This means that market share estimates are based on both the taste parameters and the ASCs. With individual-level data, the estimated probability of the *i*th respondent choosing the *h*th option from a given choice set is calculated by substituting the appropriate attribute levels and socio-economics into the estimated utility functions. Ideally, market share ms(*h*) is estimated by summing predicted choice probabilities across respondents, as follows:

$$ms(h) = \frac{\sum_{i=1,N} P_{ih}}{\sum_{j \in C}\left[\sum_{i=1,N} P_{ij}\right]} * 100 \qquad (6.1)$$

An approximation to this equation is obtained by estimating market share as the choice probability for the average respondent. This approach is adopted in this research report as it presents fewer complications. In the case of aggregate data, market shares are estimated simply as the choice probabilities for the brands in question.

Table 6.6 SP market share estimates (%)

	Individual	Aggregate
Sorbent	37.1	35.1
Homebrand	4.5	5.1
Delsey	0.6	0.7
Safe	8.0	10.0
Purex	6.1	5.5
Kleenex	20.5	20.1
Wondersoft	7.2	6.8
Naturale	5.1	6.7
Bouquet	1.6	1.5
Tenderley	4.8	4.4
Symphony	4.5	4.0
Total green products	13.6	17.5

Market shares for each of the 48 different toilet paper products on offer at the supermarket have been estimated as the choice probabilities for the average respondent. Market shares for an equivalent aggregate data SP model were also estimated. The market share estimates, aggregated here into the 11 brands available at the supermarket, are presented in Table 6.6.

The share estimates shown in Table 6.6 could hence be recomputed for an alternative set of products on offer and any share differences observed. Alternatively, the estimates in Table 6.6 can be compared with the true market share statistics obtained from the supermarket scanner data. This comparison is made in Chapter 9.

6.6 CONCLUSION

This application of CM differs from the other applications described in this book in so far as it involves a product category that is wholly or largely traded in the market place. Consequently, respondents are likely to be more familiar with some aspects of these products than they are with those of the environmental goods typically considered in passive use or state of the world surveys. In some respects, this familiarity may be beneficial in terms of the validity and reliability of the results that emerge. For example, a respondent in the present study is likely to have a fairly clear understanding of what is meant by terms such as single ply, double ply, made from recycled paper, number of rolls, special and so on. Respondents are also unlikely to object to the notion that they have to pay money to obtain the benefits that toilet paper provides. One might expect such familiarity effects to be associated with reduced variance and/or less biased estimates of willingness to pay and market share.

However, these potential advantages of applying choice experiments to real market goods are to some extent offset by some of the disadvantages identified in the present study. First, the high number of brands and stock keeping units on offer in many product markets means that choice sets with a relatively large number of alternatives and/or brands may be required. In the present study, eleven alternatives and seven attributes were presented in each choice set in order to encompass the fifty-odd stock keeping units already on offer at the supermarket. Such choice sets are likely to be more cognitively burdensome for respondents than the typical three alternative choice sets used in non-market valuation studies. Studies of recreation site choice may also require larger choice sets when preliminary research indicates that alternative-specific labels and/or levels are required.

A second consequence of higher respondent familiarity concerns the occurrence of belief perseverance whereby individuals are inattentive to information contradicting the 'hypotheses' they have learned in the market.

One manifestation of this phenomenon was observed in focus groups when participants did not readily put aside their learned brand–benefit associations when completing questionnaires. Once respondents have formed a belief that a particular brand uses soft, strong or environmentally friendly toilet paper, they may either ignore or discount contradictory information presented in choice sets in a CM questionnaire. In the present study, these problems were reduced by emphasising in the scenario that 'the products shown mostly have different features from those you currently see at the supermarket' and that 'features of the products change from one question to the next'.

The existence of well constructed brand–benefit associations also creates a trade-off for researchers between preserving brand–benefit associations, and hence brand equity within the experiment, and allowing it to dissolve as respondents discover that their brand–benefit assumptions no longer hold. Thus, respondents who normally assume that Wondersoft is a brand of toilet paper that has soft paper may be forced to discard this assumption when confronted with a choice set in which Wondersoft is shown to have low softness. Several measures were taken in the present study in an attempt to preserve some of this 'critical' brand equity. This involved the inclusion of several constant alternatives within choice sets, the inclusion of a constant attribute pertaining to softness, allowing some of the attributes to be correlated in the choice sets, and employing alternative-specific levels for some brand-attribute combinations.

A final difference between the study described in this chapter and most non-use value CM studies is that the product category under examination involves regular repeat choices. Because toilet paper is regularly purchased, it is important to distinguish between consumer responses to temporary and permanent changes in the market. Mis-specification biases will occur if respondents indicate their choices for a different time horizon to that intended by the researchers. For example, when confronted with an unusual array of toilet paper products, respondents may choose a smaller number of rolls or rolls that are less expensive than they would usually buy with a view to re-establishing their normal purchasing patterns when the market returns to normal. Such temporary behaviour would constitute a mis-specification bias when researchers are seeking to predict longer term changes in market share. In order to reduce such problems in the present study, respondents were asked to 'assume that from now on, the products shown are the only ones available at the supermarkets in Canberra'. Similar issues might be expected to apply to recreation studies.

NOTES

1. Many of the respondents revealed a 'deep ambivalence' regarding the value of the green consumer behaviour in which they engaged. Not only did they distrust environmental claims made by manufacturers, but they questioned the meaning and influence of their behaviour when other members of the community could be relied upon to do likewise

2. A number of other studies have observed public scepticism and distrust associated with environmental product claims (Carlson *et al.* 1996; Kangun *et al.* 1991; Thomas 1989). Ellen *et al.* (1991) found that the extent to which a consumer believes that the efforts of an individual acting alone can make a difference (perceived consumer effectiveness) has a significant influence on behaviour (see also Berger and Corbin 1992). Another study showed that whilst the ranks of green consumers is growing, 'consumers most apathetic to the environment are also growing in number, indicating a backlash against environmentally friendly goods' (Anonymous 1995, p. 31). According to a representative of Roper Starch Worldwide, consumers in the 1990s are 'falling into disparate categories. Some regularly buy environmental products, while others feel they do not need to worry because others are doing it' (ibid).

3. Finding an experimental design large enough to handle such an experiment proved difficult, and the resultant task complexity may have compromised the quality of the data arising.

4. Exceptions include a three ply product recently introduced by Kleenex and a double roll product also introduced by Kleenex.

5. These strategies had occurred in a draft questionnaire in which respondents were asked to assume that the products shown were the only ones available, and that this was the only opportunity to purchase.

PART THREE

Exploring Some Methodological Issues

7.   Choice Set Design

Russell Blamey, Jordan J. Louviere and Jeff Bennett

7.1 INTRODUCTION

Correct specification of the choice set from which individuals choose is critical to the successful conduct of choice experiments. A choice set consists of the alternatives available for choice, together with the attributes of these alternatives, 'brand names', labels or other descriptors (including images) associated with them.

Although choice sets can appear to be fairly simple in some choice experiments, they often require more thought and research effort than other stages of the choice modelling process. This reflects the importance of sound choice set design as well as the flexibility of choice experiments in so far as there are typically a large number of ways to design the choice sets for a given study.

In the next section we briefly overview the various facets of choice set design, which leads to a more detailed examination of two design issues that characterise the two main sections of this chapter:

- a discussion of the effects on model parameters, marginal attribute values (that is implicit prices) and willingness to pay, including alternative-specific policy labels in choice sets rather than generic labels; and
- a discussion of the effects of including causally prior indicator attributes in choice sets. The results of an empirical study designed to test these two effects are presented, followed by some brief conclusions.

7.2 AN OVERVIEW OF CHOICE SET DESIGN ISSUES

The researcher must consider issues relating to the alternatives making up the choice sets, the attributes used to describe those alternatives and the ways in which the experimental design impacts on the choice set. Once these issues have been addressed, the physical appearance of the choice sets must be considered. A reasonably comprehensive (but not exhaustive) list of choice set design issues is presented in Table 7.1. It is not possible to discuss all of these issues in detail; hence we provide a brief and selective overview that highlights some of the key issues and associated research design decisions.

In any empirical application there are a number of objectives but, as with all multi-criteria objective problems, it is not possible to optimise them all simultaneously. Thus, a typical application represents a compromise among the objectives such as those listed below that pertain to choice set design:

- to maximise attribute and task plausibility and realism from the respondents' perspective;
- to identify and use attributes and choice alternatives that are relevant and determinant from the respondents' perspective (under low and high awareness conditions);
- to create and implement meaningful and acceptable tasks;
- to balance task complexity with realism and response reliability and validity;
- to identify attributes, choice alternatives and tasks that are relevant and determinant from a client's or user's perspective; and to develop and implement tasks with appropriate incentive properties.

Perhaps the most obvious features of choice set design are the number of alternatives in each choice set and the number of attributes that describe each alternative. Typically, the design of choice sets and choice tasks involves trade-offs between completeness and complexity. As the number of attributes increases, the number of profiles increases exponentially, and the cognitive demands of fully evaluating choice sets also increase, although the exact extent of this increase is as yet unknown. The size of experimental designs also increases, and design requirements become more complex, which in turn limits the effects that can be estimated in many applications. A similar situation obtains as the number of alternatives increases. For example, Svenson (1979) analysed the results of several studies and found that the proportion of choice set 'aspects' considered by respondents decreased as the number of attributes and alternatives increased, with the former having greater effect.[1]

The complexity of choice tasks also may influence the strategies that respondents use in formulating responses (Swait and Adamowicz 1997; Saelensminde 1998; Johnson, Mathews and Bingham 2000). For example, it may be that more complex tasks lead to greater use of heuristics and more

Table 7.1 Facets of choice set construction

Choice set construction	Choice set presentation
Alternatives • number of alternatives • generic or alternative-specific labels • fixed or variable choice sets • competitive relationship among alternatives • whether or not to include an opt-out option • definition of the opt-out option • other fixed alternatives • self-explicated alternatives	• should options be presented as rows or columns? • should columns or rows be highlighted or should each receive equal attention? • should labels be presented as words or images? • should the order of presentation of attributes and alternatives be systematically varied? • should attribute levels be presented as words or images?
Attributes • number of attributes • level at which attributes are defined in cause–effect hierarchy • level of attribute disaggregation (that is, degree of specificity) • relevance/ meaningfulness/ plausibility/ determinance of attributes to consumers • relevance/ deliverability/ actionability of attributes to policy/decision makers • metrics used to describe attribute levels • number, spacing, range and definition of levels in absolute or relative terms • generic, overlapping or unique attribute levels • correlated relationships among attributes • causal relationship among attributes • fixed attributes	• should attributes be defined by words or images? • should stimuli be presented in word strings, paragraphs, virtual displays, pictorial images, physical models or mockups, and so on? • should font, font size, shading and so on, be varied? • should choices (responses) be recorded by ticking boxes, circling labels and so on?
Interactions with experimental design • respondent efficiency versus task complexity • dominated alternatives • implausible attribute combinations	

inconsistent and random choices. Such effects might manifest themselves in higher response variability and smaller scale parameters in choice models. In addition to the number of alternatives and attributes, task complexity is likely to be a function of the correlational structure of the attributes, and hence the number and type of trade-offs that respondents face. For example, in many markets attributes are negatively correlated due to market forces that drive the sets of options toward a Pareto frontier. If respondents are aware of such correlations and make use of them in their decisions, this may impact task complexity and response variability. Inclusion of dominant or dominated alternatives within choice sets also impacts complexity, as do reductions in the numbers of attributes that differ across alternatives and numbers of choice sets included within surveys. For example, Mazzotta and Opaluch (1995) considered the effect of increasing the number of attributes that vary between alternatives. They found that where four or more attributes were varying, respondents consistently eliminated one or more attribute from their consideration in order to reduce the task complexity.

Choice sets typically contain what researchers believe to constitute a minimal set of choice alternatives relevant to the population of consumers and/or decision makers of interest. Although one can match choice sets to each individual's awareness or consideration sets (Peters *et al.* 1995), it is more common to present all respondents with the same set of alternatives (see also Horowitz and Louviere 1995; Jedidi *et al.* 1996). Numbers of alternatives and attributes have varied across empirical applications in environmental contexts, but most applications have used three alternatives (including an 'opt-out' option) and five or six attributes. In alternative-specific designs, the number of alternatives is often larger because different brands or policy options represent separate alternatives. Tourism destination and recreation site choice studies often involve more possible destinations or sites than can be listed in choice sets. In such circumstances one has to categorise choice alternatives in a meaningful way, rely on a comprehensive list of generic, determinant attributes, or possibly individualise the design and use of choice sets (see, for example, Peters *et al.* 1995). Another possibility is to vary the presence/absence of brands, locations and so on in choice sets by means of so-called 'availability designs' that vary presence/absence using types of fractions of 2^J factorials (Louviere and Woodworth 1983).

The decision about which alternatives and attributes to include within a choice set requires one to consider how choices can be 'framed' to reflect appropriately the competitive environment of alternatives available to consumers and/or decision makers. 'Framing' refers to the effects of the ways a situation is described or defined on 'ways in which people involve themselves with and experience that situation' (Reber 1985, p. 286). For example, estimates of market share and willingness to pay for a given alternative are likely to be more accurate if respondents are aware of substitute and complement alternatives. Choice sets in the green product study discussed in Chapter 6, for example, included nearly all available brands available at the particular supermarket studied, not just the green products of primary interest. Framing issues in non-market valuation studies are considered in more detail in Chapter 10.

Inclusion of constant 'do-nothing' or 'opt-out' options avoids forced choices that may bias estimates of demand, and hence willingness to pay. In any particular application, one may need to consider several alternative ways of defining opt-out options. For example, in passive-use value studies, one may need to distinguish between a current policy or state of change and the current state of the environment. For studies of market and recreational goods, distinctions between 'no purchase' and 'choose some other alternative' often may be required (see Chapter 8). In the case of 'some other alternative', respondents might be asked to report the attributes of the 'other' alternative to allow attributes of that alternative to be included in model estimation (that is, a 'self-explicated' alternative). Constant base alternatives that pertain to a status quo or current situation provide a convenient reference point in terms of utility and attribute levels for respondents. However, one needs to assess carefully if respondents choose this alternative because it's the highest utility alternative or whether they use it to avoid a difficult choice or are confused, sceptical or opposed to one or more aspects of the scenario or choice set (see, for example, Adamowicz *et al.* 1998b; and Blamey *et al.* 2000). Although opt-out options are common constant or fixed alternatives in choice experiments, other fixed alternatives also are possible. For example, in alternative-specific choice set designs one or more brands with low market share might be fixed at their true attribute values and treated as constants to reduce task complexity whilst at the same time enhancing plausibility. Refer to Chapter 6 for an example.

Another important issue that arises in choice experiments is whether to present choice alternatives as generic or labelled choice options (see, for example, Blamey *et al.* 2000). Generic choice options are unlabelled and/or the label conveys no additional attributè or relevant information about the choice alternative per se, such as 'Alternative A', 'Alternative B' and so on Labelled choice options have names or assigning labels that potentially communicate information to respondents directly or indirectly about tangible and/or intangible qualities of each alternative. Labels in marketing applications tend to be brand names and/or logos that consumers may associate with different product characteristics and free-standing emotions. In environmental policy contexts labels tend to refer to sites, locations, policy names or other descriptors.

One advantage of alternative-specific labels is that responses may be more reflective of the information context in which preferences are ultimately constructed and revealed. For example, a respondent may be predisposed to visit a particular recreation site because he or she has fond memories from a past visit. To the extent that experiences and expectations play a role in decisions, and economic theory suggests that they should, such effects may not be revealed by CM tasks that describe sites purely in terms of tangible attributes involving recreation opportunities, camping facilities, proximity and cost. Thus, labels often provide a convenient and plausible way to include such information about choice alternatives. Such information not only increases predictive validity, but may also make the task less cognitively demanding. However, the potential advantage of labelled choice alternatives may be offset if generic labels and information encourage more discerning and discriminating responses. That is, the use of generic labels and attribute information discourages respondents from basing responses wholly or largely on alternatives with the most superficially attractive label or descriptor; instead, respondents must consider differences in policy options described by the attributes. Thus, more informed and deliberated preferences may be elicited from generic tasks, which may be desirable from a non-market valuation perspective.

Identification and selection of attributes also require careful thought and also usually research. For example, attributes should be meaningful and determinant for respondents, relevant and actionable for policy/decision makers, analytically and theoretically sound, and measurable. Determinant attributes are 'attitudes toward features which are most closely related to preferences or to actual purchase decisions' (Myers and Alpert 1968).[2] Lancaster distinguishes between *relevant* and *irrelevant* characteristics. A characteristic is 'relevant to the situation if ignoring its existence would change our conclusions about choice or ordering of the goods by the consumers' (Lancaster 1991, p. 56). It is irrelevant if ignoring its existence would not change our conclusions. Lancaster observes that characteristics may be irrelevant from either a technical supply perspective or a human demand perspective. Attributes that are irrelevant are typically excluded from choice sets in CM studies, although those that are technically irrelevant but demanded by consumers when evaluating products sometimes may be included for reasons of plausibility and completeness.[3] When considering whether an attribute is relevant, or determinant, it is important to have a clear idea of the purpose of the study. Attributes that are demand irrelevant given current levels of consumer awareness and involvement may become relevant and determinant under higher awareness conditions. For example, choice models can provide valuable information regarding how customers will choose if they are informed about attributes and associated benefits. Similarly, if properly designed, choice experiments can also provide insights into how consumer choices may change as they gradually become aware of changes in the attributes of competing products. Finally, attributes that are relevant in the long term may not be in the short term (Huber 1998).

Sometimes it is useful and realistic to fix the levels of attributes across all choice sets to their current values or levels. For example, weather typically is fixed for any particular recreation destination, but usually varies across destinations within a choice set. To the extent that weather plays a role in choice, and subjects may misperceive the true weather levels of destinations, it may be useful to include a fixed attribute for weather to describe each. This has the advantage of avoiding correlations between respondents' weather perceptions and the site's random component, and also separates this effect from others in the mean of the random component. Thus, fixed attribute levels can facilitate plausibility and the maintenance of brand–benefit associations[4] as well as help to reduce the number of attributes in designs. However, if there is concern over numbers of attributes, there are ways to handle such problems, including hierarchical choice experiments (Louviere *et al.* 1993a).

The preceding considerations often produce a short list of environmental attributes that includes subsets which may be causally related. For example, the attributes 'endangered species lost' and 'non-threatened species lost' may be perceived to be causally 'downstream' to attributes such as 'loss in area of native vegetation'. In this case, the CM practitioner must decide whether to include all three attributes, just the two 'downstream' attributes, or just the 'upstream' attribute. These decisions matter because, depending in part on how a CM task is framed, inclusion of causally related attributes may stimulate some respondents to seek to understand the causal relations to assign greater meaning to alternatives, and potentially also simplify the decision making process. If respondents use such causal heuristics, this may affect the weights assigned to each attribute when they choose preferred alternatives, which in turn may impact marginal values and/or welfare estimates.[5] For example, some respondents also may assign greater weight to attributes of a more fundamental, causally prior, nature, as discussed by Blamey *et al.* (1997) and Morrison *et al.* (1997).

There is some question as to whether the order or position of attributes and/or alternatives influences results. For example, Kumar and Gaeth (1991) found larger attribute order effects when consumer's familiarity with product classes is low. However, such effects may merely reflect differences in random component variances, and not real differences in preferences (see Chapter 2 for an explanation of the role of the random component on choice model parameters). In virtually all studies, an important initial consideration is whether to use qualitative (discrete) or quantitative (continuous) levels for attributes. For example, a quantitative approach might result in levels of 20, 50 and 100 for the attribute 'number of whales harvested'; whereas a qualitative approach might define the levels as low, medium and high. Many attributes such as 'colour', 'location' 'type of campsite' or 'type of forest' cannot be defined quantitatively. Additionally, quantitative attribute levels can be defined in absolute terms, such as 'number of whales remaining', or in relative terms, such as 'percentage loss in whale populations'. The range of attribute levels should be chosen to encompass the full range of alternatives with which respondents are familiar and which matter to those who will use the study results. The number of levels that one uses for a particular attribute is primarily a function of:

- the number of levels needed to simulate the actual or hypothetical market of interest;
- the size of the experimental design that one can afford; and
- the need to specify non-linear attribute effects.

Levels typically are chosen to be equally spaced in original units or equally spaced in some transformed units such as logarithms of levels. The latter is a statistical consideration because equal spacing enhances one's ability to orthogonalise the effects of interest in model estimation.

Finally, Carson *et al.* (2000) show that in studies concerned with consumer preferences regarding government provision of public goods, or single quasi-public goods, choice sets containing two alternatives are less susceptible to strategic bias from the perspective of incentive compatibility theory than those containing more alternatives. In the case of private and quasi-public goods, larger choice sets may be 'close to' incentive compatible when the perceived number of goods that are likely to be provided is relatively high. Thus, from the standpoint of maximising the incentive compatability of choice tasks, one needs to take this issue into account in task and study design. For example, it may be that some public goods such as wetlands are unique, and consumers know or believe that there probably will be no more than one or two of them provided at the study area, whereas boat launch or other recreational sites may be provided in much larger numbers.

7.3 EMPIRICAL STUDY

In this section the results of an empirical study that bears on differences in results due to differences in task and choice set design are presented. Specifically, one design condition involved the use of an alternative-specific (instead of a generic) experiment, and the second condition included a causally prior indicator attribute with the other attributes. The objective of the empirical study was to test the effect of these choice tasks/choice set design conditions on estimates of choice model parameters, marginal values and willingness to pay (WTP). To test for differences in these two conditions, three versions of a survey were developed as follows:

- version 1 (v1): generic choice set without causally prior 'ecosystem' attribute;
- version 2 (v2): alternative-specific choice set without 'ecosystem' attribute;
- version 3 (v3): generic choice set design with causally prior 'ecosystem' attribute.

The effect of employing an alternative-specific rather than generic choice set design thus involves comparing choice model parameters, marginal rates of substitution involving the monetary attribute and WTP for versions 1 and 2. The effect of including a causally prior indicator attribute pertaining to ecosystem health involves comparing the results for versions 1 and 3.

7.3.1 Methods

The study context was a case study involving the protection of remnant vegetation in the Desert Uplands region of central Queensland, Australia. Further details of this study are provided in Chapter 5.

The survey design phase involved extensive background research and two rounds of focus groups with potential respondents (details in Blamey *et al.* 1997). Generic and alternative-specific choice tasks were pretested, as were choice sets with and without causally prior ecosystem attributes. The issue of whether to include an ecosystem attribute in the choice tasks emerged in the first groups where participants commonly cited the state of ecosystems as important and, when asked why, they nearly always cited other 'attributes' like impacts on endangered and other species.

Table 7.2 lists the attribute levels assigned to each choice alternative in the three survey versions and Figure 7.1a illustrates the main differences between the choice tasks. The labels shown in Figure 7.1b are based on those actually discussed in policy circles. The capacity to incorporate associations between attribute values and labels within the design of the second survey version might be considered an advantage of the alternative-specific approach to choice task design because this minimises implausible combinations of attributes and labels.[6]

Fractional factorial designs were used to assign attribute levels to alternatives and reduce the number of alternatives to a manageable level. Choice sets were constructed in such a way that orthogonality both between and within alternatives was ensured. To reduce implausibility problems whilst at the same time increasing the balance between environmental and economic variables, an eight-level attribute was used to allow correlation between jobs lost and income lost. The design produced 64 choice sets, and an extra, orthogonal eight-level column was used to allocate the 64 sets to eight blocks of eight choice sets in each of the three versions. Thus, there were 24 total survey sub-versions (three main versions, each blocked into eight sub-versions).

Statements were included in the scenarios of all sub-versions to try to further diffuse perceptions of implausible attribute combinations that might have encouraged non-rational response strategies. Respondents were told to 'consider carefully the implications of each tree-clearing option, by looking at the numbers in the table. To keep matters simple, we do not describe how each option would work. Some implications which may seem a little odd are in fact quite possible ... You will find some questions easier than others.'

Table 7.2 Attributes, levels and corresponding variables

Attribute (variable in model)	Levels in versions 1 and 3	Levels in version 2
Levy on income tax (levy)	Option A: $0 (base) Options B & C: $20, $60, $100, $140	Option A: $0 (base) Option B: $20, $40, $60, $80 Option C: $80, $100, $120, $140
Income lost to region in $ million (inc)	Option A: 0 Options B & C: 5, 10, 15	Option A: 0 Option B: 5, 7, 9 Option C: 11, 13, 15
Jobs lost in region (jobs)	Option A: 0 Options B & C: 10, 15, 20, 30, 40	Option A: 0 Option B: 10, 14, 18, 21, 24 Option C: 26, 30, 34, 37, 40
Number of endangered species lost to region (end)	Option A: 18 Options B & C: 4, 8, 12, 16	Option A: 18 Option B: 10, 12, 14, 16 Option C: 4, 6, 8, 10.
Reduction in population size of non-threatened species (pop)	Option A: 80% Options B & C: 30%, 45%, 60%, 75%	Option A: 80% Option B: 60%, 65%, 70%, 75% Option C: 30%, 35%, 40%, 50%
Loss in area of unique ecosystems (ecos)	(version 3 only) Option A: 40% Options B, C: 15%, 22%, 28%, 35%	

Implications	Option A Current guidelines	Option B	Option C
Levy on your income tax	none	$60	$20
Income lost to the region ($ million)	none	5	10
Jobs lost in region	none	15	40
Number of endangered species lost to region	18	8	4
Reduction in population size of non-threatened species	80%	75%	45%
Loss in area of unique ecosystems	40%	15%	28%

Figure 7.1a Example of a generic choice set with ecosystem attribute (v3)

Implications	Option A Current guidelines	Option B	Option C
	Graziers to leave at least 20% of trees	Graziers to leave at least 30% of trees	Graziers to leave at least 50% of trees
Levy on your income tax	none	$20	$100
Income lost to the region ($ million)	none	9	11
Jobs lost in region	none	18	30
Number of endangered species lost to region	18	16	10
Reduction in population size of non-threatened species	80%	70%	40%

Figure 7.1b Example of an alternative-specific choice set without ecosystem attribute (v2)

A C Neilsen McNair administered the survey using a census style 'drop-off and pick-up' procedure. They first selected 30 nodal points in the

Brisbane metropolitan area at random. Each nodal point was used as a starting point to select households randomly. The final data set contained 720 valid responses, approximately one-third of which corresponded to each survey version.

7.3.2 Testing for Differences

Choice model attribute taste vectors, marginal attribute values and compensating surpluses were compared for each version (v1 vs v2 and v1 vs v3). Differences in parameter vectors were tested using the method proposed by Swait and Louviere (1993). Compensating surplus was estimated using the approach proposed by Hanemann (1984) and differences in compensating surplus and marginal values across treatments were tested using a Poe *et al.* (1997) test. With regard to the v1 vs v2 comparison, if respondents chose the option with the label that most closely aligned with their held values and attitudes, and ignored the outcomes described by the attributes, one might expect significant differences between attribute parameters across treatments, and some attribute parameters in the labelled model might not be statistically significant. To the extent that inclusion of policy labels reduces the importance of attributes, one also might expect a decrease in their marginal values. For compensating surplus, inclusion of alternative-specific policy labels and levels may simply redistribute the source of the utility in terms of attribute marginal utilities or alternative-specific constants (ASCs). Thus, inclusion of policy labels might shift respondents' attention from attributes to labels.

With regard to the v1 vs v3 comparison, whether including a causally prior environmental attribute changes the behavioural relationship between dependent and common independent variables was tested first. On the one hand, it may be that adding an attribute increases the variance of the random component of utility by increasing the cognitive burden of the task. Alternatively, random component variance may decrease if including an attribute leads to greater preference homogeneity; for example, more meaningful interpretation of alternatives and/or widespread use of a causal heuristic may increase homogeneity.

To the extent that inclusion of a causally prior attribute results in use of causal heuristics, one would expect respondents to assign lower value to less fundamental, downstream attributes, such as impact on endangered species. Thus we hypothesised that including a causally prior attribute would reduce the marginal values for downstream environmental attributes. It also may be that adding a causally prior attribute simply redistributes the source of the utility in terms of the attribute marginal utilities and/or ASCs, but produces no overall difference in compensating surplus. A test of the latter hypothesis requires one to specify the attributes of the proposed policy option, including the causally prior attribute. Hence, the results may be sensitive to the assumed level of the prior attribute.[7]

7.3.3 Results

Variables included in the choice models discussed below are defined in Tables 7.2 and 7.3. In contrast to the variable *envatt*, which provides a measure of respondents' general stances on environmental issues, the *confuse* and *object* variables relate to respondents' reactions to the survey instrument.

Table 7.3 Non-attribute variable definitions

Variable	Definition
const	Alternative-specific constant taking on a value of 1 for options 2 and 3 in the choice sets, and 0 for the base option.
const1	Alternative-specific constant taking on a value of 1 for option 2 in the choice sets, and 0 for the base option.
envatt	Dummy variable taking on a value of 1 for respondents indicating that, over the years, when have heard about proposed conflicts between development and the environment, they have tended to 'More frequently favour preservation of the environment'; 0 otherwise.
confuse	Five point Likert scale response indicating extent of agreement with the statement 'I found questions 3 to 10 [the choice set questions] confusing'.
object	Five point Likert scale response indicating extent of disagreement with the statement 'A tree levy is a good idea'.
version	Dummy variable depicting version of questionnaire. In the case of v1 versus v3, equals 1 when the ecosystem attribute is excluded, 0 otherwise. In the case of v1 versus v2, equals 1 for the labelled treatment and 0 otherwise.

Determination of an appropriate model specification to test the hypotheses requires the issue of appropriate model specification to be addressed. The Hausman and McFadden (1984) test for IIA violations was used. IIA violations were found in the generic, but not the labelled tasks. These violations were addressed by using a nested logit model with the two environmental improvement alternatives grouped in one branch and the status quo or do-nothing option in the other. This specification suggests that respondents may first choose between 'doing something' and 'doing nothing'. The utilities of these two branches depends on an ASC and its interaction with environmental attitudes, self-reported confusion and self-reported levy protest. Respondents choosing one of the pro-environment options might be expected to have greener attitudes, and lower levels of confusion and object, than those who prefer to continue current tree clearing guidelines.[8] At the second level of the nest, the model assumes that respondents choose on the basis of the attributes of the alternatives. Although the labelled task did not exhibit significant IIA violations, the same nested structure was used for all model comparisons.

Another issue germane to model specification is whether a generic model is appropriate for the alternative-specific task. For example, different labels and/or attribute ranges for different alternatives might give rise to different marginal utilities for the same attributes for different alternatives. Thus, we tested whether restricting the utility function to be generic in the taste parameters was appropriate (that is, $\beta_{j=1} = \beta_{j=2} = \beta_{j=3} = \beta$). A likelihood ratio test for the more general compared to the restrictive specification resulted in a LR statistic of 2.1, which is well below the critical value of 11.1 (5 degrees of freedom, 5 per cent significance level). This result suggests that a generic specification is appropriate for all three treatments.[9]

7.3.4 The Effect of Alternative-Specific Policy Labels and Attribute Levels (v1 vs v2)

Results for the nested logit specifications described above for v1 and v2 (and v3) are in Table 7.4. At the top level of the nest, all interactions with the ASC have the expected signs and most are highly significant. Taken as a whole, respondents with pro-environment orientations were more likely to choose one of the improvement options than those with a pro-development orientations. Those who reported confusion were more likely to choose the status quo, as were those who had a problem with the idea of a tree levy.

Parameter vectors
The grid search technique of Swait and Louviere (1993) was applied to the v1 and v2 data sets that were pooled and stacked. Results shown in Tables 7.4 and 7.5 permit the hypothesis of equal attribute taste parameters across the two treatments to be tested. All ASC terms were allowed to differ between treatments and only common attribute parameters were included in the rescaling test. The test proposed by Swait and Louviere (1993) was used to infer whether the parameter equality restriction provided as good a fit as allowing each version to have separate parameters (see Table 7.4). The

estimated variance-scale ratio was 0.365, which implied that the generic task had lower response variability. The likelihood ratio test statistic for this comparison was $-2*[-3254.518-(-1547.388 + -1704.261)] = 5.74$. The critical chi-square value is 11.07 at the 5 per cent significance level (5 degrees of freedom); hence we fail to reject the hypothesis that the vector of common attribute parameters is equal across data sets.

Table 7.4 Nested logit results for separate data sets

Utility functions	Generic choice set with out ecos treatment (v1)		Labelled choice set treatment (v2)		generic choice set with ecos treatment (v3)	
	coeff.	s. error	coeff.	s. error	coeff.	s. error
const1	0.1152***	0.0694	0.1691	0.3218	0.1644**	0.0663
levy	−0.0099*	0.0012	−0.0067*	0.0018	−0.0107*	0.0011
jobs	−0.0372*	0.0054	−0.0083	0.0092	−0.0324*	0.0053
inc	−0.0857*	0.0143	−0.0130	0.0271	−0.0597*	0.0138
end	−0.1705*	0.0124	−0.0518*	0.0184	−0.1214*	0.0111
pop	−0.0246*	0.0031	−0.0028	0.0061	−0.0180*	0.0029
ecos	na		na		−0.0392*	0.0065
Branch choice equations						
const	−0.0650	0.5557	3.1205*	0.7698	−1.9738*	0.5913
envatt*const	1.1820*	0.1173	0.7691*	0.1234	1.1344*	0.1105
object*const	−0.6958*	0.0528	−0.9770*	0.0554	−0.5750*	0.0501
confuse*const	−0.5009*	0.0517	−0.0700	0.0509	−0.1550*	0.0477
Inclusive value parameters						
do something	0.2811*	0.0735	0.8663***	0.4872	0.1904**	0.0795
do nothing	1.0000	0.0000	1.0000	0.0000	1.0000	0.0000
Model statistics						
n (choice sets)	1840		1806		1826	
Log L	−1547.388		−1704.261		−1685.564	
adj ρ^2 (%)	26.7		18.2		20.1	

Notes:
*** denotes significance at the 10% significance level
** denotes significance at the 5% level
* denotes significance at the 1% level

Table 7.5 Nested logit results for pooled data sets (optimally scaled)

Utility functions	v1 and v2		v1 and v3	
	coeff.	s. error	coeff.	s. error
const1	0.1153***	0.0693	0.1725*	0.0660
const1*version	0.2761**	0.1081	−0.0637	0.0957
levy	−0.0103*	0.0011	−0.0114*	0.0009
jobs	−0.0365*	0.0053	−0.0390*	0.0042
inc	−0.0843*	0.0141	−0.0821*	0.0111
end	−0.1695*	0.0120	−0.1648*	0.0093
pop	−0.0243*	0.0031	−0.0240*	0.0024
ecos	na		−0.0389*	0.0064
Branch choice equations				
const	0.0243	0.5471	−1.9217*	0.4615
const*version	2.1165*	0.4840	1.8378*	0.3966
envatt*const	1.1830*	0.1173	1.1375*	0.1106
envatt*const*version	−0.4134**	0.1702	0.0422*	0.1610
object*const	−0.6963*	0.0528	−0.5759	0.0502
object*const*version	−0.2802*	0.0765	−0.1185	0.0727
confuse*const	−0.5013*	0.0517	−0.1552	0.0478
confuse*const*version	0.4319*	0.0725	−0.3452	0.0703
Inclusive value parameters				
do something	0.2929*	0.0729	0.2434	0.0540
do nothing	1.0000	0.0000	1.0000	0.0000
Model statistics				
optimal scale ratio	0.365		0.78	
n (choice sets)	3646		3667	
Log L	−3254.518		−3236.586	
adj ρ^2 (%)	22.4		23.3	

Notes:
***   denotes significance at the 10% significance level
 **   denotes significance at the 5% level
  *   denotes significance at the 1% level

To test if the random component variances (or equivalently, scale parameters) were equal across versions required a subsequent test. We re-estimated the model in Table 7.5 with the restriction that the variance-scale ratio was the same across versions. The LR statistic for this test was LR = −2[−3273.947−(−3254.518)] = 38.91, which significantly exceeds the critical value of 3.84 at the 5 per cent confidence level.[10] Thus, we reject the hypothesis of equal random component variance while retaining the hypothesis of equal utility parameters. Thus, the versions appear to differ in the degree of random component variability, which is likely to be associated with the task differences. However, the task differences did not lead to mean model parameter differences.

Marginal values

The above results indicate no differences in attribute parameters across versions v1 and v2, but it may be that one or more differences in marginal willingness to pay exist. In particular, the insignificance of several non-monetary parameters in the labelled model suggests that there could be lower implicit values. Marginal values were calculated as the marginal rates of substitution between the monetary attribute and each of the non-monetary attributes (that is marginal attribute values), and are in Table 7.6 for each version. Note that the signs of the differences across versions are as expected a priori in all cases because the labelled tasks exhibited reduced importance for all non-monetary attributes. For example, a $1 million increase in regional income is valued at $1.7 in the labelled task, but is $8.8 in the generic task. Indeed, averaged over all four non-monetary attributes, the generic task produced marginal values that were more than four times higher than corresponding labelled marginal values. A Poe *et al.* (1997) test suggested that the differences were statistically significant at the 5 per cent level for both environmental attributes, and differences in regional income and jobs were significant at approximately the 10 per cent significance level.

Table 7.6 Marginal values (implicit prices)

	Generic treatment v1 ($)	Policy-label treatment v2 ($)	Generic treatment v3 ($)	Prob $(MRS_{v1} - MRS_{v2} > 0)$	Prob $(MRS_{v1} - MRS_{v3} > 0)$
Jobs	3.81	1.19	3.04	0.895	0.80
Inc	8.80	1.66	5.60	0.925	0.93
End	17.32	8.05	11.39	0.965	0.99
Pop	2.51	0.39	1.69	0.965	0.92
Ecos			3.68		

Compensating surplus

Now consider how the two treatments compare in terms of the overall welfare estimates generated for two specific policy options, corresponding to a movement from 20 per cent tree retention to 30 per cent, and 50 per cent, retention. These environmental improvements are associated with higher opportunity costs in the form of forgone regional income and jobs. Table 7.7

specifies the attribute levels associated with each of the policy options under consideration.

Table 7.7 Policy options used in welfare estimation (v2)

	20% tree retention	30% tree retention	50% tree retention
Inc	0	5	12
Jobs	0	10	30
End	18	16	10
Pop	80	50	35

Mean welfare estimates corresponding to an increase to 30 per cent tree retention are $119 and $83 per respondent household (one-off) respectively for the labelled and generic treatments. These values are calculated at the mean values for *envatt, confuse* and *object*. Both the ASCs and the attributes are included when calculating the utilities. A Poe *et al.* test found no significant difference between these values (p = 0.41).

An examination of the magnitude of the ASC terms indicates considerable unobserved and systematic utility. For example, in the generic task the environmental improvement options have an unobserved utility of −2.9 relative to the current guidelines. This is suggestive of the occurrence of status quo biases similar to those reported by Adamowicz *et al.* (1988b). When minimum rather than average levels of *object* and *confuse* are substituted, the unobserved utility of the improvement options increases to − 0.66.[11] In the labelled task, the improvement options have an unobserved utility of +0.4175 relative to the current guidelines, at the average levels of *confuse* and *object*, and +2.4 at the minimum of these variables. Thus, the environmental improvement alternatives are associated with greater unobserved utility in the labelled rather than the generic task.

The above welfare estimates represent net improvements in the mean welfare of Brisbane residents resulting from tighter tree clearing guidelines in the Desert Uplands. They are net values in the sense that they take into account the losses experienced by Brisbane residents resulting from changes to the economy of the Desert Uplands region. It is possible to recalculate the estimates for the case in which only the above environmental improvements are considered. When employment and income effects are held constant and at the levels specified for the 20 per cent tree retention scenario, the welfare estimates become $106 and $108 respectively.[12] Again, the difference is not statistically significant (p = 0.49).

In the case of 50 per cent rather than 20 per cent tree retention, the mean welfare estimates are $107 and $84 respectively for the labelled and generic tasks. The difference relating to the tasks was not found to be significantly different using the Poe *et al.* test (p = 0.44). When the employment and income impacts associated with the environmental improvement are set to zero, the estimates increase to $146 and $155 respectively. These are still not statistically different.

It appears that the labelled and generic tasks do not produce significantly different estimates of consumer surplus for the scenarios considered in this section.

7.3.5 The Effect of Including a Causally Prior 'Ecosystem' Attribute (v1 vs v3)

Parameter vectors
An examination of a plot of the parameter vectors for versions 1 and 3 in Table 7.4 indicated quite high proportionality between the two vectors, with the exception of the parameters for *const* and the interaction of *const* with *confuse*. The ratio of 'without ecosystem' to 'with ecosystem' parameters appeared to be greater than 1, implying lower variance when the ecosystem attribute is present. It may be that the addition of the ecosystem attribute had no systematic influence on the main taste parameters, only affecting results via differences in variance. If inclusion of the causally prior attribute results in greater homogeneity with respect to choice strategies (including heuristics), one would expect variance to decrease.

The Swait and Louviere (1993) grid search technique was applied to the stacked data sets for two different model specifications. In the first, rather ambitious model (not shown in Table 7.5), all parameters, including the ASC terms, were constrained to be equal across the two tasks, providing an unqualified test of equality in parameter vectors. The hypothesis of equal parameter vectors was rejected, which is not surprising, given the above noted observations regarding the graph. The second model, which is shown in Table 7.5, allowed all ASC terms to differ between versions and rescaled only the common attribute parameters. The Swait–Louviere procedure was used to test whether this reduced set of equality restrictions provides as good a fit as the separate models shown in Table 7.4. The estimated variance-scale ratio for model 2 was 0.78, which yields a likelihood ratio test statistic of 7.32. The critical chi-square value is 11.07 at the 5 per cent significance level (5 degrees of freedom); hence we fail to reject the hypothesis that the vector of common attribute parameters is equal across data sets. To test if scale parameters are equal across data sets we re-estimated model 2 in Table 7.5 with the restriction that the scale parameters are equal across data sets. The LR statistic for this test was 7.638, which exceeds the critical value of 3.84 at the 5 per cent confidence level. Thus, inclusion of the ecosystem attribute significantly reduced the scale parameter, and hence increased the random component variance. Inclusion of the ecosystem attribute did not seem to have a significant effect on the taste parameters, but rather it affected the variance and the alternative-specific utility component.

Marginal values

Although the above results indicate no overall difference in the vector of attribute parameters across versions, it may be that differences in marginal values exist. The marginal attribute values or willingness to pay for the common non-price attributes are in Table 7.6. The signs of the differences in versions 1 and 3 are as expected a priori in all cases. Hence, inclusion of the causally prior ecosystem attribute reduced the importance of downstream attributes reflected in their marginal values. The endangered species attribute difference was statistically significant at $p < 0.01$, but regional income and population of non-threatened species differences were significant at the 0.10 level and not the 0.05 level. Thus, the Swait–Louviere test found no globally significant differences in model parameters, but more detailed local tests suggest that there are some differences in the marginal attribute value that have the expected sign. Specifically, inclusion of the causally prior ecosystem attribute reduced the marginal value of endangered species.

Compensating surplus

The final test takes on increased importance given the previous result. Versions 1 and 3 were compared in terms of the overall welfare estimates generated for two specific scenarios. First, compensating surplus was estimated for a movement from current tree clearing guidelines, with the outcomes listed under Option A in Figure 7.1, to a new set of guidelines under which less endangered and non-threatened species would be lost (end = 16; pop = 50). Associated with the tighter tree clearing guidelines would be additional losses in jobs and regional income (jobs = 10; inc = 5).

The corresponding mean welfare estimates are $76 and $71 respectively for versions *with* and *without ecos*. These values were calculated at the mean values for *envatt, confuse* and *object*. Thus, inclusion of the causally prior ecosystem attribute only slightly increased WTP. A Poe *et al.* test suggested that the $76 estimate was not significantly higher than the $71 estimate ($p = 0.54$).[13] Recalculating these welfare estimates for the case in which the above environmental improvements are achieved at no cost in the form of lower regional employment and income increases the welfare estimates to $87 and $94 respectively.[14] Again, the difference was not statistically significant ($p = 0.47$).

An advantage of incorporating measures of perceived confusion and levy appropriateness within the choice model is that WTP measures can be computed for any level of these variables. For example, if we assign both these variables values of 1.5, corresponding to relatively low levels of confusion and objection, the WTP measures rise substantially. When reductions in employment and income are assumed, as specified above, WTP increases to $175 and $247 respectively. In this case, the hypothesis that the latter is higher than the former is rejected at the 5 per cent significance level, but not the 10 per cent level ($p = 0.08$).

7.4 CONCLUSIONS

Central to the design of any choice experiment is a well thought out choice task, and particularly the choice alternatives and attributes that describe them in each choice set. As discussed, there are many issues involved in proper design of choice experiments, hence selecting the most appropriate mix for a given study can be challenging. We cannot overly stress the importance of spending as much time as possible on focus groups, in-depth interviews, literature reviews, workshops with key stakeholders and other pilot and pre-testing methods to evaluate and review strengths and weaknesses of alternative designs. Indeed, due to the inseparable relationship between the variance of the random component and the quality of the estimates of the systematic component of utility, it behoves all researchers undertaking choice modelling studies of whatever type to spend as much time and resources as possible in advance of formulating final tasks and designs, not to mention in advance of data collection in the field. The latter prescription stands in stark contrast to the practice of many academics and practitioners who think that choice modelling research can be done quickly using 'off-the shelf software'. The foregoing discussion makes it clear that such practice is not only risky, but is counter to the basic theory itself.

A key issue that arises when conducting CM studies is whether to design choice tasks to be generic or alternative-specific. To the extent that the inclusion of policy or other labels increases correspondence between the emotional triggers embedded within surveys and those embedded in true market situations, the latter approach should lead to higher predictive validity. On the other hand, the generic approach has the potential to elicit more discerning trade-off information, which some might view as desirable.

Results of a study reported in this chapter indicate that whilst the mean unobserved utility component differed across the generic and alternative-specific treatments, as reflected in ASCs and their interactions, the vectors of attribute taste parameters did not differ significantly when random component variance differences were taken into account. However, the inclusion of policy labels appears to have reduced the attention respondents give to the attributes. Respondents appear to have anchored their responses to what they perceived to be their most preferred policy label. The results suggest that respondents may have adopted the strategy by which they choose the alternative with the preferred label unless it seemed unacceptable in terms of the one or two most important attributes (*levy* and *impact on endangered species*). Importantly, however, no statistically significant differences in welfare estimates were found when estimated for two different environmental improvement options. This further suggests that inclusion of alternative-specific policy labels and levels may redistribute the source of the utility in terms of the attribute marginal utilities and ASCs.

When selecting attributes in environmental choice modelling studies, we suggested that preference should be given to attributes that are demand-relevant, policy-relevant and measurable. However, these criteria often may yield lists of environmental attributes that include some that are causally related. Depending in part on how the CM task is framed, inclusion of causally related attributes may encourage some respondents to try to understand the causal relations among attributes to assign greater meaning to alternatives and, potentially, simplify their decision making process. Should this occur, there may be implications for the weights assigned to each attribute, and in turn the marginal WTP for the attributes and/or welfare estimates. The latter may be undesirable from a practitioner's perspective if respondents are requested to view attributes as *final* outcomes. In turn, this raises questions about whether causally related attributes should be included in choice sets, and if so, how to present and explain them to respondents. Future research designed to isolate and determine the locus of any such effects as well as their generality would be beneficial.

Thus, we found only limited support for the hypothesis that including causally prior attributes such as area of unique ecosystems affects the importance of downstream attributes. No significant difference in attribute parameter estimates was found, but the implicit value of a single endangered species fell by 34 per cent when the ecosystem attribute was included. As previously indicated, this may be due to part of the utility associated with endangered species being transferred to the ecosystem attribute. If replicable, this result would suggest that marginal rates of substitution, and hence marginal WTP, should not be interpreted without understanding the roles played by different attributes in choice processes. Like attributes, marginal WTP can be causally related and not readily interpreted in isolation to other choice set elements. Yet, it is significant that estimates of compensating surplus did *not* differ significantly across the two treatments for a given policy package. This suggests that to the extent that inclusion of causally prior ecosystem attributes reduces marginal WTP for one or more downstream attributes, the associated loss in utility may be approximately offset by utility associated with the new attribute. If this is true, it would suggest that marginal utilities were repackaged in such a way that the overall welfare implications of a policy proposal are unchanged. On balance, our findings suggest that using CM to estimate welfare effects in this case study produced logical and empirically meaningful results that were not significantly affected by framing tasks as generic or alternative-specific choices or by inclusion of causally prior attributes. The latter provide additional positive support for the choice experiment and modelling approach to environmental valuation.

NOTES

1. Blocked experimental designs can be used to address such problems. Respondents are assigned to one of *m* blocks, with respondents in different blocks receiving different subsets of the total number of choice sets. Respondents within the same block are presented with identical questionnaires.
2. Piggott and Wright (1992, p. 238) observe that a 'potentially important implication ... is that characteristics which are the focus in economics, such as price, may not be determinants of choice among products ... The role of price may be primarily to eliminate substitutes prior to formation of the final choice set ... Among the final choice set, price may not be a determinant attribute because all products exceeding acceptable price have been defined out of the set.'
3. A characteristic is also held to be *dominant* 'within some group of characteristics, in some sets of situations, if the consumer always prefers a collection with more of the dominant characteristic, whatever the amounts of other characteristics' (Lancaster 1991, p. 64–5). Dominance will often vary considerably from one consumer group to the next: 'the calorie content of food may be the dominant characteristic in a starving African society and, negatively, in a wealthy American society, while being irrelevant in a moderate-income European society' (p. 67).
4. Refer to Chapter 6 for an example.
5. Tversky and Kahneman (1982, p. 117) observe: 'It is psychological commonplace that people strive to achieve a coherent interpretation of the events that surround them, and that the organisation of events by schemas of cause-effect relations serves to achieve this goal.' Kelley (1972) originally proposed the notion of a causal schema, defining it as 'a conception of the manner in which two or more causal factors interact in relation to a particular kind of effect. A schema is derived from experience in observing cause and effect relationships ... It enables a person to perform certain operations with limited information and thereby to reach certain conclusions'.(p. 2). Einhorn and Hogarth (1985, p. 313) observe that 'one must have some hypothesis or theory for selecting relevant from irrelevant variables. Indeed, relevance can only be understood in relation to some model (usually implicit) of what generates the variable[s]' in question.
6. Whether or not alternative-specific attribute levels are required clearly depends to a large extent on the nature of the information communicated by the labels. For example, labels based on biogeographic differences such as 'The Desert Uplands' and 'The Brigalow' may not require alternative-specific attribute levels if respondents do not have strong a priori expectations regarding the relative magnitude of attribute levels for these regions.
7. A further caveat is that interactions between the causally upstream and downstream attributes are not tested in this chapter, as the experimental design employed in this study did not permit these interactions to be properly estimated. Future research might consider,

for example, whether the effect of downstream attributes on the odds of an alternative being chosen depends on the level of the upstream attribute.

8. Exploratory analysis indicated that the same model specification could be applied across the two treatments.

9. This implies that the marginal attribute values are equal across options in the labelled treatment, even though the range of levels represented in each option is alternative-specific. It would appear that marginal utility is not diminishing at a significant rate over the range of attribute levels included in the questionnaire (Table 7.2).

10. An examination of results in Table 7.3 suggests that equality of parameter vectors is unlikely to remain if the ASC terms are included in the test. A Swait–Louviere test of equality in entire parameter vectors confirms this suspicion, with the LR test not close to statistical significance (LR = 49.7 on 10 df, Critical Value = 18.3).

11. Specifying confusion and object in the utility function thus permits the majority of the systematic unobserved component to be controlled for.

12. These latter estimates should only be considered approximations. Whilst contributions to utility of the job and inc attributes can be controlled, the ASC terms will to some extent reflect attitudes to employment, which cannot be isolated.

13. Plugging envatt=1(pro-environment orientation) into the model results in respective WTP estimates of $140 and $158 for the two treatments. Plugging envatt=0 (pro-development orientation) into the model results in estimates of $33 and $39 respectively. Respondents' general stances on environmental issues clearly play an important role in how they respond. Some of this effect may involve yea-saying and/or symbolic responses.

14. These latter estimates should only be considered an approximation. Whilst contributions to utility of the *job* and *inc* attributes can be controlled for, the ASC terms will to some extent reflect attitudes to employment which cannot be isolated.

8. Opt-out Alternatives and Anglers' Stated Preferences

Melissa Ruby Banzhaf, F. Reed Johnson and Kristy E. Mathews

An important methodological issue in stated preference (SP) choice experiments is the inclusion and format of an op-out alternative. Opt-out alternatives avoid a 'forced choice' by allowing respondents to select another alternative if they do not prefer any of the hypothetical goods in the choice set. A split-sample design is used in a saltwater angling SP survey to test how including a 'no-trip' option influences attribute salience, relative to an option which allows respondents to choose their customary site.

8.1 INTRODUCTION

Stated preference (SP) surveys increasingly are applied to a variety of environmental economic contexts. SP methods have been used as an alternative to contingent valuation (CV) and advanced travel cost models to value recreational trips.[1] For example, Gan and Luzar (1993) use SP to value hunting trips in Louisiana. Mackenzie (1993) values hunting trips in Delaware using SP analysis. Roe et al. (1996) use SP to value the effects on sport fishing of implementing alternative management plans to restore runs of Atlantic salmon in Maine. SP methods also have been used to elicit preferences for other public goods. Opaluch et al. (1993) use SP to describe public preferences for siting a noxious facility. Johnson and Desvousges (1997) use SP to estimate electricity customers' willingness to pay for environmental and other attributes of electricity generation. In addition, SP methods are increasingly combined with revealed preference (RP) methods to obtain a richer view of environmental preferences. Adamowicz et al. (1994), Boxall et al. (1996), and Adamowicz et al. (1997) combine SP and RP approaches to evaluate site characteristics and to explain recreational site-choice selection. Finally, the National Oceanic and Atmospheric Administration recently has endorsed the use of SP to determine the scale of in-kind compensation for lost natural resource services. Thus, SP techniques are playing a more prominent role in many areas of environmental economics.

Many methodological issues associated with non-market applications of SP techniques remain unresolved. One of these issues is the decision to include an opt-out alternative in discrete choice SP questions. Employing an opt-out option avoids a 'forced choice' by allowing respondents to select another alternative if they do not prefer any of the hypothetical goods in the choice set (Olsen and Swait 1997). There are two main forms of opt-out options used in market research: the 'no-purchase' option and the 'my current brand' option. Little attention has been given to determining under which circumstances each format should be used. Yet the type of opt-out option may have a substantial impact on results because the format may induce respondents to evaluate the choice sets in different ways.

In this study, we evaluate the effect of opt-out options on the choices of recreational saltwater fishing sites. We use a split-sample design in which one group receives SP choices that include a 'no-trip' option. The other group evaluates SP choices in which the opt-out option is specified as an alternative fishing site of the respondent's choice. For this second subsample, respondents indicate at which site they would fish instead of the two hypothetical alternatives. We incorporate the characteristics of these alternative fishing sites into estimation and compare the results of this opt-out option with the results of the no-trip option for attribute salience. Because of the panel nature of the data, we estimate the data using random parameters logit (RPL) techniques recently developed by Revelt and Train (1998) and Train (1998), in addition to standard conditional logit models.

8.2　SP SURVEYS AND OPT-OUT OPTIONS

One SP format that is becoming increasingly popular is the discrete-choice format (Adamowicz *et al.* 1994, 1997; Opaluch *et al.* 1993). With the discrete choice format, respondents are presented with several alternatives, differing in attribute levels, and asked to select the most preferred alternative. Much of this approach's appeal lies in its resemblance to the way individuals normally purchase goods in the market place, as opposed to ranking or rating methods in which respondents rank all the available alternatives or rate their desirability using a scale. Proponents argue that because SP choice experiments mimic real choice environments, they more accurately predict actual choices (Louviere 1988a; Louviere and Woodworth 1983; Elrod *et al.* 1992).[2]

One aspect of discrete choice experiments that has received little attention in environmental applications is the use of an opt-out option and what form it should take. Opt-out options are alternatives that do not vary from one choice set to another (Batsell and Louviere 1991). These non-varying options are useful for several reasons. First, and most importantly, including an opt-out option prevents a forced choice in the experiment. In reality, many consumers when faced with the decision of which brand to purchase of a particular good can choose not to purchase the good at all on that occasion, or choose to purchase their usual brand. Restricting respondents only to hypothetical alternatives in an SP experiment may change the salience of attributes relative to a real market choice (Olsen and Swait 1997; Huber and Pinnell 1994). For instance, customers could be asked which of two brands of orange juice they prefer. The forced choice question will overstate the likelihood that they actually would purchase one of the two alternatives if, in fact, purchasing nothing or an alternative brand is preferred to purchasing one of the two offered brands.[3]

Including an opt-out option also has other advantages. Surveys which include opt-out options may reveal information about total demand, or market participation information, as well as share information (Batsell and Louviere 1991). They also may facilitate aggregating different data sets that use the same non-varying alternative (Louviere and Woodworth 1983). Lastly, incorporating an opt-out option into each choice set makes generating an efficient experimental choice design easier (Anderson and Wiley 1992).

There also are several potential disadvantages to incorporating an opt-out option into the experimental design. Respondents may select the opt-out option not because it provides the highest utility among the alternatives but to avoid making a difficult decision (Huber and Pinnell 1994). Additionally, allowing respondents to select an opt-out option provides less information on respondents' relative preferences for the attributes in the hypothetical alternatives. Also, opt-out options can create econometric challenges when researchers do not know what attribute levels are associated with the opt-out option. For example, in Adamowicz *et al.* (1997), respondents can choose not to go moose hunting on their next hunting occasion rather than hunt at the two hypothetical alternatives presented to respondents. If respondents decide not to hunt moose on their next trip, it is unclear what they are deciding to do instead (stay home, fish and so on) and thus it is unclear how to model this opt-out alternative.[4] Thus, an opt-out option may not be appropriate for every discrete choice study. If the objective is to mimic real market situations as closely as possible, however, then including an opt-out option may be warranted for many situations.

This analysis focuses specifically on what format of opt-out option should be implemented and what the implications are of using that format for the study's results. As noted above, the two most common forms of opt-out option are the 'no-purchase', also sometimes called 'delay purchase', and the 'my current brand' format. The equivalent formats in a recreation context are 'no trip' and 'my current site', respectively.

In the recreation literature, only one type of format has been used. Adamowicz *et al.* (1994) used the no-trip format in their study of recreators' choices of water-based recreation sites. Adamowicz *et al.* (1997) also applied the no-trip format in a study of moose hunters' choices of hunting sites. To our knowledge, no studies have employed a current-site format in an environmental economics context.[5]

The market research literature provides some guidance on this issue. Batsell and Louviere (1991) state that 'ideally one wants choice experiments to mimic the actual choice situations faced by individuals as closely as possible'. Their statement implies that whichever format may most accurately reflect the real situation faced by respondents in the study context is the appropriate one to use. Carson *et al.* (1994) suggest that the no-purchase format may be appropriate when including it would enhance task realism or when an objective is to measure market penetration, or in the case of recreation, participation. Alternatively, Carson et al. (1994) suggest that the current-brand format may be more relevant when the research objective is to determine which attributes a new product must have to induce consumers to switch to the new product over their current brand. Situations which fall into this category include products that are almost universally purchased, such as toothpaste or toilet paper, or decisions which must be made, such as mode choice for work trips, in which the trip must occur and the only question is which mode will be used. Thus, discussion in the market research literature suggests that different formats may be pertinent in different contexts.

The purpose of our SP study is to identify the most important features of a saltwater fishing experience along the central Gulf Coast of Texas. The results of this analysis will be used to inform the selection of restoration alternatives in a natural resource damage assessment. The SP analysis allows us to identify salient characteristics that increase angler utility. Estimated preferences help identify suitable restoration options that can be implemented to compensate for losses in fishing opportunities related to natural resource injury.

Respondents to the survey were prescreened saltwater anglers. In addition, this central coast region of the Texas coastline supports significant amounts of recreational fishing and offers numerous fishing sites. In this case, excluding the respondent's preferred actual site from the choice set may impose an unrealistic forced choice. Confronted with the choice among two hypothetical sites and not taking a fishing trip on their next choice occasion, respondents may indicate that they would prefer one of the hypothetical sites to not fishing at all. In fact, they might prefer their customary site even more, so their SP response overstates their likelihood of visiting a site with the hypothesised characteristics. Conversely, selecting 'not go fishing' rather than fishing at one of the two hypothetical sites on their next choice occasion would understate their likelihood of taking a fishing trip if they preferred their customary site overall. Thus, the argument for including a current site opt-out option appears to apply in this context.

Because the appropriate choice of opt-out format has not been explored in the recreation literature previously, we include both formats in a split sample design. This design allows us to test what effect, if any, the opt-out format may have on individual attribute salience. In addition, the results of this analysis can help identify recreation contexts in which one format may be more valid than the other.

8.3 EXPERIMENTAL DESIGN

The experimental design consists of the specific attributes, attribute levels and fishing-site profiles that appear in the SP questions. Determining the relevant attributes and the specific attribute levels required balancing several factors. First, the attributes used in an SP design must be meaningful to respondents in describing saltwater fishing experiences on the central coast of Texas. Second, the SP portion of this study was part of a joint RP–SP application. Therefore, at least some of the attributes must correspond to attributes in the RP models.[6] Furthermore, with certain attributes, the SP attribute levels are designed to provide more independent variation than is present in the RP data to enhance estimation and to facilitate evaluation of restoration options that are not prevalent at existing fishing sites. Finally, the attributes must correspond to practical restoration options. Thus, the objectives of the study governed the appropriate attribute and levels used in the SP design.

Table 8.1 contains the attributes and levels used in our SP survey. We developed this list based on site visits, a review of the SP and RP recreation literature, and two pretests. The first attribute is fishing mode (with boat and pier as the levels), which allows respondents' preferences to vary by mode. It is hypothesised that different respondents may have preferences for the two fishing modes, especially because boat fishing requires a capital investment.

The second attribute is the additional distance to the fishing or launch site.[7] This marginal difference in travel distance is the key to making this attribute meaningful to respondents. In this application, there are many saltwater opportunities within a couple of miles of some population centres. However, there is also a large inland population of anglers who live more than 40 miles from saltwater sites. To make the attribute equally realistic to both kinds of anglers, the distance attribute represents the number of additional miles from the closest saltwater site rather than an absolute number of miles. The specific levels are based on estimated distances to saltwater fishing sites from major population centres within the survey area.

Table 8.1 Attributes and levels used in SP survey

Attribute	Levels
Fishing mode	Pier
	Boat
Additional distance to fishing or launch site	5 additional miles
	15 additional miles
	30 additional miles
Species and catch rate	1 Red Drum
	3 Red Drum
	2 Flounder
	10 Flounder
	2 Speckled Trout
	10 Speckled Trout
Surroundings	No view of industrial plants
	View of industrial plants
Congestion	Many people or boats in sight
	Some people or boats in sight
Amenities	Limited parking
	Good parking
	Good parking and restrooms
	Good parking, restrooms and bait shop
Fish consumption advisory	No advisory (fish can be eaten)
	Fish should not be eaten

The next attribute is the number and type of fish caught, because these characteristics are likely to be an important part of the fishing experience. Practical limitations require that the number of species be limited to three and that the catch be limited to two different levels for each species. The largest number represents the bag limit, or the maximum number of fish that may be kept, for each species.

The surroundings for the fishing trip, the level of congestion and site amenities can also influence site selection. The surroundings attribute includes a two-level view of industrial plants, which captures a noticeable feature of fishing sites in this somewhat industrial area of Texas. The congestion attribute is included because this characteristic affected site selection in pretests. Because minimal visitation is not realistic when viewed from a restoration perspective of providing attractive fishing opportunities for anglers, the lowest level of congestion describes the presence of at least some other anglers. The final design also includes four levels of site amenities. This attribute and the associated levels are important in terms of restoration alternatives because these amenities represent specific projects that may be feasible to implement.

Finally, the design includes the presence or absence of a fish consumption advisory to ensure enough variation in site characteristics for econometric estimation. Because there is insufficient variation across actual fishing sites with respect to a consumption advisory, the SP data supplements the RP data and enables more variation for this particular site characteristic to be included in the design.

The experimental design consists of a main-effects, nearly orthogonal array sorted into 30 choice sets. This study adapted a search procedure from Zwerina *et al.* (1996) to develop an optimal choice experimental design. In addition to the SP questions, respondents were asked to answer questions on RP fishing trips and monthly fish consumption. Thus, given the large amount of information elicited from respondents as well as respondents' attention constraints, we blocked the SP experimental design into two sets of 15 SP questions each. We randomly assigned a 15 question choice set to each respondent.

In addition to the two different design blocks, we included an experimental treatment on the opt-out alternative in each choice set. In the first treatment, the opt-out option is comparable to a no-purchase option. This treatment asks respondents to assume that Site A and Site B are the only two sites available for their next fishing trip. These two hypothetical sites are described using the attributes and levels in Table 8.1. In this treatment, respondents who do not like either of the two hypothetical fishing sites offered can select the third alternative of 'Neither Site A nor Site B, I will not go saltwater fishing'. In the second treatment, the survey instructions ask respondents to think about what they would do if these two sites were available in addition to existing fishing sites. Respondents who do not like either of the two hypothetical fishing sites may opt-out by selecting the third choice of 'Neither Site A nor Site B, I would go saltwater fishing at another site'. These respondents are asked to provide the name of that fishing site. Figure 8.1 provides an example of an SP question for the second treatment.

Assuming that the following two saltwater fishing sites were available, in addition to your usual saltwater fishing sites, which one would you choose on your next saltwater fishing trip? If neither appeals to you, then choose the third box, and write in the space provided below where you would go saltwater fishing instead.

	Site A	Site B	Neither
Type of fishing	Boat	Pier	
Additional distance to fishing or launch site	30 miles from your closest saltwater fishing site	15 miles from your closest saltwater fishing site	
Catch rate	3 red drum	10 spotted sea trout	
Surroundings	View of industrial plants	No view of industrial plants	Neither Site A nor Site B
Congestion	Some people or boats in sight	Some people or boats in sight	
Facilities at site	Good parking	Limited parking	I would go saltwater fishing at another site
Fish consumption advisory	Fish should not be eaten	No advisory (fish can be eaten)	

Check only ONE box

☐   ☐   ☐

Prefer Site A   **Prefer Site B**   **Prefer another site**

Write name of site here

Figure 8.1 Example of an SP question

The two opt-out treatments were administered to respondents randomly across the two different design blocks. Thus, the SP survey consisted of four versions of the experimental design: block one combined with the not go fishing opt-out treatment, block two combined with the not go fishing treatment, and two similar combinations for the prefer another site opt-out treatment.

The questionnaire was administered to licensed anglers from three counties on the central coast of Texas. The study used a combination mail–telephone mode for survey administration. The incentive payment for respondents was $10, and respondents who completed the survey were automatically entered in a lottery for angling-related prizes. The period of survey administration lasted from December 1996 to March 1997. Depending upon how unable-to-contact households are treated, the response rate ranges from a low of 68 per cent to a high of 83 per cent. In total, nearly 2 000 anglers participated in the study. Respondents who did not answer all 15 SP questions were eliminated from the analysis reported here. Thus, this analysis includes 1 345 respondents.

8.4 CONCEPTUAL FRAMEWORK

The SP survey included a series of choice judgements with three alternatives in each choice set. The linear specification of utility for the three alternatives is:

$$U^i_{jt} = V^i_{jt} + \varepsilon^i_{jt} \equiv X_{jt}\beta + \varepsilon^i_{jt} \qquad (8.1)$$

where U^i_{jt}, $j = 1, 2$, is the utility of each of the two hypothetical sites and U^i_0 is the respondent's utility for the opt-out option in all t choice sets. X is a vector of site attributes, β is a vector of marginal utility parameters, and ε designates stochastic errors.

Assuming ε follows a type one extreme value error structure, the probability that alternative j will be selected from choice set t is the standard conditional logit expression:

$$\text{Prob}\left(C^i_t = j\right) = \frac{\exp\left(\mu^i \cdot V^i_{jt}\right)}{\displaystyle\sum_{k=0}^{2}\exp\left(\mu^i \cdot V^i_{kt}\right)} \qquad (8.2)$$

where C^i_{jt} is the selected alternative in each of 15 choice sets, μ^i is the scale parameter, and V_j^i is the determinate part of the utility of alternative j.[8] Note that individual characteristics fall out of this expression unless interacted with site attributes. The scale parameter μ^i also generally is not identifiable in such models and is normalised at one.

Conditional logit models are known to be subject to violations of the irrelevance of independent alternatives assumption (IIA). This condition requires that the ratio of probabilities for any two alternatives be independent of the attribute levels in the third alternative. Conditional logit parameter estimates are biased if IIA is violated. Furthermore, conditional logit does not account for correlations within each respondent's series of choices. Revelt and Train (1998) have proposed using random parameter logit (RPL) for SP data similar to ours. RPL is not subject to the IIA assumption, accommodates correlations among panel observations and accounts for uncontrolled heterogeneity in tastes across respondents.

Modifying equation (8.1) to introduce respondent-specific stochastic components for each β:

$$U_{jt}^i = V_{jt}^i + \varepsilon_{jt}^i \equiv X_{jt}\left(\beta + \eta^i\right) + \varepsilon_{jt}^i \qquad (8.3)$$

Equation (8.2) now becomes:

$$\text{Prob}\left[C^i = \left(C_{j1}^i, C_{j2}^i, \ldots C_{j15}^i\right)\right] = \prod_{t=1}^{15} \left\{ \frac{\exp\left[\mu^i \cdot X_{jt}\left(\beta + \eta^i\right)\right]}{\sum_{k=0}^{2} \exp\left[\mu^i \cdot X_{kt}\left(\beta + \eta^i\right)\right]} \right\} \qquad (8.4)$$

In contrast to conditional logit, the stochastic part of utility now may be correlated among alternatives and across the sequence of choices via the common influence of η^i. McFadden and Train (1997) show that any random utility model can be approximated by some RPL specification. We compare both the standard logit and the RPL estimates of the SP model in this study.

Treating preference parameters as random variables requires estimation by simulated maximum likelihood. Procedurally, the maximum likelihood algorithm searches for a solution by simulating m draws from distributions with given means and standard deviations. Probabilities are calculated by integrating the joint simulated distribution. In the following analysis, we assume parameters are independently normally distributed. Distribution simulations are based on 500 draws.[9]

8.5 ANALYSIS RESULTS

The 1 345 respondents in the SP portion of the survey each answered 15 SP questions, producing a total of 20 175 observations. Splitting these observations into their respective treatments yields 10 410 for the not go fishing opt-out treatment and 9 765 for the prefer another site opt-out treatment. We estimate separate models for each treatment and base the statistical analysis of the data on the discussion in the previous section.

Table 8.2 Variables used in analysis

Variables	Description
REDDRUM	Number of red drum caught and kept
FLOUNDER	Number of flounder caught and kept
TROUT	Number of trout caught and kept
BOAT	Dummy variable = 1 if mode of fishing is boat trip
GOODPARK	Dummy variable = 1 if site amenities include good parking
RESTROOMS	Dummy variable = 1 if site amenities include rest rooms
BAITSHOP	Dummy variable = 1 if site amenities include bait shop
NOVIEW	Dummy variable = 1 if there is no view of industrial plants at site
LOWCONGEST	Dummy variable = 1 if there are some boats or people in sight at site
NOADVISORY	Dummy variable = 1 if there is no fish consumption advisory at site (that is, fish can be eaten)
LNMILES	Natural log of total distance to site from home
EST_STD	Estimate of the standard deviation of the site characteristic random parameter
ASD_AB	Alternative specific dummy for alternatives A and B in each choice set
ASD_CMISS	Alternative specific dummy for alternative C in the prefer another site treatment if the respondent never provided an alternative site in all 15 questions

Table 8.2 contains a list of the variables used in this analysis. Many of these variables are the same attribute levels described earlier. EST_STD is estimated standard deviations of the random parameters for the RPL models. In addition, we include two alternative specific dummies. In the not go fishing treatment, in which the alternative C choice was defined as 'Neither Site A nor Site B, I will not go saltwater fishing', utility is normalised on this third alternative. No site characteristics are included for this option. However, for the prefer another site treatment, in which respondents have the alternative of specifying an existing site if they do not like alternatives A or B, we include actual site characteristics in alternative C for the sites respondents specified. An alternative specific dummy, ASD_CMISS, is used for respondents who never provided an alternative site in their 15 SP questions (that is, these respondents selected the hypothetical sites A or B for each question) in the prefer another site treatment.

The first model shown in Table 8.3 is a standard conditional logit model for the not go fishing treatment that does not account for within-subject error correlation. The results of this model indicate that almost all of the site characteristics are highly significant in influencing site choice, with the exception of BAITSHOP which is significant at the 10 per cent level. In addition, all of the site attributes, except for RESTROOMS and LNMILES, are positive, indicating that the presence of these attributes increases the probability of site selection, other things remaining equal. The three site amenity levels are interpreted relative to the omitted category of limited parking. Initially, the negative sign on RESTROOMS at first appears counter-intuitive because one might think that the presence of restrooms would enhance the site attractiveness relative to limited parking. However, the public restrooms in this area of Texas are perceived to be dirty and unattractive to many anglers. Thus, respondents appeared to have imputed their current perceptions of the restrooms in the study area to the hypothetical attribute levels in the survey. The negative coefficient on the distance variable suggests that anglers derive less utility from a fishing trip when they have to drive further, which is consistent with expectations.

The relative magnitude of the coefficients indicates that being able to eat the fish caught at a site (NOADVISORY) is the most important attribute to anglers in our sample. This variable is over seven times larger than the next most important attribute, boat fishing. Of the fish species, catching one red drum yields twice the utility of catching either a trout or a flounder. This result is not surprising because red drum is a highly sought sport fish in the area. Also, boat fishing is significantly preferred to pier fishing. Examining the parameters of the site amenities reveals that good parking is the most highly desired amenity, relative to limited parking. A priori, we expected bait shops to be the most desirable amenity to anglers, so the result is somewhat surprising. The aesthetic attributes of no view of industrial plants and low congestion at the fishing site appear to be somewhat important to anglers and provide slightly more utility than catching one flounder or trout. Finally, the alternative-specific constant on alternatives A and B (ASD_AB) accounts for the proportion of choices of A or B relative to alternative C not otherwise explained by the model.

The conditional logit model for the prefer another site treatment, also shown in Table 8.3, reveals similar patterns. For instance, the NOADVISORY coefficient is the largest in magnitude and by approximately the same magnitude as in the not go fishing treatment. In addition, all of the site characteristic coefficients are positive except RESTROOMS and LNMILES. However, fewer variables are significant in this model. The site amenities of restrooms and bait shops are not significant, suggesting that these amenities do not enhance site attractiveness relative to limited parking in this treatment model. Also, the aesthetic variable NOVIEW is not significant, indicating that aesthetics did not influence site selection.

The conditional logit models of each treatment shown in Table 8.3 are based on statistical procedures widely used in the market research and recreation literature. Nevertheless, there is the potential for bias in such estimates. First, we have assumed that the utility weights for site attributes are the same across all respondents. Second, unbiased conditional logit estimates require IIA. If this IIA assumption does not hold, parameter estimates are biased. Finally, conditional logit estimates assume that errors in each respondent's series of answers are uncorrelated.

As discussed in the previous section, the RPL technique avoids all three of these potential sources of bias. Table 8.3 reports RPL results corresponding to the conditional logit models. However, in the RPL models, the site characteristic parameters are treated as random variables. In this case, each parameter includes both a systematic and a random component, and thus, the model estimates a mean and a standard deviation for each distribution. Treating the site characteristics as random parameters allows us to test for the degree of heterogeneity in preferences across respondents by examining the significance of the standard deviation (EST_STD) and comparing its magnitude with the mean. The only site characteristic that is fixed is LNMILES in order to provide a basis for normalising utility scales.

Comparing the RPL model to the conditional logit model in the not go fishing treatment reveals some changes in significance levels. Both BAITSHOP and NOVIEW become insignificant, and RESTROOM decreases significance to the 10 per cent level. In addition, some parameters change in magnitude between the two specifications. The parameters on the fish species and NOADVISORY are significantly higher in the RPL model than in the conditional logit model, whereas NOVIEW and BOAT shift somewhat in the

Table 8.3 Comparing model results between conditional logit models and random parameters logit models for the opt-out treatments

Variables	Not go fishing treatment				Prefer another site treatment			
	Conditional logit coefficient	T-ratio	Random parameters logit coefficient	T-ratio	Conditional logit coefficient	T-ratio	Random parameters logit coefficient	T-ratio
REDDRUM	0.1192 ***	9.71	0.2600 ***	8.87	0.1799 ***	9.60	0.3682 ***	13.46
EST_STD			0.3033 ***	9.36			0.2931 ***	8.02
FLOUNDER	0.0803 ***	14.64	0.1121 ***	14.03	0.0703 ***	13.12	0.1353 ***	16.36
EST_STD			0.0888 ***	9.29			0.1118 ***	11.08
TROUT	0.0883 ***	15.71	0.1418 ***	19.51	0.0850 ***	15.52	0.1491 ***	20.08
EST_STD			0.0640 ***	7.14			0.0936 ***	8.45
BOAT	0.2762 ***	8.55	0.2506 ***	3.80	0.2555 ***	8.34	0.5332 ***	7.17
EST_STD			1.5941 ***	30.19			1.8785 ***	27.52
GOODPARK	0.2415 ***	4.98	0.2449 ***	2.61	0.1635 ***	4.06	0.1965 ***	3.00
EST_STD			1.0879 ***	18.07			0.7805 ***	8.68
RESTROOMS	-0.1489 ***	-3.06	-0.1394 *	-1.91	-0.0439	-0.99	-0.1042 *	-1.68
EST_STD			0.0124	0.08			0.4212 ***	5.47
BAITSHOP	0.0884 *	1.73	0.0983	1.29	0.0157	0.35	0.1581 **	2.28
EST_STD			0.0616	0.31			0.6645 ***	7.98

	Model 1		Model 2		Model 3		Model 4	
NOVIEW	0.1360 ***	4.18	0.0501	0.75	0.0411	1.42	0.0735	1.45
EST_STD			0.9016 ***	14.81			0.7933 ***	13.66
LOWCONGEST	0.1127 ***	3.25	0.1452 ***	2.63	0.1540 ***	4.41	0.2917 ***	3.42
EST_STD			0.5035 ***	6.50			1.1740 ***	16.97
NOADVISORY	2.0916 ***	60.78	3.3684 ***	36.52	1.9018 ***	53.53	4.2528 ***	32.16
EST_STD			2.2590 ***	25.16			2.8301 ***	25.84
LNMILES	-0.1954 ***	-6.98	-0.5212 ***	-16.86	-0.2193 ***	-8.60	-0.3754 ***	-14.99
ASD_AB	-1.2307 ***	-10.65			0.5829 ***	15.78	1.0117 ***	21.84
ASD_CMISS			-0.9158 ***	-7.46	0.6033 ***	4.75	-1.4226 ***	-28.86
No. of observations	10 410		10 410		9 765		9 765	
Madalla's pseudo R-square	0.398		0.556		0.410		0.556	
McFadden's pseudo R-square	0.237		0.378		0.242		0.372	

Notes:
*** significant at the 1% level
** significant at the 5% level
* significant at the 10% level

opposite direction. Thus, these results suggest that the conditional logit model estimates are somewhat biased, although the direction of bias varies.

Allowing preferences for site attributes to vary across respondents shows that there is considerable unexplained heterogeneity in respondent preferences. Most of the EST_STD variables are highly significant, indicating statistically different preferences for these characteristics across respondents. The only ones that are not significant are RESTROOMS and BAITSHOP, implying that this treatment elicits general consensus regarding the unattractiveness of restrooms and the lack of importance of bait shops. Interestingly, although the mean parameter on NOVIEW is insignificant, the estimated standard deviation is significant, suggesting that the lack of significance in viewing industrial plants may be more a result of balancing out bimodal preferences than a general lack of salience across all respondents.

Although there appears to be significant heterogeneity across respondents for many of the site attributes, we can assess differences in the amount of heterogeneity across attributes by comparing the relative magnitude of the standard deviation coefficient with the mean parameters. For instance, there are five variables for which the standard deviation coefficient is larger than the mean estimate, suggesting relatively large variation in preferences across respondents. These variables include REDDRUM, BOAT, GOODPARK, NOVIEW and LOWCONGEST. Of these variables, NOVIEW exhibits the largest difference between the mean and standard deviation with the standard deviation being 18 times larger than the mean. This result supports our conclusion mentioned above regarding the large disparity in preferences accounting for the lack of significance of the mean.

It is not surprising that preferences for boat trips vary so widely across respondents. Anglers in this area seem to belong to one of two groups: those who do most of their angling by boat and those who fish from piers or the shore. Most anglers in this area prefer boat fishing. However, because there is a substantial capital investment to pursue this mode of angling, those who do not fish from boats probably would not prefer boat trips in the SP questions. The differences among the remaining variables may reflect differences in demographics across the sample area. This area supports a mix of blue-collar, rural and professional jobs. In addition, there is wide variation in distances to fishing sites, with some anglers living directly on the coast and other anglers living 40 miles inland. The anglers who live further inland are less frequent anglers who tend to visit more widely known fishing sites. Because GOODPARK, NOVIEW and LOWCONGEST reflect aesthetic attributes, it is not surprising that anglers with different demographic as well as distance characteristics would value different types of fishing experiences. This variety is captured in the standard deviation estimates of these coefficients.

Comparing the RPL model to the conditional logit model in the prefer another site treatment yields somewhat different disparities between the two models. For the RPL model, no variables lose significance and some gain significance. The variables RESTROOMS and BAITSHOP gain significance, and NOVIEW remains insignificant in this treatment. Many variables increase significantly in magnitude between the conditional logit and RPL models, and the increases in magnitude tend to be larger than in the not go fishing treatment. For example, the coefficients of REDDRUM, BOAT, and NOADVISORY more than double between the two models, far greater than any change in the other treatment. Only one variable, RESTROOMS, decreases in magnitude, which indicates a stronger, negative effect. Thus, the conditional logit model in this treatment shows more bias than did the conditional logit model in the not go fishing treatment and in the direction of suppressing attribute salience for most characteristics. One reason for this difference could be that the prefer another site model incorporates site characteristics from alternative sites that respondents specified. We would expect respondents' favourite sites to differ greatly from other respondents' favourite sites based on differences in location and preferences. Thus, the prefer another site models involve greater preference heterogeneity and much of this variation is not controlled for in the conditional logit model.

This last conclusion is supported further by the significance of the estimates of standard deviation of the parameter distributions. All of the EST_STD variables are significant at the highest level. In addition, there are six variables that have standard deviations greater than their means. Four of these six are the same as in the not go fishing treatment (BOAT, GOODPARK, NOVIEW, LOWCONGEST). In this treatment, the ratios of standard deviation to mean for RESTROOMS and BAITSHOP also are greater than 1, showing more variation of preferences for these amenities than in the not go fishing treatment.

Comparing the fit of these RPL models to their conditional logit counterparts shows that the RPL models appear to do a much better job of capturing preferences by several measures. Both the Madalla and McFadden pseudo R-square statistics, already high in the conditional logit models compared with most cross-sectional data, increase between 30 and 60 per cent when the parameters are assumed to be random variables. Thus, for both conceptual as well as empirical reasons, we use only the RPL models in subsequent analysis as more accurate and unbiased measures of angler preferences.

The two RPL models in Table 8.3 are fairly similar in terms of significance of variables and signs of coefficients. However, the prefer another site model has more variables that are statistically significant and appears to do a better job of capturing the heterogeneity across respondents.

Because the models may reflect different underlying scales, we cannot compare the coefficients directly across models. Consequently, to understand how treatment of the opt-out option affects attribute salience, each model must be rescaled by a common coefficient. In this case, we rescale all of the attribute level mean parameters by distance, or more specifically, the negative of the coefficient on LNMILES.

Table 8.4 Comparing rescaled coefficients across the opt-out option treatments and testing for significant differences

Parameters	Not go fishing rescaled coefficient	Prefer another site rescaled coefficient	T-ratio of differences
REDDRUM	0.4988	0.9808	−3.99 ***
FLOUNDER	0.2151	0.3604	−3.91 ***
TROUT	0.2721	0.3972	−3.30 ***
BOAT	0.4808	1.4204	−3.59 ***
GOODPARK	0.4699	0.5234	−0.20
RESTROOMS	−0.2675	−0.2776	0.03
BAITSHOP	0.1886	0.4212	−1.03
NOVIEW	0.0961	0.1958	−0.60
LOWCONGEST	0.2786	0.7770	−1.89 *
NOADVISORY	6.4628	11.3287	−5.36 ***
LNMILES	−1.0000	−1.0000	
ASD_AB	−1.7571	2.6950	−10.86 ***

Notes:
*** significant at the 1% level
** significant at the 5% level
* significant at the 10% level

Table 8.4 contains the rescaled parameters for each treatment, as well as the t-statistic for differences in attribute coefficients across the two treatments.[10] This table illustrates some interesting results with regard to treatment. First, the variables NOADVISORY, REDDRUM, FLOUNDER, TROUT, BOAT and LOWCONGEST have significantly higher coefficients in the prefer another site treatment than they do in the not go fishing treatment. These results suggest that when respondents are given the choice of specifying an alternative site, they are more likely to specify sites with these characteristics, thus increasing the salience of these attributes. For example, if anglers prefer to target red drum when they fish, then they may choose hypothetical alternatives involving red drum catches. However, when presented with an SP question that describes two trips in which the target species are trout and flounder, they may opt out of the two hypothetical sites and specify an actual site known to have a high probability of catching red drum. Doing so increases the salience of the red drum attribute. Therefore, when given a choice of specifying an existing site, respondents tend to choose boat sites, sites that have higher catch rates of red drum, flounder and trout, sites that have lower congestion and sites that do not have a fish consumption advisory.

Another interesting result of this comparison is the number of site attributes that are *not* significantly different between the two treatments. None of the site amenities or the surroundings attribute is statistically different between the two treatments. This result supports the lack of robustness observed with these variables in Table 8.3. Thus, treatment of the opt-out option does not seem to affect variables that are less important to anglers. This result again is not surprising. Opt-out selections are simply not driven by variations in the levels shown for less salient attributes.

Therefore, treatment does seem to affect the salience of key site characteristics. When given the choice, respondents do opt-out in favour of actual sites with their preferred site attributes. Including the characteristics of these opt-out sites increases salience, sometimes as much as double, for the more important characteristics. However, for less important characteristics, treatment does not seem to have a significant effect.

8.6 CONCLUSIONS

The results of this study show that the opt-out treatment can influence results under certain circumstances. The effect of the opt-out treatment appears to be most influential on site characteristics that are the most salient to respondents. We therefore expect to find differences between the two treatments in policy situations in which changes in these characteristics are likely to be important determinants of welfare.

These results suggest that it is important to consider in which situations each treatment would be applicable. In this context, our sample consisted of anglers in a study area which contains many substitutes. Thus, it seems that, in this context, applying a prefer another site treatment is more appropriate than a not go fishing treatment because in reality anglers are frequent 'purchasers' of saltwater fishing sites. Including their preferred sites from the choice set is consistent with Batsell and Louviere's (1991) recommendation to mimic the actual choice situation as closely as possible. In addition, by including the site characteristics of these anglers' preferred sites in estimation, we obtain a more accurate picture of the salience of site attributes.

Although the prefer another site treatment seems to be more appropriate in this situation, other policy contexts may govern the use of the not go fishing, or similar 'non-participation,' opt-out treatments. For example, in situations when the sample does not consist of usual recreators, applying a 'no purchase' opt-out treatment may be more appealing conceptually.

NOTES

1   Terminology has not been standardised across various disciplines. In this analysis, we will use the term 'stated preference' to refer to a group of techniques primarily used in market research studies to measure consumer preferences. The term 'conjoint analysis' also has been used to describe some of these techniques. Although CV could also be called a stated preference technique, CV was developed independently by environmental economists and relies on a different set of elicitation formats and analytical approaches.

2.   However, Huber (1997) notes that choice, rating and ranking SP formats trigger different cognitive responses. For example, with a choice task, respondents are more likely to consider fewer attributes and put the greatest weight on the least attractive attribute levels. Huber concludes that choice tasks are most appropriate when simulating short-term responses when consumers make decisions on the basis of competitive differences among attributes. Ratings tasks draw attention to differences in the attribute levels and are most appropriate when modelling longer-term market adaptations. Finally, ranking exercises encourages respondents to evaluate each profile individually. This elicitation approach is most appropriate when the focus of a choice is within the profile, not across profiles. Thus, selection of the appropriate SP elicitation technique depends on the specific context and remains a research issue.

3.   Freeman (1991) demonstrates the need for a 'status quo' alternative in SP experiments.

4.   This problem can be avoided by specifying the attribute levels of the non-varying alternative as in Swait *et al.* (1994) which specified the attribute levels for a constant freight carrier in a shipping study. However, including this type of non-varying alternative could still constitute a forced choice if respondents would rather select their current freight carrier over the alternatives included in the choice sets.

5.   Both types of formats have been used in the market research literature. Louviere and Woodworth (1993) discuss several studies which have used a no purchase opt-out format, including studies evaluating the use of airline tickets to predetermined destinations, analysing the selection of lunch menus, and assessing characteristics that induce travellers to travel to the US from Australia. Huber and Pinnell (1994) incorporate a delay purchase option in a study on the decision of business managers to purchase computers, and Olsen and Swait (1997) examine the decision to purchase frozen concentrate orange juice. Studies using a current brand or 'other' opt-out option include Elrod *et al.*'s (1992) study analyzing the decision to rent apartments and Swait *et al.*'s (1994) study examining freight shippers' choice of carrier.

6.   The RP analysis associated with the study is not discussed here.

7.   In this study, there is not a cost attribute per se, but we have incorporated a distance attribute which may be converted into a travel cost attribute. Because our focus is on attribute salience to satisfy in-kind compensation analyses, we do not report willingness to pay values.

8.   The basic exposition of the properties of this model can be found in McFadden (1981).

9. Estimation was accomplished using an adaptation of Kenneth Train's Gauss program available from the Berkeley Econometrics Laboratory web site at emlab.berkeley.edu/Software/abstracts/train0296.html.
10. The utility scale is arbitrary, so coefficients are divided by LNMILES to standardise the scales for the two treatments. Standard errors of the differences are obtained from 1 000 draws on each multivariate normal parameter distribution.

9. Yea-saying and Validation of a Choice Model of Green Product Choice

Russell Blamey and Jeff Bennett

9.1 INTRODUCTION

Numerous studies have examined the extent to which stated preferences (SP) diverge from revealed preferences (RP). While the majority of these studies appear to have involved marketing and transport applications, recreation and environmental applications are becoming more common. Examples of the former include Ben-Akiva and Morikawa (1990), Hensher and Bradley (1993), Swait et al. (1994),[1] and examples of the latter include Adamowicz et al. (1994, 1996), Champ et al. (1997), Cummings et al. (1995), Duffield and Patterson (1991), Loomis et al. (1996), Navrud (1992), Polasky et al. (1996) and Seip and Strand (1992).

Validation studies involving environmental SP applications have been limited by the absence of market data with which to compare results. Those that have been conducted vary in terms of the nature of the environmental good under consideration, the preference constructs that are compared[2] and the extent to which the RP data are collected in a 'normal' setting.[3] Studies conducted to date have considered a range of environmental goods and behaviour, including recreation site choice (Adamowicz et al. 1994) donations to environmental funds (Champ et al. 1997), and voting behaviour (Polasky et al. 1996).

We are unaware of any SP–RP comparisons regarding green product[4] choice. This is perhaps surprising given that green products provide benefits in the form of non-use values and preferences for these products are revealed in markets. Green product choice thus presents an opportunity to validate stated and revealed preferences regarding environmental values with a non-use component. The results of such an SP–RP validation exercise are presented in this chapter. The relative ease of conducting validation exercises with respect to existing market products is exploited here to compare what people say they will buy with what they actually buy in a product category with a socially desirable environmental dimension.

This validation exercise is conducted in the context of the toilet paper case study described in Chapter 6 of this volume. The first objective is to compare the results of the choice experiment described in Chapter 6 with RP data obtained in the form of supermarket scanner data for the same shopping location and purchase period. Results are also presented of a test for the effect of yea-saying. One concern with the use of SP methods is that they are susceptible to biases such as social desirability bias (SDB) and pro-environmental yea-saying, which may give rise to SP–RP divergences. A second choice experiment was therefore run in parallel with the experiment described in Chapter 6 in order to test for these effects. The only difference between the two surveys was that the second included 'green product' social desirability prompts in the covering letter. To the extent that SDB and yea-saying affect environmental choice experiments, one would expect these prompts to increase their extent.

The two SP treatments are compared in terms of marginal rates of substitution (implicit prices) for the environmental attribute, overall taste parameter vectors and predicted market shares. SP choice models and associated market share estimates are then compared with corresponding RP models and actual and estimated shares.

This chapter is structured as follows. A review of factors likely to underlie RP–SP divergences is presented in the next section, focusing on the social desirability and yea-saying explanations. An outline of the methods used to test the hypotheses is then provided, followed by the results in section 9.4. Some conclusions are drawn in the final section.

9.2 FACTORS UNDERLYING RP–SP DIVERGENCES

A number of factors may give rise to divergences between SP and RP estimates of market share, marginal rates of substitution and willingness to pay. An awareness of these factors is important when designing any RP–SP comparison.

One explanation for divergences is the occurrence of social desirability bias (SDB), whereby respondents have a tendency to present themselves in a favourable position with respect to social norms (Edwards 1957; Nunnaly 1978; Sudman and Bradburn 1974; Jo *et al.* 1997). The tendency to give answers that make oneself look good (Paulhus 1991) is a particular concern in research utilising self-report questions, where the object of the questions has a significant desirability component. In the context of SP surveys with an environmental component, the social norms are likely to relate to perceived expectations of the interviewer, sponsor, friends, family and/or society as a whole. To the extent that respondents perceive that a 'green' response is socially desirable, they may implicitly or explicitly overstate the importance of green attributes and/or brand or policy labels when formulating their responses. In such cases, SDB may pose a threat to construct validity.

Only one study of SDB in this area was found when reviewing the literature for this research. Connelly and Brown (1994) tested for SDB in reported contributions to a wildlife income tax check-off programme. Respondents were asked in a mail survey if they were aware of the programme, if they had contributed, and whether they intended to contribute in the future. Responses regarding stated contributions were then validated against official tax records. After allowing for recall errors, the estimated percentage of non-contributors who stated they had contributed was no less than 5.8 per cent. Because this was almost twice the actual contribution rate, Connelly and Brown (1994, p. 84) conclude that this result 'poses a major validity problem in any analysis of self-reported contributors based on survey results'.

Closely related to SDB is the occurrence of yea-saying. Yea-saying has traditionally been defined as the tendency to agree with questions regardless of content (Cronbach 1946, 1950; Couch and Keniston 1960; Arndt and Crane 1975; Moum, 1988). In the context of in-person contingent valuation (CVM) interviews, Mitchell and Carson (1989, pp. 240–1) define it as 'the tendency of some respondents to agree with an interviewer's request regardless of their true views'. In this sense, yea-saying is essentially a form of social desirability bias. However, Blamey *et al.* (1999c) argue that such a definition is unnecessarily narrow and raises the question of whether yea-saying occurs at all in mail surveys. They suggest that yea-saying (and nay-saying) be defined as the tendency to subordinate outcome-based or 'true' economic preferences in favour of expressive motivations when responding to CVM questions. These expressive motivations may be either socially motivated, as in the case considered by Mitchell and Carson (1989) where social pressure or desirability considerations motivate respondents to yea-say, or internally motivated, where respondents simply seek to express their attitudes and/or held values.

A question that arises when considering the yea-saying concept is how to distinguish it from other choice processes and biases. The answer depends on the extent and nature of information that the yea-sayer is assumed to attend to or ignore. Virtually all definitions of yea-saying require the respondent to attend to some information. For example, one can only agree with a request if it is understood that a *request* of some kind is made. Suppose you are asked to choose between two options, A and B, but are not told anything about them. Without more information, it is impossible to say whether, as a yea-sayer, you would choose A or B. Whether or not an individual categorises a 'request' in an SP survey as being pro-environmental, pro-developmental or even objectionable is likely to have a bearing on the relative likelihood of yea, and nay-saying. Is not the environmentalist who says 'yes' to all environmental requests a yea-sayer and the developer who says 'no' to all such requests a nay-sayer? And what about the individual who responds 'no' to each question as a protest against the payment vehicle? In each case, the respondent attends to some information and ignores the rest.

Yea-saying is perhaps most clearly defined in dichotomous choice CVM studies where failure to attend to and process the magnitude of payment is probably the single most defining characteristic. It is unclear whether the CVM yea-sayer is also assumed to ignore other key elements of the questionnaire, such as information pertaining to the nature and magnitude of environmental improvements, although the answer is probably affirmative. In choice experiments, yea-saying is most likely to occur at the brand or option level, for example, when a respondent always chooses the green, or greenest, brand of toilet paper. Yea-saying becomes more complex when choice sets contain more than two alternatives. While one can always nay-say when there is a single 'do nothing' option, the form yea-saying takes when there is more than one superficially attractive option in a choice set is less clear. It can also be argued that lexicographic behaviour with respect to any one attribute constitutes a case of yea-saying, particularly when motivated primarily by expressive considerations. A fine line may exist between a yea-sayer in a survey and someone who chooses the option with the greenest brand name or attributes in both questionnaires *and* real life.

Whilst SDB and yea-saying may explain a significant percentage of SP–RP divergences in the environmental context, a number of other factors may be operative, thereby preventing a 'clean' test of these specific motivations. Another explanation which may have some overlap with yea-saying in SP data is strategic bias. This occurs when respondents give responses that differ from their true preferences in an attempt to influence provision of the good or policy. Variety-seeking behaviour may result in a bias of this type if respondents state that they would choose options perceived to involve new product developments in an attempt to increase the variety of products available, even though they may not purchase them in reality (Carson, personal communication; see also Carson *et al.* 1997).

A further, related, factor contributing to divergences in RP and SP estimates of market share and value may be the occurrence of habitual behaviour and inertia effects. People have habits and may not notice that a new product exists or that it is better in some sense until some perceptual threshold is exceeded (Ben-Akiva and Morikawa 1990). Those who do notice may not be willing to pay the transaction costs associated with brand-switching. Blamey (1998) observed that whilst behavioural commitments are easy to make in questionnaires, in reality changing established behaviour patterns in order to make an environmental contribution can involve significant transaction costs.[5]

A fourth explanation for SP–RP divergences is a difference in knowledge and awareness. Carson *et al.* (1994) observed that '[g]ermane to [the] issue of comparing revealed and stated choice data is the need to understand and predict differences in awareness and knowledge among consumers and to find ways to incorporate such differences directly in choice models'.[6]   A further related reason for divergences in RP and SP estimates is the existence of measurement error associated with the inclusion of objective attribute definitions and levels in SP questionnaires rather than those perceived by respondents. Although such effects may not result in systematic biases, the possibility exists.

A sixth factor is the occurrence of justification bias in SP surveys. This involves a desire to rationalise choices actually made by the respondent (Morikawa 1994, p. 164). One might expect this bias to be particularly prevalent when both RP and SP data are collected in the same questionnaire, or when SP respondents expect researchers to know through some other means how they really behave. A seventh reason is differences in RP and SP task demands. Whilst consumers in real markets are typically required to make only one choice in a product class during a single shopping experience, SP exercises can require up to 16 such choices. Respondents may thus use different heuristics in an SP survey than in the real market. Other possible task differences relate to the number of attributes, levels and so on. Finally, divergences in SP and RP estimates may occur due to poorly specified SP and/or RP choice models. Some possible reasons for this are outlined in subsequent sections.

It appears that a range of factors can explain differences in RP and SP estimates of market share and/or value. The above list is not claimed to be exhaustive. An examination of the literature on green product choice indicates that SP research regarding such products may be susceptible to biases such as those listed above. Bennett (1992, p. 4), for example, observes that 'consumer's claims that they were willing to pay more for green products have not been matched by their actions'. Several studies have hinted at problems arising from the use of self-report measures (Schwepker and Cornwell 1991; Kangan *et al.* 1991). Pickett *et al.* (1993) acknowledge the possibility of 'inaccurate reporting'. Schwepker and Cornwell (1991) suggest that researchers need to take care to design questions in a way that clearly delineates the attitudinal from the behavioural.

It appears that studies directed at estimating the demand for green products are susceptible to some similar biases to those directed at estimating the demand for non-market environmental goods. In particular, biases pertaining to social desirability and yea-saying can be expected to be operative across both contexts. Green product choice is, therefore, a suitable context in which to explore the sensitivity of choice modelling studies to such influences.

9.3 METHODS

Two SP treatments are employed in this study. The questionnaire and sampling strategy for the first of these (SP1) was described in detail in Chapter 6 in this volume. The title of the SP1 questionnaire was 'Consumer Shopping Survey' and the covering letter stated inter alia that 'By completing this survey, you will assist our understanding of what people do when they go shopping'. The second (SP2) treatment contained a green priming condition. This questionnaire was titled 'Consumer Shopping Survey: Green Products' and the covering letter stated that 'By completing this survey, you will assist our understanding of what people do when they go shopping, and how they go about choosing among products that claim to have different implications for the natural environment'. All other aspects of the questionnaire and its administration were equivalent for SP1 and SP2.

One hundred and twenty-eight choice sets were allocated to 16 blocks of eight choice sets in each of the two treatments, producing a total of 32 versions of the questionnaire. Interviewers alternated the questionnaires they handed out. Thus, having handed out version 1 to the first individual, version 2 would be handed to the next, version 3 to the next and so on. A total of 2200 questionnaires were handed out over a two-week period. The results reported here are based on the information provided by 904 respondents, corresponding to a response rate of approximately 41 per cent.

These two treatments were compared both with each other and with the RP data. In Table 9.1, the basis of the comparisons is shown. Consider each of the three criteria in turn.

9.3.1 Implicit Prices

The occurrence of social desirability, yea-saying and related biases in the SP treatments might be expected to result in higher implicit prices for green attributes in the SP treatments compared with the RP. To the extent that the green priming condition shifts respondents' choices in favour of products that have environmentally friendly paper, these implicit prices might also be expected to differ between SP treatments.

Implicit prices (IP) for a given attribute are calculated as the marginal rate of substitution between the price attribute and the attribute in question. The method outlined by Poe *et al.* (1994, 1997) is used to test for differences in implicit prices across SP treatments. The Krinsky and Robb (1986) procedure is first used to simulate the distribution of the IP measures. For each version of the questionnaire, multiple parameter vectors are drawn randomly from a multivariate normal distribution with the mean and variance-covariance matrix of the sample logistic distribution. Each of these vectors is used to calculate the IP of interest. Following Poe *et al.* (1994), the simulated MRSs are then paired across the two treatments and differences taken. Finally, a one-sided approximate significance level is estimated by calculating the proportion of the differences with the hypothesised sign. Because the scale factors cancel when dividing coefficients, estimates of IP are essentially independent of differences in error variances.

Table 9.1 Summary of comparisons

Data sets compared	Comparison criteria		
	Implicit prices	Attribute parameters	Market share estimates
RP vs SP1 and RP vs SP2	Not possible, due to confounding of green product alternative specific constants (ASC) and green attribute variables.	Swait–Louviere test applied to aggregate data RP and SP models.	Compare true share with shares predicted from: • RP model • SP models • sequential SP–RP model.
SP1 vs SP2	Poe *et al.* test for differences in implicit prices derived from model employing individual level data.	Swait–Louviere test applied to taste parameter vectors in individual level model.	Compare share estimates from individual level SP models.

Whilst the same procedures can in principle be used to compare IP between SP models and across RP and SP models, collinearities between

ASCs and attributes in the RP data can confound the latter. In the present study, the green attributes were confounded with the green ASCs in the RP data, preventing a valid comparison of RP and SP IP for the green attribute. Hence the IP criteria was used only to compare the SP models.

9.3.2 Attribute Parameter Vectors

Differences in attribute taste parameters across data sets implies different choice processes. Any consideration of differences in the β vectors across two data sets first requires differences in the scale parameter to be taken into account. A likelihood ratio test is used to test for such differences. Following Swait and Louviere (1993), the LR test statistic is:

$$LR = -2[LogL_{\lambda 1|2} - (LogL_{X1} + LogL_{X2})] \qquad (9.1)$$

where $LogL_{\lambda 1|2}$ is the log-likelihood obtained from the stacked $[\lambda^{1|2}X1]$ and $[X2]$ data sets,[7] and $LogL_{X1}$ and $LogL_{X2}$ are the log-likelihoods corresponding to separate estimations on the original data sets $X1$ and $X2$. This test statistic is asymptotically chi-square distributed with $[Z-1]$ degrees of freedom, where Z is the number of common parameters across the two treatments, the additional degree of freedom arising because $\lambda^{1|2}$ is allowed to vary under the alternative hypothesis.[8] The estimated relative scale factor can only be interpreted as a measure of the heterogeneity of the error variances across the two treatments if the hypothesis of equal taste vectors is rejected (Swait and Louviere 1993).

It is important when applying the Swait–Louviere test that the utility functions be specified as completely as possible. Failure to do so can result in erroneous conclusions. Consequently, the SP treatments are compared using the individual level data, which incorporates selected respondent attitudes within the model. Because RP data were only available at the aggregate level in the present study, comparisons with the RP model necessarily involve simpler model specifications. The implications of any collinearities between the ASCs and attributes in the RP case also need to be considered when applying this test.

9.3.3 Market Share

If the market share estimated for the green products in either of the SP treatments is not statistically different from the true market share for these products, the SP results can be presumed valid from a predictive market share perspective.

Estimates of market share are based on predicted probabilities, which are calculated on the basis of a set of values for the explanatory variables. This means that market share estimates are based on both the taste parameters and the ASCs. This contrasts with the above two tests, which focus on taste parameters only. Several authors have suggested that the ASCs may incorporate the effect of biases pertaining to strategic responses, inertia effects, errors in measurement, differences in opportunity and so on (Ben-Akiva and Morikawa 1990; Swait *et al.* 1994).[9]

Whilst the RP data are more likely to represent current market behaviour than the SP, the SP data are characterised by a well-conditioned design matrix and a less constrained decision context (Swait *et al.* 1994). Consequently, Swait *et al.* (1994) propose a sequential approach to market share prediction in which the parameters for the attribute variables in the RP model are fixed at the values estimated in the SP model. The RP data are simultaneously rescaled to correct for differences in the way the RP and SP data are perceived by consumers and measured for the purpose of analysis.

In the present study, the true market share for each brand of toilet paper, calculated using scanner volume data, is compared with the market share estimated from the two individual data SP models, and the sequential SP–RP model. The SP models are also compared with each other. Whilst a Poe *et al.* test is used to test for differences between share estimates from the two SP treatments, and the SP estimates and the true shares, the sequential nature of the Swait *et al.* (1994) method does not readily lend itself to the use of this test. Conclusions regarding the sequential share estimates are hence qualitative in nature.

With individual-level data, the estimated probability of the *i*th respondent choosing the *h*th option from a policy-relevant choice set is calculated by substituting the appropriate attribute levels and socio-economics into the estimated utility functions. Ideally, market share is estimated by summing predicted choice probabilities across respondents. However, an approximation can be obtained by estimating market share as the choice probability for the average respondent. This approach is adopted in this chapter as it presents fewer complications in hypothesis testing. Because the RP and sequential SP–RP models involve the use of aggregate data, market shares are estimated simply as the choice probabilities for the brands in question.

9.4 RESULTS

9.4.1 Comparison of SP Treatments

The socio-economic, attitudinal and attribute variables included in the choice models presented in this chapter are described in Tables 6.2 and 6.3 in Chapter 6 and are not reproduced here. Table 9.2 presents the two discrete choice models that were estimated for the SP data. Preliminary investigations indicated that a common MNL specification across the two treatments provided an acceptable fit.[10] For most brands, the ASCs are approximately similar between the two models. The vast majority of attributes are highly significant, the exceptions being selected levels of the paper type and colour attributes. For most attributes, the two models yield very similar parameter estimates. As one would expect, cheaper products and price specials are preferred when other attributes are held constant. Respondents in both treatments had a general preference for more toilet rolls per pack, and two-ply paper with 250 sheets. The focus groups indicated that ply and sheets were highly correlated with perceived paper strength.

Both sets of results in Table 9.2 indicate a significant increase in the utility provided by toilet paper that is both recycled and unbleached among those who are committed to green product choice. The interaction of 'Green' with the ASCs for the three green brand-names, Safe, Naturale and Delsey, indicates an increase in the unobserved utility component of approximately 1.65 units for each of these brands. This has an equivalent effect on utility to a price reduction of $3.27. The magnitude of the coefficient for 'Both' is also five times higher for these respondents.

Implicit prices

The importance of different paper types is now compared across the two SP treatments. The basis for the comparison is the implicit price of specified changes in the 'paper type' attribute. The qualitative nature of this attribute requires that specific changes in paper type be specified in order to calculate implicit prices. Furthermore, the interaction of green attitudes and the attribute variable 'Both' in the regression implies that implicit prices depend on the level of the variable 'Green'.

The implicit prices associated with obtaining each of the three environmentally friendly types of paper considered in the experiment, rather than standard paper, are presented in Table 9.3. These results are calculated for the average value of 'Green'. The average respondent is willing to pay no more for paper that is unbleached, but not recycled, than standard paper. However, paper that is recycled is valued more highly than standard paper, particularly when it is also unbleached. The average respondent is prepared to pay between 60 and 70 cents extra to obtain paper that is both recycled and unbleached, other factors held constant. Those respondents with a preference for environmentally friendly toilet paper appear to value paper that is both recycled and unbleached. Recomputing the estimates in the last row of Table 9.3 for Green = 1 increases the implicit price to $1.57 for SP2 and $1.69 for

SP1. By contrast, the respective prices for Green=0 respondents are $0.36 and $0.39.

Table 9.2 SP results on individual data

	SP1			SP2		
	Coeff.	Std. err	P-value	Coeff.	Std. err.	P-value
ASC_BOUQUET	−0.823	0.125	0.000	−0.383	0.122	0.002
ASC_DELSEY	−1.682	0.306	0.000	−2.164	0.331	0.000
ASC_HOMEBR	−1.348	0.257	0.000	−2.475	0.283	0.000
ASC_KLEEN	0.743	0.110	0.000	0.926	0.110	0.000
ASC_NATURE	−0.864	0.151	0.000	−0.540	0.149	0.000
ASC_PUREX	−0.497	0.119	0.000	−0.074	0.116	0.527
ASC_SAFE	−0.567	0.147	0.000	−0.341	0.145	0.018
ASC_TENDERLY	−0.694	0.125	0.000	−0.435	0.130	0.001
ASC_SORBENT	0.682	0.110	0.000	0.764	0.112	0.000
ASC_WONDERS	−0.357	0.116	0.002	−0.011	0.115	0.925
PRICE	−0.418	0.022	0.000	−0.504	0.022	0.000
SPECIAL	0.179	0.024	0.000	0.140	0.024	0.000
ROLL	0.240	0.014	0.000	0.303	0.013	0.000
PLY250	0.290	0.024	0.000	0.229	0.024	0.000
WHITE	0.136	0.038	0.000	0.054	0.038	0.159
OWHITE	−0.046	0.039	0.239	−0.061	0.039	0.114
COLOURED	0.045	0.039	0.253	0.112	0.038	0.004
STAND	−0.070	0.049	0.150	−0.056	0.048	0.251
UBLEACH	−0.100	0.094	0.290	−0.227	0.096	0.019
BOTH	0.094	0.048	0.050	0.120	0.047	0.011
SCENT	−0.166	0.024	0.000	−0.098	0.023	0.000
BOTH*GREEN	0.546	0.072	0.000	0.616	0.075	0.000
IRRITATE	−0.594	0.225	0.008	−0.770	0.292	0.008
CHEAP1	0.886	0.135	0.000	1.099	0.144	0.000
CHEAP2	−0.675	0.087	0.000	−0.460	0.085	0.000
GREEN	1.631	0.104	0.000	1.669	0.106	0.000
DECOR	−0.762	0.130	0.000	−0.782	0.126	0.000
AGE	0.014	0.005	0.004	0.034	0.005	0.000
CLEAN	−0.643	0.101	0.000	−0.493	0.104	0.000
% correct predict	17.5			18.1		
Choice set obs	3143			3192		
LogL (final)	−6331.862			−6368.056		
Adjusted ρ^2	15.9			16.7		

However, the results in Table 9.3 indicate that the implicit prices of environmentally friendly toilet paper are not significantly higher under the green prime condition, using a Poe *et al.* test. This suggests that any differences in cognitive processes are not driven by an increased importance of the green attribute listed in the choice sets. It is possible that the effect of the prime has been to focus respondent attention more on perceived environmentally friendly brand names.[11]

Finally, it is noted that the implicit prices reported in Table 9.3 require careful interpretation. Whilst these prices indicate willingness to pay for environmentally friendly toilet paper, it is assumed that all other attributes, and brand, are held constant. In reality, some respondents with positive implicit prices for environmentally friendly paper may actually choose products with standard paper, because only these products satisfy their preferences for other attributes or qualities. None the less, implicit prices give an indication of how much people would be willing to pay to obtain a product that is environmentally friendly, but equivalent in all other respects to an existing product that is made of standard paper.

Table 9.3 Implicit price comparison

Change in paper type	Implicit price		Is difference significant at 5% or 10%?
	SP1	SP2	
standard→ unbleached only	$-0.04	$-0.36	No
standard→ recycled only	$0.09	$0.18	No
standard→both unbleached and recycled	$0.66	$0.61	No

Parameter vectors

Differences in parameter vectors across the two individual-level SP data sets, after allowing for differences in scale, are now tested. The attribute parameter vectors corresponding to the two treatments are plotted in Figure 9.1. An examination of the figure suggests moderate proportionality between the two taste vectors, with no one or more parameters differing dramatically across treatments.

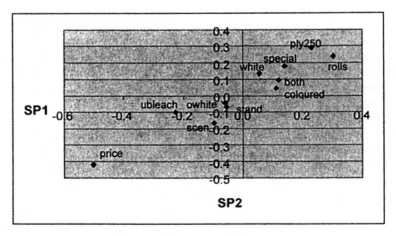

Figure 9.1 Plot of SP parameter vectors

The Swait–Louviere grid search technique mentioned earlier was applied to the stacked data sets, with attribute data for the base SP data set being multiplied by different values of λ. All parameters pertaining to terms involving the ASCs were free to vary across treatments. The maximum log-likelihood of −12729.34 corresponded to λ = 0.91. The test statistic for the likelihood ratio test described above is thus:

$$LR = -2[-12712.70-(-6368.056+-6331.862)] = 25.6.$$

The critical value of the chi-square distribution is 18.3 at the 95 per cent significance level and on 10 degrees of freedom. We thus reject the hypothesis of equal attribute parameter vectors, concluding that scale differences do not account for all of the differences in the two SP data sets. It thus appears that the social desirability prompt has resulted in qualitatively different cognitive processes, although the result is only marginally significant at the 95 per cent level.

Market share

Each SP model presented in Table 9.2 was used to predict the market share of each of the 48 different toilet paper products on offer at the supermarket. These market shares were estimated as the choice probabilities for the average respondent. Differences in market share across SP treatments were tested using the Poe *et al.* test described earlier. Market shares for aggregate data SP models were also estimated.

The market share estimates, aggregated here into the 11 brands available at the supermarket, are presented in Table 9.4.

An examination of predicted market shares for the three green product brands, Safe, Naturale and Delsey, indicates that whilst the share for Delsey is constant across treatments, the shares for the other two are slightly higher under the green priming condition (SP2). However, the difference is only significant using a Poe *et al.* test in the case of Naturale. The final row in the table indicates market share for the green product category as a whole, calculated as the sum of the shares for the above three brands. Predicted share is significantly higher under the green priming condition.

Table 9.4 SP Market share estimates (%)

	SP1		SP2	
	Individual	Aggregate	Individual	Aggregate
Sorbent*	37.1	35.1	31.0#	29.8
Homebrand	4.5#	5.1	3.7 #	4.4
Delsey	0.6#	0.7	0.6 #	0.9
Safe	8.0#	10.0	9.0	10.8
Purex*	6.1	5.5	7.9 #	7.0
Kleenex*	20.5#	20.1	18.4 #	18.1
Wondersoft*	7.2#	6.8	8.7 #	8.0
Naturale*	5.1#	6.7	9.4 #	10.1
Bouquet*	1.6#	1.5	2.1 #	2.0
Tenderley	4.8#	4.4	5.0 #	4.7
Symphony	4.5#	4.0	4.3#	4.0
Total green products*	13.6#	17.5	19.0	21.8

Notes:
Brands for which share estimates from the two individual-level SP models differ significantly at the 95% confidence level are indicated by * in the first column.
Brands for which estimated share differs significantly from the true share (Table 9.8) according to a one-sided Poe *et al.* test (95%) are indicated by # in the relevant SP column.

These results suggest that the green priming condition has resulted in significantly higher estimates of market share for the green product category as a whole, and the Naturale brand in particular. Whilst Safe is a more popular brand, the Naturale brand name may have stronger environmental associations among those respondents with lower product and category familiarity.

9.4.2 Comparison of SP and RP Estimates

The RP choice model estimated on aggregate scan data, along with the comparable SP models, are presented in Table 9.5. Note that no ASCs are estimated in the RP model for the Delsey and Naturale brands. Perfect collinearities between these ASCs and the effect-coded green attribute variables rendered these ASCs redundant. Including both the ASCs and the attribute variables consequently resulted in a Hessian singularity problem. Although analysis indicated that the two ASCs could be omitted from the model without loss of overall fit, this had the effect of confounding both the attribute and ASC utility component. Hence the RP parameter estimates for 'Stand', 'Ubleach' and 'Both' in Table 9.5 cannot be compared with the SP results for these same variables.

Implicit prices
A comparison of implicit prices for environmentally friendly paper across RP and SP data sets was not possible due to collinearities between the green brand ASCs and the effect-coded variables associated with the paper type attribute. Hence, the SP and RP models are largely compared in terms of market share predictions.

Parameter vectors
An examination of the results presented in Table 9.5 reveals considerable divergence in the ASCs, and to a lesser extent the taste parameters, between the RP model and the SP models. For example, the ASC for Homebrand is +0.7 in the RP data set and –0.7 in the SP base data set. A substantial difference in the mean unobserved utility component thus exists across data sources for some brands. In terms of taste parameters, price appears to have a similar coefficient across data sources, but most parameters differ by at least 50 per cent, and in most cases 200 per cent across sources. Whilst for some variables such as 'Special' and 'Scent' the RP parameters exceed the SP parameters in magnitude, in others, such as 'Roll' and 'Ply250', the reverse applies. This suggests that differences in scale parameters across RP and SP models are unlikely to account for the different results obtained.

Two pooled RP–SP models were estimated in order to provide a formal test of the hypotheses of equal parameter vectors between each SP model and the RP model. Results for the optimally scaled joint models are presented in Table 9.6. As observed by Adamowicz *et al.* (1997), joint models of this kind can be sensitive to the way in which RP observations are weighted relative to SP observations. For example, while each SP respondent contributes eight choices to the SP data set, the number of choices made by each supermarket shopper during the 10-week period is highly uncertain, although probably less

Table 9.5 RP and SP results on frequency data

	RP		SP1		SP2	
	Coeff.	Std err.	Coeff.	Std err.	Coeff.	Std err.
ASC_BOUQUET	0.352*	0.163	−0.656**	0.119	−0.294*	0.117
ASC_DELSEY			−0.155	0.197	0.367	0.199
ASC_HOMEBR	0.709**	0.176	−0.702**	0.120	−0.784**	0.128
ASC_KLEEN	0.813**	0.169	0.669**	0.101	0.882**	0.103
ASC_KLEEN (3PLY)	−0.275	0.215				
ASC-KLEEN (UNSCENTED)	−0.608*	0.246				
ASC_NATURE			−0.592**	0.128	−0.313*	0.128
ASC_PUREX	−0.114	0.163	−0.373**	0.114	0.011	0.112
ASC_SAFE	0.542**	0.150	−0.302*	0.122	−0.123	0.124
ASC_TENDERLY	−0.882**	0.171	−0.508**	0.120	−0.303*	0.126
ASC_SORBENT	0.859**	0.162	0.576**	0.102	0.707**	0.104
ASC_SORBENT (HYPOALLERG.)	−0.088	0.227				
ASC_SORBENT (SILK)	−0.934**	0.226				
ASC_WONDERS	−0.355*	0.167	−0.204	0.111	0.090	0.111
PRICE	−0.360**	0.053	−0.397**	0.021	−0.482**	0.021
SPECIAL	0.457**	0.022	0.176**	0.023	0.133**	0.023
ROLL	0.154**	0.025	0.229**	0.013	0.290**	0.013
PLY250	0.165**	0.052	0.274**	0.023	0.217**	0.023
WHITE	0.240**	0.055	0.109**	0.036	0.041	0.037
OWHITE	0.011	0.081	−0.052	0.038	−0.071	0.037
COLOURED	−0.119**	0.046	0.052	0.038	0.116**	0.037
STAND	−0.171	0.136	−0.066	0.047	−0.056	0.047
UBLEACH	1.087**	0.149	−0.117	0.089	−0.252**	0.091
BOTH	−0.128	0.118	0.233**	0.041	0.265**	0.042
SCENT	−0.310**	0.039	−0.154**	0.023	−0.088**	0.022
% correct pred (J=no. alterns)	3.5 (J=49)		14.8 (J=11)		15.6 (J=11)	
LogL (final)	11758.68		−6945.651		−6976.020	
Adjusted ρ^2	4.9%		9.3%		10.3%	

Notes:
*   indicates that parameter is statistically significant at the 5% level
**   indicates significance at the 1% level.

than eight. Assigning equal weighting to each choice across both the SP and RP data sets would likely result in each SP respondent receiving greater weight than each RP shopper.

Another way of looking at the weighting issue is to consider the weight that each data set receives during model estimation. The RP scanner data are based on 136 712 product purchases, compared with the SP data sets which pertains to 3 248 choices in SP1 and 3 297 in SP2. The RP data set thus contains approximately 42 times the number of choices as each SP data set. Simply pooling the RP data set with one of the SP data sets will thus result in the RP data dominating during model estimation. One way of avoiding this dominance is to assign lower relative weight to each observation in the RP data set during model estimation. Preliminary analysis indicated that results for the joint model were sensitive to the weight assigned to each of the data sets. For the purposes of this research report, each choice in the RP data set was assigned a weight of 1/42 relative to each SP choice. This means that the RP data set has been given equal weight in model estimation to the SP data set.

Applying the Swait–Louviere likelihood ratio test to the results presented in Tables 9.5 and 9.6 produces test statistics of 77.6 and 164.4 respectively for the base and primed SP treatments. The critical value of the chi-square distribution is 18.3 at the 95 per cent significance level and on 10 degrees of freedom. For both SP treatments, we thus reject the hypothesis of equal attribute parameter vectors across RP and SP data sets, concluding that scale differences do not account for all of the differences in the two data sources. It thus appears that the choice model has generated significantly different taste parameters to those implicit in actual choice behaviour.

Market share

True market shares were calculated using the scanner data provided by the supermarket. These can be compared with the shares estimated from the separate SP and RP choice models presented in Tables 9.2 and 9.5, and the sequential SP-RP choice model presented in Table 9.7.

The relevant market share estimates are shown in Tables 9.4 and 9.8. A comparison of the true market share data in Table 9.8 with the shares estimated from the two SP models (Table 9.4) indicates mixed results. Although the share for Naturale has been over-estimated in both SP treatments, the shares for Safe and Delsey have been under-estimated. For example, the estimated market share for Safe in SP2 is not significantly less than the true share. However, the difference is significant in SP1. The share for Naturale is significantly over-estimated in both SP treatments, whilst the share for Delsey is significantly under-estimated in both cases.

Table 9.6 Joint RP-SP models

	RP+SP1			RP+SP2		
	Coeff.	Std err.	P-value	Coeff.	Std err.	P-value
RP_BOUQUET	0.471	0.161	0.003	0.532	0.161	0.001
SP_BOUQUET	−0.802	0.108	0.000	−0.508	0.107	0.000
RP_DELSEY	1.860	0.281	0.000	2.167	0.284	0.000
SP_DELSEY	−0.558	0.181	0.002	−0.167	0.182	0.360
RP_HOMEBR	0.772	0.152	0.000	0.796	0.152	0.000
SP_HOMEBR	−0.850	0.109	0.000	−1.003	0.118	0.000
RP_KLEEN	1.111	0.150	0.000	1.317	0.149	0.000
SP_KLEEN	0.523	0.088	0.000	0.669	0.091	0.000
RP_KL_3PLY	0.155	0.192	0.420	0.419	0.191	0.028
RP_KL_UNSCENT	−0.313	0.233	0.180	−0.090	0.233	0.700
RP_NATURE	−0.838	0.201	0.000	−0.974	0.201	0.000
SP_NATURE	−0.754	0.117	0.000	−0.540	0.117	0.000
RP_PUREX	−0.135	0.158	0.390	−0.065	0.157	0.681
SP_PUREX	−0.521	0.102	0.000	−0.197	0.101	0.052
RP_SAFE	−0.029	0.180	0.872	−0.013	0.179	0.940
SP_SAFE	−0.461	0.111	0.000	−0.346	0.113	0.002
RP_TENDERLY	−0.860	0.165	0.000	−0.762	0.165	0.000
SP_TENDERLY	−0.628	0.100	0.000	−0.611	0.106	0.000
RP_SORBENT	1.145	0.144	0.000	1.330	0.144	0.000
SP_SORBENT	0.426	0.089	0.000	0.494	0.092	0.000
RP_SO_HYPO	0.231	0.211	0.274	0.462	0.211	0.028
RP_SO_SILK	−0.618	0.213	0.004	−0.392	0.212	0.065
RP_WONDERS	−0.320	0.159	0.044	−0.218	0.159	0.169
SP_WONDERS	−0.351	0.099	0.000	−0.122	0.100	0.220
PRICE	−0.532	0.028	0.000	−0.605	0.028	0.000
SPECIAL	0.399	0.019	0.000	0.375	0.019	0.000
ROLL	0.262	0.015	0.000	0.305	0.015	0.000
PLY250	0.359	0.030	0.000	0.300	0.029	0.000
OWHITE	0.016	0.046	0.728	−0.014	0.045	0.750
WHITE	0.189	0.035	0.000	0.165	0.035	0.000
COLOURED	−0.049	0.036	0.170	−0.005	0.035	0.886
SCENT	−0.306	0.026	0.000	−0.268	0.026	0.000
STAND	−0.107	0.076	0.160	−0.086	0.076	0.261
UBLEACH	−0.166	0.145	0.254	−0.393	0.149	0.009
BOTH	0.436	0.062	0.000	0.518	0.063	0.000
Rel. scale param		0.61			0.61	
LogL (final)		−18743.11			−18816.90	
Adjusted ρ^2		24.5%			24.8%	

Table 9.7 Sequential SP–RP estimation

	RP on green SP condition		RP on base SP condition	
	Coeff.	Std err.	Coeff.	Std err.
ASC_BOUQUET	0.703**	0.158	0.593**	0.158
ASC_DELSEY	2.668**	0.155	2.466**	0.146
ASC_HOMEBR	1.078**	0.133	0.961**	0.134
ASC_KLEEN	1.756**	0.133	1.422**	0.133
ASC_KL_3PLY	1.091**	0.174	0.611**	0.169
ASC-KL_UNSCENT	0.447*	0.221	0.002	0.221
ASC_NATURE	−1.083**	0.164	−1.155**	0.188
ASC_PUREX	0.098	0.150	−0.166	0.157
ASC_SAFE	0.230	0.139	0.044	0.143
ASC_TENDERLY	−0.312*	0.156	−0.712**	0.167
ASC_SORBENT	1.664**	0.131	1.415**	0.131
ASC_SO_HYPO	0.953**	0.197	0.532**	0.193
ASC_SO_SILK	0.161	0.200	−0.275	0.197
ASC_WONDERS	−0.016	0.149	−0.294	0.154
PRICE	−0.627	fixed	−0.397	fixed
SPECIAL	0.172	fixed	0.176	fixed
ROLL	0.377	fixed	0.229	fixed
PLY250	0.281	fixed	0.274	fixed
OWHITE	−0.092	fixed	−0.052	fixed
WHITE	0.054	fixed	0.109	fixed
COLOURED	0.151	fixed	0.052	fixed
SCENT	−0.114	fixed	−0.154	fixed
STAND	−0.073	fixed	−0.066	fixed
UBLEACH	−0.328	fixed	−0.117	fixed
BOTH	0.344	fixed	0.233	fixed
% correct pred.	3.0		3.1	
Optimal Rescaling	1.56		1.3	
LogL (final)	−11983.48		11979.68	
Adjusted rho2 %	3.7		3.0	

Notes:
 * indicates that parameter is statistically significant at the 5% level.
 ** indicates significance at the 1% level.

For the green product category as a whole, share is significantly under-predicted in the base condition, and does not differ significantly from the true share in the priming condition. Factors unrelated to desirability considerations may have reduced the choice probabilities of the green brands below their 'true' values in both SP treatments. For example, Safe and Naturale are typically packaged in distinctive recycled paper and plastic, which clearly triggers some consumers to purchase these products. However, in the CM questionnaire, where the nature of the packaging was not conveyed to respondents, this triggering may not have occurred to the same extent, and market share estimates may have thus been reduced. The greater occurrence of social desirability biases under the priming treatment may have offset this reduction such that resultant share estimates do not differ significantly from the true shares. Whilst the results presented in Table 9.4 are consistent with the notion that social desirability biases may have produced some degree of desirability bias with respect to green products, the results are not consistent and no firm conclusions can be drawn.

Table 9.8 RP market share comparison (%)

	RP data		Sequential SP–RP	
	Raw scanner	RP model	Base SP	Primed SP
Sorbent	37.4	32.7	35.2	31.1
Homebrand	18.4	15.4	15.0	16.8
Delsey	4.1	3.6	5.7	3.8
Safe	9.9	13.8	7.8	10.3
Purex	5.4	5.6	3.8	4.9
Kleenex	10.5	14.0	19.8	16.9
Wondersoft	4.7	3.3	3.4	4.2
Naturale	3.1	4.7	2.1	4.0
Bouquet	2.8	2.2	2.9	2.8
Tenderley	2.2	2.0	2.0	2.8
Symphony	1.5	2.6	2.3	2.5
Total green products	17.1	22.1	15.7	18.1

Whilst the SP share predictions for most products provide reasonable first order approximations of the true shares, the share for Homebrand is substantially under-predicted in both treatments. It may be that this 'generic' brand is itself susceptible to negative desirability considerations: respondents may not want to be seen to be buying this brand.

Now consider the performance of the RP choice model. As might be expected, the RP model out-predicts the SP models more often than not. However, both SP models predict the share for the green product sub-category better than the RP model. Both SP market share predictions for Safe are also closer to the true share than the RP model estimates. Whilst the SP share estimates are sometimes grossly over- or under-estimated, as in the case of Homebrand, the RP estimates generally deviate by less than 50 per cent of the magnitude of the true estimates.

An examination of the results in Tables 9.4 and 9.8 indicates that the sequential SP–RP model (Table 9.7) is clearly superior to the SP only models. Although the SP models provide marginally superior predictions in a small number of cases, the sequential approach always predicts reasonably well, suffering from none of the major errors of the SP models (for example, Homebrand). These results support Swait *et al.*'s (1994) contention that the sequential approach has considerable practical value.

A comparison of the sequential predictions with the RP-only model predictions reveals that the sequential model predicts at least as well as the RP-only model. Indeed, the sequential approach produces share predictions that are closer to the true values for the majority of brands. This result is obtained despite the relatively poor rho square for the sequential model.

Whilst it was possible to estimate an RP model in the present study, the model was limited by the confounding of effects due to collinearities. Such problems are common when estimating RP models. The sequential approach is particularly useful in such cases, since all parameters are estimable.[12]

Finally, it is important to note that the market share estimates considered in this chapter correspond to the set of products available at the study supermarket during one of the ten weeks for which scanner data were obtained. Ideally, the predictive performance of the different approaches would be assessed for choice sets different to those represented in the RP data set. This would provide a stronger test of predictive validity. Suppose, for example, that several months after the period for which scanner data were collected in the present study, two new green products were introduced at the study supermarket and two others were removed. Model forecasts could then be validated against scan data corresponding to these new market conditions.

9.5 CONCLUSIONS

Concerns regarding the validity of value estimates derived in SP studies have given rise to numerous studies designed to compare SP with RP data. In this chapter, a novel approach has been taken to deriving such a comparison. Choice modelling data have been generated to predict market shares for toilet paper products, some containing environmentally friendly brand names and/or attributes. One might expect SP surveys of these 'green' products to be susceptible to some of the same biases as non-market environmental valuation surveys, such as yea-saying and social desirability bias (SDB). The difference is that results of SP studies of green product choice can be validated against observed market data, whereas non-market results typically cannot. In this study, the green product SP results were compared with corresponding RP data provided by a supermarket in the form of scanner data. To investigate further the potential for discrepancies, two SP data sets were developed, one of which was sourced from a questionnaire which included an environmental prompt and the other which did not.

Results of the two SP treatments indicated that the choice model corresponding to the SDB prompt is the outcome of a different cognitive process to that of the unprompted model. The market shares for the green product toilet paper category as a whole were also higher under the SDB green prompting condition, suggesting that the prompt was effective in triggering choices in favour of green products. However, an examination of the implicit prices of different types of paper suggests that this effect is not clearly reflected in the importance assigned to green levels of the environmental attribute.

Rather, the differences in market share appear to be associated with differences in the way respondents generally went about their choices, particularly in relation to the brand names. For example, the green prompting condition appears to have resulted in greater unobserved utility for each of the environmentally friendly brands. Overall then, it appears that the SDB prompt has had an influence on the way respondents formulate their responses, and that this effect has involved brand names more than attributes. These results are consistent with the claim that SP environmental valuation surveys are susceptible to biases such as yea-saying and SDB. However, the implications for a given environmental valuation study will depend on whether the unobserved utility associated with the policy options under consideration is to be included within the value estimates. Whilst the unobserved utility will to some extent be associated with the omission of attribute information from the choice set, it is also likely to reflect biases such as yea-saying and SDB. Whilst the former is considered valid from an economic valuation perspective, the latter is not generally considered valid. Refer to Blamey *et al.* (1999b) for a related discussion.

Perhaps the most important results pertain to the comparison of results for the revealed and stated preference data. The results of the Swait–Louviere test suggest that the cognitive processes employed by respondents in the SP context are different to those employed by consumers in the real market. Whether this is more a function of the context described in the SP questionnaire, the SP task or the SP and/or RP model specification is unclear.

In neither of the SP treatments did the predicted market share for the green product sub-category significantly exceed the true share. Although the green priming condition appears to have resulted in some degree of social desirability bias, this bias only serves to bring the SP share estimates for the green product sub-category closer to the true share. This suggests that other factors may be causing a downward bias in the share estimates, which is largely offset by the upward desirability bias in the priming condition.

Whilst the share predicted for the 'green' product category as a whole is within 20 per cent of the true share, the share predictions for individual brands, green and non-green, are somewhat mixed. Indeed, the estimates for several brands can only be considered poor. Delsey, for example, is predicted to have a share of 0.6 per cent when in fact the true share is 4.1 per cent. Similarly, the share for homebrand products is predicted to be in the vicinity of 4 per cent when in fact it is closer to 20 per cent. Such results raise doubts about the ability of SP methods to predict accurately true market data in the absence of some means of calibration. These concerns flow through to the non-market valuation context where the accuracy of value estimates derived in SP CM studies must be questioned. Of course, it is possible that some of these errors may be reduced or removed through the use of more sophisticated modelling methods than were employed in this chapter.

The research presented here also highlights the problems that are often encountered when relying solely on RP data. Collinearities between the green attributes and brands meant that the two effects could not be separated. Such collinearities often require simplifying assumptions that ultimately compromise overall model fit. The limited variation of RP products relative to those that can be presented in SP experiments also limits the ability of the RP model presented in this study to predict the market share for products with attributes and/or values not currently existing.

Whilst the goodness of fit measures for the sequential SP–RP approach to market share prediction were unimpressive, the approach predicted shares at least as well as the RP only approach, and far better than either of the SP approaches. When considered together with the less restrictive nature of the sequential approach, it appears that this approach may have considerable practical value, as suggested by Swait *et al.* (1994).

NOTES

1. Louviere, Hensher and Swait (forthcoming) review a number of such studies.
2. SP and RP data are typically compared in terms of market share and implicit or explicit estimates of marginal rates of substitution and willingness to pay.

3. Controlled experiments (for example, Bennett 1987) have the advantage of being able to control for some of the less interesting explanations for RP–SP divergences, but the external validity is often questionable.
4. Green products are marketed goods that involve an environmental attribute. For instance, dishwashing liquid may be 'biodegradable', paper may be manufactured from recycled stock and so on.
5. For instance, respondents in a CVM survey involving a voluntary donations payment vehicle may have little idea of how the payments would be collected. Would they be collected via a door knock appeal, in which case they may not have the cash on them, or would credit card payment be acceptable? Perhaps they may have to return a cheque to the address mentioned in a newspaper advertisement, in which case they may simply forget about it. Alternatively, they may need to get in the car and drive to the local shopfront of a conservation organisation. This can involve time, fuel and parking costs.
6. This point cannot be emphasised enough. It is unreasonable to expect convergence in RP and SP estimates without endeavouring to control for differences in the marketing context, and most notably the four 'P's of the marketing mix (Blamey 1998).
7. Data set X1 is multiplied by a parameter $\lambda^{1|2}$ to allow for differences in the scale of the X1 data relative to that of X2.
8. If the hypothesis of equal taste vectors cannot be rejected, we proceed to test for equivalence in the scale parameters across the two datasets, as follows: LR = $-2[\text{LogL}_{X1,2} - \text{LogL}_{\lambda 1|2}]$, where $\text{LogL}_{X1,2}$ is simply the log likelihood for the same model specification as previously, estimated over the stacked dataset without rescaling. This test statistic is asymptotically chi-square distributed, with a single degree of freedom (Swait and Louviere 1993).
9. Overall then, predictive validity with respect to market share may be a stronger test than predictive validity with respect to implicit prices and taste vectors.
10. Several nested logit and heteroscedastic extreme value models were run in an attempt to relax the assumption of independence of irrelevant alternatives. While neither of these approaches suggested that a departure from MNL was necessary, this result was not entirely conclusive.
11. Results not shown indicate that several of the ASCs are statistically different between treatments.
12. The joint models shown in Table 9.7 could also be used to predict market share whilst avoiding many of the problems associated with estimating RP-only models.

10. Framing Effects

John Rolfe and Jeff Bennett

10.1 INTRODUCTION

One of the key issues faced by researchers employing non-market valuation techniques is framing. This refers to the way that survey respondents might view or 'frame' the trade-offs being presented to them. In one sense, framing effects are a standard component of everyday choices that people make. The psychological make-up of a person, together with influences from culture, society and a variety of other influences will help to determine that person's choices about lifestyle, purchases and so on. These influences can be thought of as providing a frame within which people find many choices easy and efficient to make.

In applications of stated preference, non-market valuation techniques, the researcher has a great deal of choice about the ways in which information and trade-offs are presented to people. In effect, the researcher presents a trade-off to survey respondents that has already been framed in a particular way, and then analyses the results in the understanding that choices have been framed in the manner that the researcher intends. Failure to understand that choices may have been 'framed' by respondents in a different context can lead to misleading results.

Framing effects cannot be viewed in a simplistic 'present/not present' manner. All responses to a non-market valuation application are framed in a variety of different contexts. The aim of an application is to mirror as closely as possible the choices that people would make if they were faced with the same situation in a real world setting. Satisfaction of this goal implies that the stated preferences are matched by the same constraints that affect preferences revealed in market transactions, and that the results are directly relevant to policy makers. In effect, the aim is to replicate or match framing effects between an experiment and the corresponding real-world situation.

Given this goal, though, the determination of the most appropriate way to frame particular choices remains problematic for a number of reasons. A major focus of the National Oceanic and Atmospheric Administration (NOAA) inquiry into the contingent valuation method (CVM) in the early 1990s was the possibility that respondents to stated preference surveys framed their answers differently to choices in real markets. To minimise effects relating to factors such as substitutes and budget constraints, the NOAA panel made a number of specific recommendations about how surveys should be conducted (Arrow *et al.* 1993).

There has been continued debate over the effectiveness and appropriateness of the NOAA recommendations (Randall 1997). One reason is that practitioners are developing a better understanding of framing influences, and are suggesting new ways of minimising them. It is also because the NOAA panel effectively set limits to the application of CVM. As a result, researchers have been exploring other ways of using stated preferences to develop valuation estimates (ibid.) and minimise framing difficulties. One of the outcomes has been growing understanding that framing effects are pervasive in stated preference applications, are complex and multi-faceted, and are only problematic when the frame effectively differs between stated and revealed preferences.

In the past, the main framing issues of concern relate to ensuring that survey respondents consider appropriate budget constraints and substitute goods (Arrow *et al.* 1993). If survey respondents fail to consider these adequately when they are formulating their choices, then it is clear that subsequent values would be framed differently to how they would be when choices are framed in a 'real' setting. One potential outcome of this framing effect would be that willingness to pay (WTP) bids might be inflated. This leads to the aggregation problem outlined by Bishop and Welsh (1992), where they argued that extrapolating estimates of existence values for specific endangered species across the full spectrum of endangered species soon generates estimates that are implausible.

Parallel to these debates have been issues about how choice processes and the structure of non-market valuation experiments can influence value estimation. A prime example has been the development of the referendum model of CVM as being more incentive compatible than earlier bidding or open-ended models. Other issues of debate concern how trade-offs in complex scenarios might be modelled to respondents, what the effect of different payment mechanisms are on value estimation, and whether people employ different and varied decision structures to make choices about trade-offs.

One outcome has been the recognition that, with the CVM, it is difficult to identify empirically when particular framing effects might be present, or to identify how choices might be structured. Boyle (1989) suggests that small variations in commodity descriptions will not affect value estimates, while large variations will. However, the development of stated preference techniques has been accompanied by growing awareness that the presentation of surveys and subtle contextual cues can have significant impacts on value estimation (Ajzen *et al.* 1996). Associated with the interest in developing new approaches to non-market valuation issues has been the need to identify more precisely the impacts on choice of different framing influences.

A major rationale for the development of the choice modelling (CM) technique is that it has major strengths in relation to framing issues. To describe these strengths in detail, this chapter is organised as follows. In the next section, an overview of framing effects is presented, followed by an analysis of the strengths of CM in this area in section 10.3. In section 10.4 some of these strengths are demonstrated in relation to a sequence of CM experiments involving rainforest protection. Conclusions are drawn in section 10.5.

10.2 THE DEBATE OVER FRAMING EFFECTS

To analyse some of the complexities involving framing effects, it is convenient to separate them into the core issues of substitute goods and budget constraints, and other framing issues. The latter are mostly focused on the process that respondents use to make choices.

10.2.1 Core Framing Issues

The core issues in the debate over framing effects are the extent to which respondents consider substitute and complementary goods and how they incorporate budget implications when the trade-offs are presented to them (Boyle 1989; Mitchell and Carson 1989; Carson and Mitchell 1995). There has often been suspicion that, under survey conditions, perceptions about budget and substitute constraints vary markedly from what they would be in a 'real life' situation.

The NOAA panel recommended that reminders of substitute goods and budget constraints be included within applications of the CVM (Arrow *et al.* 1993). Since that recommendation, there has been increasing interest in the effectiveness and form of information about substitute goods, and the extent to which they help the respondent to frame the trade-off of interest.

There remains uncertainty about the effectiveness of direct reminders about substitute goods in CVM surveys. There is some evidence that the inclusion of reminders in CVM studies has little effect on the values estimated (Loomis *et al.* 1994; Kothchen and Reiling 1999), despite broad evidence that substitution effects can exist between similar environmental goods (Hoehn and Loomis 1993) and very disparate goods (Cummings *et al.* 1994). There are two broad explanations why this should be possible.

First, such reminders may do little to increase the awareness of respondents about substitute goods. This may be because they already have well-structured values for the trade-off in question, because the effect of the reminders may be small compared to other sources of variability (Loomis *et al.* 1994), or because respondents need much more detailed knowledge about substitutes than a simple reminder will provide (Whitehead and Bloomquist 1999). These latter reasons suggest that as the CVM is applied to lesser known goods, the problems relating to framing choices against substitutes intensify.

The other broad explanation is that simple reminders may not be effective in changing the structure of choice and information transfer. The position of an amenity in a queue of choices will influence values through a type of sequencing effect (Randall and Hoehn 1996), implying that reminders of substitutes which do not change the order in which items are viewed will not have substantial impact on values.

The results of Neill (1995) show that substitution effects vary according to whether respondents are simply reminded of their existence (as according to the NOAA recommendations) or whether they are directly forced to consider them. Neill reported an experiment where little difference in value estimates arose between one split sample in which respondents valued an amenity directly and another split sample in which respondents were reminded of seven potential budgetary substitutes. In contrast, significant effects on valuation estimates were reported when respondents valued the good along with the seven other substitutes.

These results suggest that the way in which choices about substitutes and budgetary constraints are framed has significant effect on resulting values. This supports the arguments advanced by Hoehn and Randall (1987), Hoehn (1991), Hoehn and Loomis (1993) and Cummings *et al.* (1994) that in order to generate unbiased estimates of value for a particular good, respondents must be asked to value simultaneously the good in question together with relevant substitutes and/or complements. As researchers wish to consider amenities that are less familiar and comprehensible to potential respondents, the need to frame choices directly in the context of substitutes intensifies, and the appropriateness of the CVM diminishes.

There has also been substantial debate over how budget constraints can be framed accurately in non-market valuation studies. Some researchers (for example, Diamond and Hausman 1993) have cited studies where the hypothetical bids made in CVM experiments do not appear to correlate well to actual behaviour. However, there have been a number of other studies reported (for example, Sinden 1988; Frykblom 1997) that report close correlation between stated and actual payment intentions, indicating that budget constraints have been accurately perceived.

Mitchell and Carson (1989), Hanemann (1994) and Carson and Mitchell (1995) show how poorly designed and administered surveys (such as those using open-ended formats, poorly defined amenities and scenarios, and the shopping-mall surveying technique) tend to result in value estimates that are biased. In these cases, apparent contradictions with budget constraints arise from other methodological problems.

More serious questions about budget constraints relate to the form of the monetary trade-off commonly employed in the CVM. For many public goods that involve private benefits (such as recreation facilities), as well as many consumer items, the use of monetary trade-offs is easily understood and accepted by survey respondents. For items that fall more closely within the definition of public goods though, there are a number of issues that often reduce the acceptance of a monetary trade-off.

One issue is that people often become uncomfortable in terms of framing trade-offs in terms of a single monetary cost. There are some arguments that preferences involving environmental amenities are lexicographic, making it impossible to compare monetary and environmental trade-offs (Sagoff 1988; Blamey *et al.* 1995). However, these arguments do little to explain how people donate to environment causes, choose to purchase environment friendly goods, or go on nature-based holidays. It appears more likely that it is the process of simplifying opportunity costs back to a simple monetary trade-off that is the problem, rather than the actual trade-off mechanism.

This may be the case because people are aware of a variety of opportunity costs associated with a particular issue. Any attempt to focus only on a monetary trade-off frames these opportunity costs in an unrealistic fashion. A common example is where there may be offsetting social losses associated with an environmental protection option, meaning that a single focus on a monetary trade-off would appear unrealistic. Framing effects might result from a stated preference survey if respondents were only asked to choose between a monetary trade-off and a protection option.

Another reason is that a single focus on a monetary trade-off firmly casts the choice to be made in WTP terms. This format is usually preferred by researchers over the alternative willingness to accept (WTA) format because it reduces opportunities for strategic behaviour, is more closely related to budget constraints, and produces more conservative value estimates. As a result, the WTP format is generally applied, even when respondents might feel that they should be compensated for accepting any further environmental losses. Knetsch and Sinden (1984) showed that a wide disparity exists between WTA and WTP estimates, which subsequently it has been argued are caused by factors such as risk aversion (Hoehn and Randall 1987) or prospect theory (Kahneman *et al.* 1991). Clearly, framing issues might arise if a WTP mechanism is employed to model a WTA situation.

Employing a variety of opportunity cost mechanisms that might be associated with environmental gains may alleviate these difficulties over a payment mechanism. The opportunity costs could involve monetary payments, a variety of social losses, and even offsetting environmental losses. Expanding the range of opportunity costs in this way would help to reduce the focus on a monetary trade-off, model actual situations more realistically, and allow the non-monetary opportunity costs to be modelled in a WTA format.

Another reason why monetary trade-offs may cause framing difficulties is that some respondents protest about the form of the payment vehicle. This is because taxes or other compulsory collection mechanisms are often employed to be congruous with the provision of a public good such as an environmental protection goal. While further research is necessary to determine forms of the payment vehicle that minimise this type of framing effect, its overall impact and importance is likely to be reduced in cases where a variety of opportunity costs can be employed.

In summary, there is substantial evidence to suggest that the single trade-off approach of the CVM is not particularly effective in minimising framing effects associated with budget constraints and substitute goods. There is little evidence that direct reminders about substitutes and budget constraints are enough. To address these core framing issues, one solution appears to be to expand the range of choices that respondents consider directly, so that the choices encompass both a range of substitute goods and opportunity costs. This solution is incompatible with the CVM format, but is consistent with the conjoint basis of the CM technique. To determine where the use of CM is preferred over the CVM, a range of other framing issues needs to be explored.

10.2.2 Other Framing Issues

Applications of the CVM appear to be valid and accurate in cases where the situation of interest can be easily represented in terms of a single trade-off, and respondents are well informed about the relevant issues (Mitchell and Carson 1989). However, for many environmental amenities involving non-use values, these conditions do not apply.

Environmental issues are often complex and multi-faceted. This means that the researcher often has to choose how the amenity should be framed. For example, the substitutes for a rainforest area might be other places for its local inhabitants to live, other recreation areas for visitors, or similar ecosystem types for the native flora and fauna to be preserved. Thus, as the complexity of the amenity to be valued increases, the 'single shot' approach of the CVM becomes less appropriate in comparison with multi-attribute approaches.

For issues that involve direct use values, such as a recreation amenity, the pool of potential respondents and their knowledge about the subject of interest are usually easy to identify. As researchers have become more interested in estimated non-use values, challenges have arisen in identifying both the relevant population group and the background level of knowledge. Conceptually, it is quite possible that people may hold non-use values for remote species about which they have little knowledge. Thus the pool of potential respondents involved in many protection and preservation choices is likely to extend across international borders.

As non-market valuation experiments are conducted across wider population groups, it becomes more likely that value estimates will vary according to specific sub-groups. Values may be framed according to regional, state or national characteristics, or other stratification indicators. More sophisticated models of choice need to be developed in light of these framing differences in order to predict values accurately.

A further issue with valuing environmental amenities that are not well known to respondents relates to the process of information transfer. Respondents to CVM surveys often gain substantial amounts of information about the amenity of interest in the process of having that amenity defined for them. There is also information transferred implicitly ('it must be important for them to run a survey'), and a queuing effect resulting from bringing the issue of interest to the forefront of an individual's attention ('I'll support this issue because it is in front of me'). The end result from a process that focuses on one particular trade-off is that respondents become 'super-informed' about the environmental amenity of interest (Rolfe 1996). While their responses might accurately reflect their revised perceptions, the respondents are no longer representative of the population from which they have been drawn. Any subsequent extrapolation of the results from a sample group across a population will be based on an inappropriate frame.

This means that as the amenity of interest becomes less familiar to respondents, the single trade-off focus represented by the CVM is likely to generate an information-framing problem. To avoid this, it may be important not only to present an environmental amenity within the context of a number of substitute goods, but to avoid identifing it specifically. The problems of 'super-information' may be avoided, or at least minimised, by framing the amenity of interest as just another member of the group of substitutes.

If framing effects vary according to the scale of the substitute goods presented to respondents, this has substantial implications for scope tests, which are routinely recommended in stated preference surveys (Arrow *et al.* 1993). Scope tests generally operate by performing a split-sample experiment, the first involving the amenity in question, and the second involving a more encompassing amenity. Higher value estimates should be derived from the latter sample.

However, reference to a more encompassing amenity is likely to produce some form of a framing effect because respondents might form their preferences differently according to which pool of substitute goods are relevant to the trade-off. This framing effect would tend to reduce specific value estimates (because they would be framed against a wider set of goods) and would thus offset any increase in values from the increased scope of the amenity. Confounding between framing and scoping effects may be commonplace in stated preference experiments. This highlights the dual needs of being able to minimise and identify framing effects.

10.3 CHOICE MODELLING AND FRAMING ISSUES

The process of framing tends to be more explicit in CM applications than with the CVM because of the number of mechanical steps involved. The ways in which a CM survey instrument can be framed include:

- the number of attributes used to describe the trade-offs of interest;
- the number of levels and range across which each attribute can vary;
- the number and form of choice alternatives. These may be generic or labelled, with the latter referring to some particular identification such as brand name;
- the presentation of the 'status quo' option to act as a base for value estimation;
- the form of the payment vehicle;
- the presentation of information about scenarios preceding the choice questions;
- the use of other questions in the survey to act as 'warm up' and framing exercises.

CM appears to offer several advantages over the CVM for framing purposes. Perhaps the most significant advantage is that it allows the simultaneous presentation to respondents of a pool of alternative and substitute goods. This explicitly requires respondents to consider complementary and substitution effects in the choice process, and the resulting choice model reveals what those effects are. In comparison, the researcher administering a CVM questionnaire has to assume that alternative and substitute goods have been considered and receives no direct evidence that they have.

An associated advantage is that problems of bias can be minimised because the amenity of interest can be 'hidden' within the pool of available goods used in a CM application. This means that problems of information transfer and 'super informing' respondents can be avoided or at least minimised in a CM application.

These strengths are demonstrated in relation to some experiments reported in the following section. The issue of interest was the estimation of non-use values held by Australians for rainforest conservation in the Republic of Vanuatu, one of the Pacific nations. Because Australians are not well informed about Vanuatu or other countries where rainforest conservation is an important issue, any potential application of the CVM for that purpose would be problematic. The more appropriate way of framing these choices was to present Vanuatu as one of a pool of countries (including Australia) where rainforests could be preserved (see Figure 10.1).

Table 10.1 IIA/IID tests for application A

Alternative omitted	Chi-squared (DoF)	Pr(C>c)	Significant
No choice	35.9283 (6)	0.000003	Yes
FNQ	46.8908 (6)	0.000000	Yes
Vanuatu	8.3572 (6)	0.213083	No
PNG	14.7594 (6)	0.022212	Yes
South America	7.9187 (6)	0.239448	No

Another major advantage of CM is that it provides a more realistic way for respondents to trade-off opportunity costs than CVM allows (Adamowicz *et al.* 1998b). This occurs in two important ways:

- the WTP attribute is only one of several attributes that define profiles, and hence is de-emphasised in importance relative to its central role in the CVM; and
- CM allows one to introduce a variety of opportunity costs, not just a WTP mechanism.

In the Vanuatu study, choices were framed against the range of attributes that respondents commonly used to make choices about rainforest conservation (Rolfe and Bennett 1996b). The attributes[1] chosen to describe the rainforest conservation profiles were:

- location (country);
- area (of the conservation proposal);

- rarity;
- potential to visit;
- effect on local populations;
- special features of the area;
- price of the proposal (framed as a donation).

Apart from the location, the attributes describing each profile could be classified as three environmental attributes (Area, Rarity and Special Features), and three socio-economic attributes (Visits, Locals and Price). This approach has a number of advantages. It de-emphasises price as a trade-off and makes the scenarios more realistic. Its results provide some indication about how people viewed trade-offs between social and environmental factors.

The varying profile sets in CM applications can make respondents aware that a large variety of possible policy options are under consideration. By varying the component attributes across levels, respondents are automatically informed that different policy options are available. This may be a more realistic representation of some choices facing governments and organisations than the single trade-off approach of CVM. It may also help to make respondents more aware of the uncertainties associated with predicting outcomes in natural resource management.

The richness of statistical data from CM experiments provides significant advantages in analysing and comparing CM applications. This allows the analyst to test whether differences in framing cause variation in the parameters of the resulting choice models. For convenience, differences in framing can be categorised into slight variations in the description of essentially the same good, and larger variations that change the structure of the choices involved (Boyle 1989).

A related issue is determining whether the attitudes and characteristics of respondents are important in the way that they make choices about the trade-offs presented to them. While there is a general expectation that factors such as household income and proximity to the issue in question probably influence choices, researchers using the CM technique are now able to develop more comprehensive models of how heterogeneous factors impact on value. For example, Bennett *et al.* (Chapter 5) report how respondent attitudes essentially determine the branches of the decision tree that respondents use to make choices about protecting remnant vegetation.

10.4 TESTING FOR FRAMING EFFECTS

There are three broad ways of testing CM results for the various framing effects that have been detailed above. The first is to determine if particular model parameters are significant explanators of choice. For example, substitute amenities may be included directly in choice sets, either as attribute levels or as alternative options. If respondents consider these substitutes when making their choices, this will be reflected in the subsequent set of model parameters. In the same way, it can be determined if attitudinal variables and individual characteristics are significant choice explanators for all (or sub-groups) of respondents.

The second type of test that can be performed is to check that violations in model assumptions have not occurred. Identifying any independence of irrelevant alternatives/independently and identically distributed (IIA/IID) violations can test the internal validity of choice models. The IIA/IID conditions mean that the error terms associated with each alternative in a CM application should be independently and identically distributed. Violations of these conditions would suggest that choices have not been consistent (independent), and therefore that respondents have had difficulty in framing choices through the course of the experiments. In some cases, IIA/IID conditions can be addressed by the use of nested logit models, which essentially group some choices together under a decision tree structure. Thus the analysis of choice variance can help the analyst to frame more accurately the structure of choice processes.

The third type of test that can be performed is to determine whether differences in framing cause significant variations in model parameters between separate or split sample experiments. These are the most commonly used tests for framing differences because the first two types of tests are only informative in certain situations. However, it is not appropriate to make direct comparisons of model parameters between models because they are confounded with the error terms specific to each model.

Differences in model parameters can be tested with log-likelihood and/or part-worth tests. Log-likelihood tests can be used to identify whether model parameters differ by any more than variations in the relevant scale parameters. Confidence intervals for part-worths can be compared to isolate any differences that might exist between models. Here, the relevant tests are described in more detail.

10.4.1 The Scale Parameter (Swait–Louviere) Tests

The Swait–Louviere test entails a proportionality restriction on the parameters of one data set relative to the second, and a test of whether the sum of the log-likelihoods for the two different data sets differs significantly from the log-likelihood for a model estimated from the pooled data sets with the parameter proportion restriction. The pathway for this analysis is through the estimation of the ratio of scale parameters for the different models.

A scale parameter (the constant of proportionality) is inversely proportional to the standard deviation of the error distribution for each data set. The ratio can be estimated by stacking two data sets X_1 and X_2, and conducting a grid search over some hypothesised region for an appropriate scalar value ϕ that multiplies the design matrix excluding the alternate-specific constant intercepts (that is, $X_1^* = \phi X_1$) (Swait and Louviere 1993). One seeks to determine the value of the scalar ϕ that optimises the log-likelihood of the multi-nomial logit (MNL) model fitted to the pooled data sets (ibid.). If both data sets have identical parameters, rescaling is unnecessary and the ratio of scale parameters is one (Blamey *et al.* 1998b). If data set X_1 has more random noise than data set X_2 the variance-scale parameter ratio $\phi^{1/2}$ will be less than one; if the opposite is true, ratios will be greater than one.

The form of the likelihood ratio test (Swait and Louviere 1993) where the MNL model parameters for the data sets X_1 and X_2 differ only by a variance-scale ratio takes the following form:

$$LR = -2(LogL_{x1/2} - (LogL_{X1} + LogL_{X2})) \qquad (10.1)$$

where $LogL_{x1/2}$ is the log likelihood value attached to the MNL model of the stacked data set at the optimum level of ϕ, and $LogL_{X1}$ and $LogL_{X2}$ are the log likelihoods of the MNL models for the individual data sets (Swait and Louviere 1993; Blamey *et al.* 1998b). The resulting likelihood ratio statistic follows an asymptotic chi-square distribution with $(P + 1)$ degrees of freedom, where P is the number of parameters across the three models involved.

10.4.2 The Part-worth Tests

The second pathway for identifying framing effects between data sets is to compare the part-worths that are available from models estimated from CM surveys. These are directly comparable between models because the scalar variance (λ) terms are cancelled out of such equations. In order to estimate whether differences between part-worths generated from different experiments are statistically robust, confidence intervals need to be generated.

This can be done using Fieller's Method as proposed by Krinsky and Robb (1986). It involves the simulation of an asymptotic distribution of the coefficients that are generated in a CM experiment, from which confidence intervals can then be computed. The distribution is achieved by taking repeated random draws of 'the coefficient vectors from a multivariate normal distribution with mean and variance equal to the β vector and variance-

Option 1 – Vanuatu
1 000 hectares
Fairly rare
No visits allowed
Protection of rainforest means local people will be worse off
Special landscapes
$5 donation required

Option 2 - Far North Queensland
1 000 hectares
Fairly rare
Easy to visit with full facilities
No local people
Special landscapes
$5 donation required

Option 3 - Papua New Guinea
100 hectares
Fairly rare
Easy to visit with full facilities
No local people
Special landscapes
$50 donation required

Option 4 - South America
10 000 hectares
Extremely rare
Easy to visit with full facilities
Protection of rainforest means local people will be worse off
No special features
$10 donation required

Option 5 - Thailand
100 hectares
Not rare at all
Visits possible but moderate access and few facilities
Protection of rainforest means local people will be worse off
Special landscapes
$5 donation required

Option 6 - Indonesia
1 000 hectares
Fairly rare
Easy to visit with full facilities
Protection of rainforest means local people will be better off
Special landscapes as well as plants and animals
$50 donation required

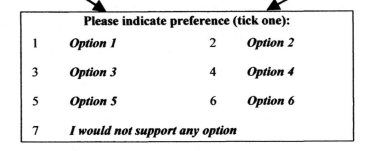

Please indicate preference (tick one):		
1	*Option 1*	2 *Option 2*
3	*Option 3*	4 *Option 4*
5	*Option 5*	6 *Option 6*
7	*I would not support any option*	

Figure 10.1 Sample choice set from the choice modelling application A

covariance matrix from the estimated multinomial logit model' (Morrison *et al.* 1998, p. 10). Implicit prices can then be calculated from each of the random draws of coefficients, and confidence intervals estimated by identifying the values at each tail of the distribution of implicit prices.

10.5 FRAMING ESTIMATES OF VALUE FOR INTERNATIONAL RAINFOREST CONSERVATION

CM applications were designed to estimate the values that Australians might hold for protecting rainforest in Vanuatu (Rolfe and Bennett 1996). An experimental design procedure was used to design the scenario choices, based on the attributes noted earlier, for presenting in questionnaires to respondents. Three successive surveys (labelled here as Applications A, B and C) were run in Brisbane, Australia in 1995 and 1996 by a market research firm. These surveys involved 100, 200 and 100 respondents respectively.

The three questionnaires used in the three applications consisted of some general ranking and choice exercises designed to remind respondents about a range of environmental issues and budget constraints, a sequence of choice sets, and questions about the characteristics of respondents. The questionnaires differed only in attributes and levels used in the choice sets.[2]

In each of the questionnaires, a labelled model format was employed. Respondents were presented with nine choice sets, each with a standard six forest protection locations on offer, as well as a *no choice* option (Figure 10.1). This meant that seven options were available in each choice set. Each location hence became a labelled alternative where a number of other unrecognised attributes specific to the locations may have contributed to choices. These effects were captured in the estimation of alternate specific constants (ASC) in the models. Holding the number of locations to six, and allowing the other attributes to vary across only three levels enabled a powerful experimental design process to be generated.

10.5.1 Application A: Framing Rainforest Preservation Measures

Some of the strengths of CM can be seen in relation to Application A. A sample choice set is presented in Figure 10.1. This demonstrates that CM can be successfully used to disguise a particular issue within a pool of substitutes and frame the choices against a range of component attributes.

In Application A, respondents were offered one Australian and five international locations for rainforest conservation. The results of the survey,

Table 10.2 MNL results for experiments with significant interactions

Variable	Application A	Application B	Application C
ASC – Vanuatu	4.76**	–5.03**	6.67**
ASC – Far North QLD	6.59**	–4.16**	3.56**
ASC – South America	5.23**	–5.48**	4.85**
ASC – Indonesia	6.08**	–5.93**	3.80*
ASC – Papua New Guinea	5.88**		
ASC – Thailand	5.10**		
ASC – Northern NSW		–3.84**	5.65**
ASC – South East QLD		–3.20**	4.38**
Area	–4.41E-05	4.10E-05**	2.89E-05**
Rarity	0.3985**	0.6621**	1.056**
Potential to visit	0.0153	–0.1736	–0.538**
Effect on locals	0.3485**	0.6357**	
Special features	0.0787	0.4691**	
Wetlands			–0.242**
Rangelands			–0.379**
Price	–0.0056**	–0.0266**	–0.017**
Area/visits	2.59E-05**		
Area/local	2.47E-05**		
Visits/locals		0.1249**	0.318**
Visits/price		0.0051**	
Locals/special		–0.1683**	
VAN _EDU	0.2628**	0.1809**	0.276*
FNQ _EDU	0.3457**		0.201**
SAM _EDU	0.2360*		0.458**
THAI_EDU			
INDO_EDU	0.2716**	0.2874**	
NSW_EDU			0.246**
VAN _ENV	–1.6895**		–3.345**
FNQ _ENV	–1.2635*		–2.382**
PNG _ENV	–2.0654**		
SAM _ENV	–2.1251**	–0.6351**	–3.147**
THAI_ENV	–2.2011**		
INDO_ENV	2.4725**		–2.500**
NSW_ENV			–2.878**
SEQ_ENV			–2.436**
VAN_TIM		0.7422**	
NSW_TIM		0.6485**	

Table 10.2 MNL results for experiments with significant interactions (continued)

Variable	Application A	Application B	Application C
SAM_TIM		1.4122**	
INDO_TIM		0.6193**	
VAN_OCC			−0.607**
FNQ_OCC			−0.394**
SAM_OCC			−0.469**
INDO_OCC			−0.454**
NSW_OCC		−0.0765**	−0.523**
SEQ_OCC		−0.1135**	−0.441**
VAN_INC	1.67E-05**	2.27E-05**	
FNQ_INC		3.03E-05**	
PNG_INC	1.58E-05**		
SAM_INC	1.54E-05**	3.87E-05**	−0.162*
THAI_INC	2.02E-05**		
INDO_INC	1.28E-05*	4.42E-05**	
NSW_INC		3.24E-05**	
SEQ_INC		3.41E-05**	
VAN_AGE	−0.0653**	−0.0290**	
FNQ_AGE	−0.0425**	−0.0173**	0.198*
PNG_AGE	−0.0637**		
SAM_AGE	−0.0612**	−0.0338**	−0.286*
THAI_AGE	−0.0553**		
INDO_AGE	−0.0560**	−0.0364**	
NSW_AGE		−0.0249**	
SEQ_AGE		−0.0154**	0.285**
VAN_SEX	−1.2171**	0.5494**	
FNQ_SEX	−1.6920**	0.4008**	
PNG_SEX	−1.2211**		
SAM_SEX	−1.0098**		
THAI_SEX	−0.8503**		
INDO_SEX	−1.2307**		
NSW_SEX		0.3509**	
SEQ_SEX		0.4380**	

Notes:
*   significant at the 10% level
** significant at the 5% level

including two significant interactions between attributes and significant heterogeneous factors, are given in Table 10.2. The relevant heterogeneous factors used were as follows:

- EDU – education level;
- ENV – membership of environmental organisation;
- TIM – associated with timber industry;
- INC – household income;
- AGE – age of respondent;
- SEX – sex of respondent.

Significant interactions were detected between *area* and *potential to visit* and *area* and *special features*. The effect of those interactions was to make the individual attributes insignificant. All other attributes in the model were statistically significant at conventional levels and their signs were as expected a priori. The overall fit of the model as measured by McFadden's rho-square (see Table 10.3) also was very good by conventional standards used to judge probabilistic discrete choice models. The coefficients for location ASCs indicate that Far North Queensland (the Australian location) was the most preferred location, while Vanuatu was the least preferred.

However, the Hausman–McPherson tests to check error distributions, displayed in Table 10.1, indicated that some IIA/IID violations occurred when an overseas location was dropped from the choice set. The lack of violations for the *no choice, Far North Queensland* and *Papua New Guinea* alternatives meant that dropping either of these alternatives did not change the ratio of choice probabilities for the other alternatives. However, when the *Vanuatu* and *South America* locations were dropped, IIA/IID violations were present in the model. This implies that the other overseas locations were viewed by respondents as substitutes, rather then as independent alternatives. The choice alternatives were not being framed consistently by respondents.

These IIA/IID tests lead to an important conclusion: framing problems may be involved in valuation experiments that otherwise appear robust. An inconsistency was identified in the CM experiment that would have remained hidden in a similar CVM approach. It was hypothesised that these framing inconsistencies occurred because the choice sets were unbalanced between Australian and overseas locations. Some respondents may have always wanted choices that involved attractive Australian profiles. From the wide selection of possible locations for rainforest conservation around the world, the six locations that were chosen were not particularly suitable in this survey format.

10.5.2 Application B: Testing for Minor Framing Effects

Application B was conducted with two location changes from Application A to give three Australian and three overseas locations.[3] All other factors were held constant in the choices sets, including the experimental design. The results are reported in Table 10.2. The main test of interest was to determine whether the minor framing changes (variations in the alternatives) had impacts on model parameters. If they did, then variations in value estimates for rainforest conservation in Vanuatu would be expected under the different models.

For the model generated from this survey, no IIA/IID violations were detected. This suggested that offering a more balanced set of locations could significantly alter the way in which respondents framed choices. To test whether differences between the models reported in Tables 10.2 and 10.3 were due to other factors apart from scale parameter differences, the confidence intervals for part-worths were estimated.[4]

These estimates were conducted by taking 200 repeated draws of the vector of coefficients, and then omitting the upper and lower tails of the distributions to identify 95 per cent confidence intervals. These tests are reported in Table 10.4. The results indicate that the only significant difference in part-worths exists for the *area* attribute and the *Far North Queensland* location. The latter result confirms the hypothesis that respondents found it difficult to frame choices in Application A where only one Australian location was offered in the choice sets. Framing the Australian choices in a different way affected the value of conservation sites in *Far North Queensland*. The results demonstrate that the part-worth tests isolate the framing effects between applications to the particular components of choice where they are occurring.

Table 10.3 Summary statistics for MNL choice models

Statistic	Application A	Application B	Application C
Log likelihood	−1296	−2920	−1308
Chi square statistic	340	790	641
No. of variables	50	51	43
Significance of Chi sq.	0.000000	0.000000	0.000000
Rho square	0.23067	0.16397	0.25285

As well, a comparison of the confidence intervals confirms that the choices expressed in Application B were more deterministic than choices expressed in Application A. The confidence intervals for the part-worths from Application B are much tighter than the corresponding part-worths from

Application A, indicating that lower levels of variation in choice occurred in that application. This meets with a priori expectations, because Application B did not have the framing issues associated with Application A.

10.5.3 Application C: The Effect of Framing Different Choices

Application C was designed to test for framing effects when a wider group of substitutes were presented to respondents. Instead of concentrating on rainforests, three types of vegetation, *rainforests, wetlands* and *rangelands*, were included in the profiles. This essentially expanded the set of substitutes for respondents to consider. Respondents were told that possible conservation sites for each type of vegetation had been identified in the locations used in the profiles.

Table 10.4 Part-worths for simple MNL models: applications A and B

Part-Worth	Application A		Application B	
	Mean ($A)	95% confidence interval ($A)	Mean ($A)	95% confidence interval ($A)
Area	0.0084	0.0047 – 0.0238	0.0025	0.0016 – 0.0036
Rare	55.61	32.79 – 124.05	39.17	30.4 – 48.6
Potential to visit	15.42	0.26 – 46.15	9.94	5.7 – 14.8
Effect on locals	64.30	37.98 – 190.92	35.20	28.6 – 44.6
Special features	11.94	−1.30 – 37.61	9.38	5.29 – 14.31
Vanuatu	−194.66	−521 – −112	−240.27	−303 – −192
Far North Qld	7.94	−58.6 – 70.1	−168.65	−211 – −132
South America	−227.72	−609 – −121	−247.44	−306 – −201
Indonesia	−272.25	−794 – −158	−251.7	−316 – −202

To enable comparisons with Application B, the same experimental design was used and the new *vegetation* attribute was substituted in place of the *special features* attribute. All the locations and other attributes used in Application B were maintained for Application C. No IIA/IID violations were detected, indicating that respondents were able to frame choices consistently. Results are reported in Table 10.2.[5]

The negative coefficients for the *wetlands* and *rangelands* attributes indicate that these are less preferred to the base level of *rainforests*. The size of the coefficients indicates that higher support exists for *wetlands* over *rangelands*.

To test for framing effects, the main issue of interest was to determine whether the influence on choice of attributes common between Applications B and C had changed. Because the coefficients are not directly comparable, the Swait–Louviere test was performed as a way of identifying whether framing effects could be isolated between the models. The data for the surveys were stacked by stripping out the attributes that were not common to each survey and then combining the sets. The survey codes for the data set from Application B were varied according to a scalar factor ϕ, while the codes for the other data set were maintained.

Table 10.5 Results for single and stacked data sets[6]

Variable	Application B	Application C	Joint B&C
Vanuatu	−3.5064	−4.5717	−3.9929
Far North Qld	−2.3741	−3.2511	−2.7754
New South Wales	−2.8238	−3.7363	−3.2401
South America	−3.5312	−4.6137	−4.0243
South East Qld	−2.5126	−3.0229	−2.7300
Indonesia	−3.6600	−4.6014	−4.0884
Rare	0.61269	0.93578	0.79047
Visit	0.15722	0.12009	0.13817
Local	0.55670	0.65376	0.61996
Area	0.00004	0.00004	0.00004
Price	−0.01469	−0.01388	−0.01468
Log-likelihood	−3056.756	−2827.778	−5911.073
Rho square	0.12730	0.19357	0.15667
Chi square (5)	549.9	863.9	1328.6

Because the data set from Application B had twice the number of observations as the data set from Application C, the latter was stacked twice to maintain consistency. Repeated MNL models for the stacked data set were calculated with varying levels of ϕ. The maximum log-likelihood value of the MNL model was achieved when ϕ assumed a value of 0.94. The MNL models for the individual data sets were also calculated, and the results for the three models are reported in Table 10.5.

This enabled the likelihood ratio test to be performed as follows:

$$\text{LR} = -2(5911.073 - (3056.756 + 2827.778))$$
$$= 26.499 \tag{10.2}$$

There are $(11 + 1)$ degrees of freedom associated with the test, implying that the chi-square statistic at a 5 per cent significance level is 21.026. This is smaller than the calculated statistic, and means that the hypothesis that the vector of parameters are equivalent across the two data sets should be rejected. The differences in the scale parameter are not enough to account for the variations in the coefficients.

The conclusion from this test is that framing effects have occurred between Applications B and C. After differences in the scale parameters had been accounted for, the variations in the coefficients were still significant. This means that the introduction of a wider choice set in Application C compared to Application B impacted on the relative values of the different coefficients. This result confirms that many scope tests that effectively expand the choice options for respondents may induce potential framing effects.

The size of the scalar factor ratio ϕ identified in the analysis also gives some indication about how respondents framed their choices. This is because the scalar factor ratio is essentially the inverse ratio of the variances of the error distributions for the different models. Because the scalar factor ratio identified is less than one, the data set from Application B has more random noise than the set from Application C. This indicates that respondents were slightly more comfortable with the wider choice than with the narrowly defined application focusing only on rainforests.[7]

More precise evidence about where framing effects have occurred can be gained by comparing the 95 per cent confidence intervals for the part-worths that are common to both applications. These are set out in Table 10.6.

Table 10.6 Part-worths for simple MNL models: applications B and C

Part-worth	Application B		Application C	
	Mean ($A)	95% confidence interval ($A)	Mean ($A)	95% confidence interval ($A)
Area	0.0025	0.002 – 0.004	0.0029	0.002 – 0.004
Rare	39.17	30.4 – 48.6	65.59	49.8 – 92.5
Visit	9.94	5.7 – 14.8	10.69	3.3 – 20.0
Locals	35.20	28.6 – 44.6	44.39	32.7 – 69.0
Vanuatu	−240.27	−303 – −192	−298.65	−347 – −222
Far North Qld	−168.65	−211 – −132	−202.88	−306 – −147
NSW	−192.89	−242 – −153	−237.65	−364 – −179
South America	−247.44	−306 – −201	−303.72	−445 – −222
South-East Qld	−175.37	−224 – −139	−185.74	−292 – −133
Indonesia	−251.7	−316 – −202	−300.21	−444 – −221

The results show that while the means for the part-worths for the attributes were higher for Application C than for Application B, the corresponding means for the part-worths for the ASCs (locations) between the same two applications were lower. However, there was no significant difference in part-worths between the applications, apart from the *rarity* attribute. For that attribute, the value derived from Application C was significantly different to the value derived from Application B. This indicates that framing effects involved in moving from the rainforest scenarios to broader vegetation conservation scenarios are centred on the *rarity* attribute.

10.6 CONCLUSIONS

The CM technique has significant strengths for estimating values for environmental goods in ways that minimise potential problems of framing. On one level, the technique offers advantages over the CVM in its ability to offer respondents choices from a wide pool of potentially substitutable goods. The ability to disguise an amenity of interest within a pool of potential trade-offs is an important way of minimising information transfer and other potential biases, and modelling realistic choices. This appears to be crucial where the amenity of interest may not be particularly familiar to respondents.

On another level, the technique has advantages in that it can frame choices according to a number of attributes, including offsetting socio-economic and environmental ones. This enables choices to be framed in more realistic contexts, as well as providing analysts with a rich information set about value trade-offs.

The CM technique allows for a more rigorous testing of framing effects than does the CVM. The evidence from three rainforest protection applications reported in this chapter suggests that framing effects in relation to substitutes are more widespread in stated preference valuation experiments than may be commonly thought. The results indicate that respondents may have difficulties in framing some choices, depending on the pool of substitutes and choice options offered. In contrast to the conclusions of Boyle (1989), it appears that small differences in presentation can influence choice consistency and also lead to significant changes in model parameters. It is notable, though, that framing effects are often concentrated on a subset of attributes involved, implying that they may not be distinguishable in a similar CVM study.

Changes in the range of substitutes that respondents have to consider may also cause framing effects. In the applications reported in this chapter, a substantial expansion of the pool of substitutes on offer led to variation in model parameters, indicating that framing and scoping effects may sometimes be offsetting. It is notable though that when the part-worths were considered, this variation was concentrated on the coefficients for one attribute (*rarity*), and that no significant differences could be found for the locations and other attributes.

One conclusion that can be drawn from these results is that framing effects may be more complex than has often been assumed by researchers. It is encouraging that framing effects do not necessarily intensify as the range of substitutes increases. There appears to be significant potential for the CM technique to be used to develop greater understanding about framing effects.

NOTES

1. These attributes (together with the levels used to represent the range of variation) were chosen after a series of focus group exercises.
2. Copies of the surveys are available from the authors on request.
3. *Papua New Guinea* was replaced by *Northern New South Wales*, and *Thailand* was replaced by *South East Queensland.*
4. It was difficult to apply the Swait–Louviere test for this purpose because the alternatives were not consistent between the choice sets.
5. To report the *vegetation* attribute in levels, the *rainforest* level has been selected to act as a base with a coefficient of zero.
6. All parameters were significant at the 1 per cent level.
7. Because the scale parameter identified was very close to a unity value, the framing differences between the two CM applications were slight.

PART FOUR

Conclusion

11. The Strengths and Weaknesses of Environmental Choice Modelling

Jeff Bennett and Russell Blamey

11.1 INTRODUCTION

Choice modelling has emerged over the last decade as a practical means of estimating the demand for environmental goods and services. The chapters of this book have demonstrated its application in a number of different contexts. Some have involved the potential introduction of new products into existing markets. Others have concerned the introduction of new products where no well defined market exists. One of the non-market applications detailed involved the estimation of use values in the form of recreational values associated with angling. Several others have focused on the estimation of non-use values. A market application in the form of green product choice has also been reported.

The chapters have shown that a number of different types of outputs can be generated from CM studies. Dollar values of the implicit prices of individual environmental attributes were estimated. The compensating surpluses associated with 'packages' of attributes that represent potential resource use outcomes were also determined. In addition, applications have been detailed where market share predictions were the outputs.

The diversity of value categories considered here and the range of estimation types produced affords an opportunity to consider the strengths and weaknesses of CM as a technique for estimating the demand for, and values associated with, environmental products, policies and programmes. Strengths and weaknesses are necessarily relative terms. The approach taken in this concluding chapter is, therefore, to assess the performance of CM relative to alternative stated preference techniques for environmental valuation, particularly the contingent valuation method (CVM) which is the most common stated preference method applied in the environmental context.

11.2 THE STRENGTHS OF CHOICE MODELLING

11.2.1 A Rich Data Set

The output of a CM application contains a wealth of detail regarding respondents' preferences. This detail enables the analyst to provide an array of information to policy makers well beyond that afforded by a CVM application. Whilst a CVM application is capable of producing an estimate of the demand for one (or perhaps two or three) potential goods, the CM approach provides a model from which the demand can be estimated for any one or more alternatives falling within the attribute and label space of the experiment. Consider a policy maker concerned with the selection of a resource management option from an array of options put forward by their various proponents. To gain estimates of the non-market, environmental values involved for each option using the CVM would require separate sample 'splits' for each option.[1] CM allows for the valuation of all options from within one sample split.[2] Cost advantages are immediately apparent.

The capacity to generate multiple value estimates from a single application is derived from CM's focus on the attributes that constitute a resource use alternative. The implicit prices or marginal rates of substitution of each attribute relative to a monetary attribute that form part of the output supplied by a CM application are also useful. These figures provide an indication of the relative importance that respondents place on the various attributes. With this information, policy makers are better equipped to design resource management strategies. Emphasis can be given to management alternatives that favour the production of the attributes with the highest implicit prices (given appropriate consideration of the units of measurement that are used for the non-monetary attribute) and reduce or eliminate any attributes that are found to detract from respondents' well being. Hence, the output of a CM application can go beyond the selection of alternatives. It can assist in the development of superior alternatives.

The 'decomposition' of value into its component, attribute, parts is also important to the process of benefit transfer. For benefit transfer of CVM generated estimates to be successful, there must be a comparability of physical environments, proposed resource use change and affected population. These requirements are particularly limiting given the small number of existing studies. CM value estimates are not so limited. For instance, where a new site shares the same attributes as a site valued in an existing study, but the changes proposed are different, CM results have the flexibility to allow for the transfer process to proceed. This potential was demonstrated in Morrison and Bennett (2000). In two CM applications involving different wetlands, the implicit prices for most of the attributes estimated did not differ across applications.

The ability of CM to provide information regarding the relative contributions made by the attributes enables some of the questions surrounding CVM applications to be answered. One concern regarding the use of CVM is that respondents include elements in their stated preferences for environmental benefits and costs other than those intended by the researcher. For instance, an environmental protection scenario presented to respondents in a CVM questionnaire may trigger respondents' concerns for the additional unemployment that it may create. The values so estimated will therefore be an amalgam of environmental and unemployment values. However, the contributions made by each remains unknown and policy makers are left with an information void. CM results, however, through the inclusion of attributes pertaining specifically to factors such as unemployment impacts and the subsequent estimation of implicit prices, enable policy makers to be more confident regarding the nature of the values held by respondents. If only environmental value estimates are sought, the impacts of the 'other factors' can be controlled for and excluded from consideration. For instance, the results of the wetlands CM application detailed in Chapter 5 show that the benefit of a designated improvement in wetland condition was reduced by between 30 and 40 per cent through the incorporation of impacts on levels of employment.

It is also worth noting that in many cases where stated preference techniques are used, the exact nature of the impacts of proposed policy initiatives are uncertain. This uncertainty may come about because policy makers are unsure themselves of the exact nature of the policy change to be made or because there is some doubt about what the consequences of a well-defined action will be. Such uncertainties are difficult for CVM practitioners to accommodate. The usual strategy adopted is to undertake separate estimation exercises for a number of scenarios that span the array of those that are possible. This is necessarily costly if independent value estimates are to be obtained because a separate sub-sample of respondents must be used for each scenario. In contrast, a CM application needs only to employ a range of attribute levels that is sufficient to cover the range generated by the potential scenarios to provide value estimates for all those scenarios. This can be achieved in a single application. The cost advantages are apparent.

An advantage of all the stated preference techniques is that their approach necessarily involves a degree of public participation in the decision making process. Hence, by undertaking a stated preference technique application, policy makers may be able to fulfil legislative requirements for public participation. Moreover, CM has a specific advantage in this respect. By presenting multiple choices to respondents, where each choice involves the consideration of alternative resource management options, CM provides a greater degree of public participation relative to the simple rejection/acceptance of a single scenario that CVM involves. In generating its rich data set, CM involves a collection process that can be put to respondents in the positive light of public participation. The wider range of options included in CM questionnaires may also lead respondents to think that they are being consulted earlier in the decision making process.

11.2.2 Framing

The CVM has been criticised frequently for its inability to provide respondents with an appropriate 'frame' in which they can consider their preferences for non-marketed goods. Because CVM questionnaires are focused on a specific case, respondents may automatically confer on that case a level of 'importance' that may be beyond its real significance. In other words, the frame within which respondents consider their preferences is inappropriate to the situation in which the resource use decision is being made. There are three parts to this concern. First, there is the problem of defining the range of substitute and complementary goods that represents an appropriate frame. Then there is the question of how this frame can be communicated effectively to respondents. Finally there is the issue of how representative the surveyed sample is of the population once they have been through the process of being surveyed. This is especially important when it is realised that through the provision of information, the questionnaire usually acts to create a group of respondents who are better informed than the population they have been selected to represent.[3] The CVM is especially prone to the framing issue because it concentrates on the estimation of the value for one environmental good.

Choice modelling offers some advantages in the development of an appropriate frame. First, the case under consideration can form just one of the alternatives from which respondents are asked to choose. As is explained in Chapter 10, by providing a 'disguise' of a number of substitute goods for the case at hand, the 'importance' of forests in Vanuatu was put into the context of being but one of a significant range of international conservation projects that could be supported. A frame was established that provided a broader context in which respondents could make a choice. Furthermore, the respondents were less likely to become unrepresentative of the population because of their exposure to the questionnaire. This is because the information provided in the questionnaire was limited to general descriptions of the attributes. No specifics regarding any of the alternatives were given.

Second, real world situations can be framed by modelling the range of simultaneous trade-offs that are often involved in many resource use issues. CM provides the opportunity to include attributes other than those of primary interest to the researcher. For example, including 'lost jobs' as an attribute may increase the face validity of the questionnaire whilst still allowing the values associated with environmental attributes to be isolated. In contrast, scenarios set up in CVM applications can often appear artificial to respondents when a simple quantity–price trade-off is involved.

What is demonstrated in Chapter 10 is that the specification of different frames within separate CM applications does have an impact on value estimates. However, the determination of what represents the appropriate frame remains problematic. This is still an issue for CM practitioners to address. However, the strength of CM in this regard is in its ability to present the frame to respondents in a way that makes it pertinent. Whilst CVM applications typically rely on a 'framing statement' at the beginning of a questionnaire to remind respondents of potential substitute and complementary goods, as well as their income constraint, CM can explicitly embed the frame within each choice set.

An added framing advantage of the CM format is that it can encourage respondents to take a more discerning approach. This is because the options from which respondents are asked to choose are set out explicitly in each choice set. The format, therefore, requires respondents to be mindful of a wide range of possible outcomes and to distinguish between them. This requirement can also entail consequences that are potentially not so beneficial to CM, which will be considered later as a potential weakness of the technique.

11.2.3 Scoping

Another frequently aired criticism of CVM is its inability in many cases to demonstrate any impact on value estimates from a change in the scope of the good involved. Where value estimates are invariant to the scope of the good, doubts must be raised as to the validity of the results involved. Tests for scope effects in CVM applications involve the comparison of value estimates for different amounts of the good involved. Arrow *et al.* (1993) have recommended that scope tests be performed on all CVM applications because of their concern regarding so called 'embedding effects'. This requirement adds to the costs of a CVM application.

Internal scope tests are automatically available from the results of a CM exercise. The contribution made by each attribute to the probability of choosing an option is an output of the multinomial logit model that is normally used to analyse CM data. The statistical significance of these individual contributions is also reported. If the contribution made by an attribute to choices and values is found to be insignificant then a priori evidence of perfect embedding is established. In other words, CM allows the researcher to check that the values for a given product or programme are sensitive to the quantity of each attribute involved. It is important to remember that value sensitivity to scope depends on respondents' sensitivities to the environmental attributes *and* the monetary attributes. Poorly defined payment vehicles and mis-specified price variables can thus lead to an apparent value insensitivity to scope (Rolfe 1998).

To some extent, the scope test afforded by the testing of the significance of the attribute coefficients must be considered 'weak'. Respondents are being offered varying levels of the attributes in the same questionnaire and are therefore able to respond in the knowledge of the relativities that are involved. A stronger test of scope is to offer different sub-samples of respondents' choices where the goods under consideration are of varying inclusiveness. Between-subject tests provide a stronger test of scope sensitivity than internal, or within-subject, tests. Such a test is detailed in Chapter 10. However, such tests are difficult to perform because the introduction of a more inclusive good also involves the provision of a different framing effect. In this regard, scope and framing effects are interrelated. This confounding is also a feature of scoping tests in CVM applications. The advantage offered by CM is that there is some potential for a better understanding of the relationship between – and hence significance of – scope and framing effects through the richness of the data sets obtained.

11.2.4 Problem Identification

The set of preference data that is generated by a CM application is, as has been noted already, far richer than that provided by a CVM application. That has advantages in terms of the amount of information relevant to resource use decision making that can be obtained. However, it also enables a better understanding of the processes underlying the statements of preferences made by respondents and the problems that may be associated with those processes.

For example, the results reported in Chapter 7 show that models generated using labelled alternatives in choice sets were significantly different from those generated using generic alternatives. Whilst such between-sample tests can also be applied to CVM studies, CM may offer greater insights regarding the source of any differences. Analysts may become more aware of the consequences of design decisions as a result. Whilst those applying the CVM may be well aware of the contingent nature of their estimates, they are less able than CM practitioners to tease out the extent to which results are sensitive to specific influences.

It is also relevant to ask if the issues proving problematic in the derivation of value estimates using CM are specific to CM or whether they are more general to stated preference methods and are simply being discovered through the development of CM. For instance, a CVM question can be construed as a single binary choice set. CM can therefore be regarded as a generalised form of the CVM. Problems of violations of certain economic and other assumptions may therefore be equally applicable to the CVM, but easier to identify in CM.

11.2.5 Incentive Compatibility

The incentive compatibility of stated preference methods is a contentious issue. Many economists and environmental managers remain sceptical of value data that are generated from statements of preferences, despite the theoretical efforts of Hoehn and Randall (1987) to show the incentive compatibility of dichotomous choice CVM questions with coercive payment mechanisms. It is not clear whether CM questions are more or less susceptible to strategic biases than such CVM questions. On the negative side, Carson, Groves and Machina (1997) have shown that the presence of more than two alternatives in a choice set provides respondents with an additional degree of freedom in strategic behaviour. In some cases, this involves respondents selecting alternatives that are not their most preferred in order to have a greater influence on the alternatives actually provided (see sub-section 11.3.3).

There are, however, several factors inherent in CM that may act to moderate the incidence of such strategic behaviour. First, it may be more difficult in CM tasks for respondents to construct a pattern of behaviour that is consistently strategic.[4] CM tasks can be cognitively demanding and some forms of strategic bias will increase these demands. Any 'uncertainty' regarding the optimal strategy may mitigate the occurrence of strategic behaviour, consistent with Bohm's (1972) hypothesis. With the exception of the most implausible (for example, dominated) alternatives, one might expect strategic behaviour based on a detailed analysis of the plausibility or popularity of each combination of attribute levels to be more cognitively demanding than that based on labels.

Second, the ability of CM to hide the purpose of an exercise and hence some of the incentives for strategic behaviour can be enhanced through the inclusion of attributes, in addition to the dollar payment, that reflect the costs of pro-environmental choices. For instance, the wetland and remnant vegetation applications reported in Chapter 5 included employment effects and regional income. The forest protection application detailed in Chapter 10 included effects of forest conservation on local people and opportunities to visit as attributes. This approach forces respondents to consider trade-offs between numerous positive and negative attributes. In a CVM application, a respondent may find it convenient to support an environmental cause without thinking too seriously about the trade-offs involved. However, in a CM application where a financial payment and, say, employment effects are both to be traded-off against an environmental goal, there is a clash between two 'external' or 'social' issues in addition to the payment trade-off. The process, therefore, is more forceful and realistic in encouraging respondents to make trade-offs. Furthermore, it may complicate the development of strategic responses. It may also act to limit the prospects of observing lexicographic preferences.

The green product application outlined in Chapter 9 provides some understanding of the extent to which strategic behaviour is problematic in CM. In that application, the demand for a marketed product, toilet paper, which incorporated socially desirable environmental attributes and brands with recycled and/or unbleached paper, was modelled. Three data sets were involved in the test. The first was supermarket sales records for brands of toilet paper. The second and third were CM data sets generated from concurrent surveys of shoppers at the supermarket. The difference between the two CM surveys was that in one questionnaire a statement was included that was designed to make respondents aware that the survey was targeted at the assessment of support for 'green' products. It was hypothesised that the inclusion of the 'green prompt' would increase environmental yea-saying and skew the results to over-predict purchases of toilet paper products that featured the green attributes and brands. The results of the two CM applications yielded models of choice that were highly significant with the majority of attributes being correctly signed. Whilst the models demonstrate strong similarities, tests show that they are derived from different cognitive processes. Despite this, no clear distinctions are evident in the market shares the two models predict. These results tend to support the contention that CM is capable of accurately reflecting respondents' preferences – at least where a familiar marketed good is involved. This represents a substantiation of results well known in the marketing literature. However, it does take the contention surrounding strategic behaviour a step further toward resolution and hence the validation of the technique in the context of non-marketed goods.

11.2.6 Data Set 'Stacking'

A technique used in the green products application (Chapter 6) involved the combining of the stated preference data collected in a CM survey with revealed preference data of shoppers' actual purchases. This procedure can enhance the effectiveness of both stated preference data and revealed preference data.

For data generated from a stated preference CM application, the calibration and re-scaling that is afforded by integrating revealed preference data can significantly improve the fit of the resultant models and hence the accuracy of the value estimates derived.

For revealed preference data, the range of circumstances that can be considered is substantially broadened with the integration of stated preference data. Hence, whilst revealed preference data may relate to only a small sub-set of attribute conditions and to one which is irrelevant to changes that are to be considered, stated preference data have no such limitations.

Whilst the advantages of data stacking are clear, they are not universally available where environmental values are under scrutiny. Where the demand for recreation in a natural environment is to be estimated, stated preference CM data could be supplemented by observations of people's actual recreation decisions (see Adamowicz *et al.* 1994 for an example). However, where environmental values are not associated with any direct use of the resource, it will not be possible to collect revealed preference data. Data stacking will therefore not be an option where non-use environmental values are to be estimated. The possibility remains that further experience in estimating joint revealed and stated preference models over a wide range of circumstances will yield knowledge regarding the extent to which CM data for non-use value estimations will require calibration and re-scaling.

11.3 THE WEAKNESSES OF CHOICE MODELLING

11.3.1 Cognitive Burden

The application of any stated preference technique requires respondents to undertake a number of tasks. These involve comprehension, construction, translation and editing. The complexity of these tasks varies from technique to technique. CVM applications require respondents to consider the details of a base case and one alternative scenario, and then to answer one dichotomous choice question. CM applications require respondents to understand, in general terms, the attributes of options, the way those attributes may vary across a number of levels and the way various combinations of attributes at varying levels may result from alternative resource use options under consideration. They also require respondents to make a number of choices between multiple alternatives.

Clearly the task complexity and cognitive burden facing CM respondents is likely to exceed that of CVM in most cases. In general, the complexity of a given conjoint task depends inter alia on the number of alternatives in each sub-task or choice set, the number of attributes used to describe the alternatives, the correlation structure of the attributes among alternatives, and the number of repetitions. The complexity of CM tasks, in conjunction with the limited cognitive abilities of respondents, may give rise to the use of simplified decision strategies, or heuristics, and any of a number of more subtle effects. To the extent that task complexity affects the use of response strategies, differences in parameter vectors and/or variance components may result.

Heuristics are often associated with non-compensatory decision strategies and elimination by aspects (Tversky 1972; Payne and Braunstein 1978). Decision heuristics can take many different forms in conjoint applications, and some of these would involve evaluation of alternatives in ways not intended by researchers. In Chapter 7, Blamey and Bennett reported evidence of use of a heuristic in which respondents seek to impose a causal structure on attributes. Payne and Braunstein (1978) found that individuals were less likely to use compensatory decision strategies as task complexity increased.

More subtle consequences of task complexity arise in relation to learning and fatigue effects. Whilst individuals may become more proficient after completing a small number of sub-tasks, a point may be reached at which fatigue sets in. This may be associated with increasing use of heuristics as well as the occurrence of status quo biases in which individuals disengage from the task and opt to simply stay with the status quo alternative. The occurrence of learning and/or fatigue effects may result in a wider variety of response strategies in some repetitions, which may lead to differences in the error component. Swait and Adamowicz (1997a) found evidence of an inverted U-shaped relationship between the variance of the latent utilities in CM exercises and the level of complexity.

Further research is required into the nature, extent and implications of the different responses individuals have to the task complexity of CM exercises. Whether respondents' use of given heuristics poses a problem for researchers depends in part on the use to which the results are to be put. While CM studies of market share that emphasise predictive validity may seek to replicate the decision strategies of a real life market counterpart, those placing an emphasis on the elicitation of trade-offs for use in non-market valuation may find some heuristics more problematic. However, it may be possible to minimise such problems by carefully designing and piloting questionnaires with this in mind. One avenue for investigation is the increased use of pictorial representation of information in choice sets. Images to represent attributes could be used to link information provided to respondents as background to the resource management decision under consideration to the choice sets. Furthermore, images may be used to represent the levels which the attributes take in the choice sets. This may assist respondents who have difficulties with numbers and, if well presented, make the choice sets more attractive for all respondents to answer. Clearly, experimentation will be required to identify improved diagrams.

The issue that must, therefore, be resolved is whether respondents' use of heuristics is inappropriate. People often employ heuristics in order to reduce the costs of all types of decision making (Rolfe 1998). It is not surprising, therefore, that respondents to CM questions would use heuristics. This is especially likely given that the costs of assimilating the information provided, and making a choice in a CM questionnaire, are current and real to respondents whereas the benefits of answering are likely to be perceived as uncertain and distant. Whilst the use of heuristics is anticipated both within CM and in the context of other choices, it can be argued that the extent to which they are employed will be different. The problem facing CM analysts is to decide on a questionnaire design that will encourage a level of heuristic use that is likely to yield reliable estimates of value. It seems that the solution to that problem is very ill defined. Certainly focus group testing of questionnaires aids the identification of the use of heuristics. However, there is really no baseline of what is appropriate to act as a guide. This type of problem is recurrent in the consideration of problems with stated preference techniques used to estimate non-market passive use values simply because there is no market or related market to act as a guide. The incentives existing in any 'markets' that might exist – for instance, the 'markets' for charitable donations – are well known to cause distortions. Similarly, the incentives in 'political markets' – as exemplified by voting in referendums – are also distorted away from giving signals that will lead to socially optimal resource allocation solutions.

11.3.2 Framing Issues

It has been argued that CM provides some advantages over the CVM in terms of its ability to establish an appropriate frame for the value being estimated. This does not, however, imply that the technique can automatically ensure that the issue is framed appropriately in a CM application. For instance, the studies reported in Chapter 5 follow an approach to the framing issue that is similar to a standard CVM approach. That is, the existence of substitutes and complements is notified to respondents through a sequence of questions at the beginning of a questionnaire. These attempt to embed the specific issue in an array of other issues. In addition, a 'framing statement' that reminds respondents of their other financial commitments and budget constraints may be included. It is in the work reported in Chapter 10, where a range of different goods was included within each choice set, that a specific framing advantage can be perceived.

However, the approach detailed in Chapter 10 is not without its difficulties. For instance, it can be argued that this approach is flawed because it only allows a respondent to choose one environment protection option from the array presented when their actual preference is to support a number of options. Furthermore, respondents might wish to divide the amount they are willing to pay overall between varying combinations of the alternatives. Providing such flexibility in choices provides a major challenge for the development of the CM process.

Ensuring that the framing of issues provided by the CM choice sets is appropriate to the context of the decision making process under consideration is also problematic. Whilst the forest protection study in Chapter 10 gave respondents choices that extended across different countries of the world and across different ecosystem types, this range contains only a sub-set of all the alternatives that a respondent may consider. At best a CM practitioner could hope to encompass goods that are strong substitutes/complements within a choice set and attempt to isolate in the respondents' thinking their budget constraint that applies to that sub-set of expenditures. Again, defining strong substitutability and complementarity and the partial budget constraint for a questionnaire setting is difficult. A final point is that the greater the number of substitute and complement goods included within the choice set, the lesser the amount of information that can be provided regarding each before the questionnaire becomes too long and complicated.

11.3.3 Incentive Compatibility

As noted above, Carson *et al.* (1997) have shown that the common CM practice of including more than two alternatives in a choice set provides respondents with an additional degree of freedom in strategic behaviour. If CM respondents make choices that are conditional on their expectations regarding the choices of other respondents, they may choose from those options they think have a reasonable chance of 'winning', even when this excludes their most preferred option. There are several ways that an alternative might be identified as an unlikely 'winner' in the CM context. For example, alternatives perceived to contain implausible or unpopular labels, levels or combinations thereof might be rejected from the late consideration set on this basis.

Respondents may also use the opportunity of answering CM questions to express their preference for variety rather than for a specific option. When the provision of one good does not necessarily preclude another, respondents may choose certain new products just to increase the choice set available to them, even though they may never (voluntarily) choose them when they are introduced to the market.

We are unaware of any specific tests of the hypotheses advanced by Carson *et al.* (1997).

11.3.4 Increased Contingencies

Value estimates generated by CM are, like CVM results, contingent on the circumstances created by the questionnaire and those otherwise apparent at the time of the survey. The goal of any stated preference technique is to establish a questionnaire scenario that is appropriate to the policy issue being considered. Because a CM questionnaire is more complex (in general) than an equivalent CVM questionnaire, it can be argued that the contingencies it contains are also expanded. This in turn implies that the task of establishing a relevant set of contingencies becomes more difficult. For example, the selection of attributes for a CM application is central to the technique. For a CVM application, a description of the alternatives between which a respondent will be asked to choose must be provided. However, there is no special significance placed on the individual components of the overall individual package, which may be many and varied. The focus placed on attributes in the CM choice sets gives their selection an increased significance. The increased task complexity of multiple response CM studies can thus necessitate greater simplification in the scenario pertaining to the choice sets and results may be sensitive to the assumptions made.

Responses to CM questionnaires are also likely to be contingent on respondents' understandings of the purpose and meaning of the questionnaires and their elements. Whilst referendum style CVM questionnaires are likely to be interpreted as simple sample referendums, it is less clear how respondents categorise CM tasks in terms of their purpose and meaning. Different categorisations may be associated with different response strategies and respondent confusion, and hence parameter estimates and scale parameters.

11.3.5 Technical Complexities

There is a substantial jump in the level of technical complexity involved in the design and analysis associated with a CM application compared to that of a CVM application. At the design stage, the most critical difference is the requirement in CM of an experimental design on which to base the structure of the choice sets. At the analysis stage, the use in CM exercises of multinomial logit analysis, and potentially more complex models such as nested and random parameters logit, involves a wider and deeper range of skills than the binomial logit model required for dichotomous choice CVM data analysis.

Many of the technical complexities of the CM technique are yet to be explored fully. Matters such as the degree to which violations of the IIA assumption impact on the technique's viability, the appropriate interpretation from a practical segmentation perspective of more complex methods such as random parameters logit, and the appropriate treatment of the alternative specific constants present challenges to CM practitioners. Further research will no doubt shed more light on these and other issues. However, whilst that research is being undertaken, there will remain an element of risk associated with the use of CM.

11.3.6 Cost

It was noted earlier that CM has a potential cost advantage over CV because of its ability to produce multiple results from a single survey instrument. This advantage particularly applies to the opportunity to run 'what if' scenarios through the resultant choice models (Blamey *et al.* 1999a). In such cases, the additional results are obtained without adding new splits or significant complications to questionnaire design. However, the use of CM to provide results for several fundamentally different goods, such as qualitatively different environmental goods, can involve significant additional costs. For example, the framing investigations detailed in Chapter 10 established that significant improvements in the performance of choice models could be achieved over a sequence of four applications. In each application, refinements were developed that enabled issues, such as the development of an appropriate frame, to be resolved.

Another matter that may require an iterative approach to survey development is the selection of an experimental design that can cope with any attribute interactions that may be present. Of course, an iterative strategy is costly both in time and money. It may be that only a test-run CM application or appropriate focus group testing can provide sufficient data to check for the presence or absence of interactions and other design problems.

The resolution of the cost issue is likely to come with the development of greater levels of experience in the application of CM. As more is known about matters such as attribute interaction and their recognition in either focus group work or in pre-tests of questionnaires, the prospects of needing iterative applications of the technique may become less likely.

11.4 CONCLUSIONS

CM as applied to the estimation of non-market environmental values – particularly non-use values – is at a formative stage internationally. The applications detailed in this book indicate that CM has both strengths and weaknesses relative to other stated preference techniques, notably the CVM.

As far as strengths are concerned, the most significant is the technique's ability to produce a rich database on people's preferences and to generate statistically robust models of choice. With that level of information, policy makers are able to make decisions about both the provision and management of natural resources that are far better informed and, hence, more likely to generate net benefits for the community at large. Some of the problems that have beset applications of the CVM are better tackled using the CM approach. The technique enables more control to be exerted over the frame that respondents use to form their preferences for the issue at hand. CM will often provide more discerning and scope sensitive responses than the CVM. The problems that CM analysts do confront are likely to be more readily understood because of the wealth of data that the technique yields.

On the other side of the ledger, CM faces some specific problems. Its ability to yield a rich data set is enabled by a more complex questioning process. That places greater strain on respondents' cognitive capacities. The heuristics respondents develop to cope with these complexities may not be appropriate to the decision making context. The complexities also mean that there are more contingencies or simplifying assumptions upon which a CM estimated value is based. The more contingencies, the more prospect there is of inappropriate contingencies being integrated into the value estimates derived. Complexities also occur in the design and analysis of CM applications. This will necessarily limit its application, as will any cost burdens associated with the complexities.

In weighing up these strengths and weaknesses it is apparent that CM is no 'magic bullet' in the profession's attempts to deal with the estimation of non-market values. But it is also apparent that the technique has some specific characteristics that make it appealing. An examination of the weaknesses indicates that some of the problems associated with the technique are amenable to research. That research should be focused on improving the accessibility of the technique to practitioners and policy makers alike. It should work toward the development of experience in the use of CM so that some of its technical hurdles are lowered. In other words, there are potential benefits associated with the application of CM and the costs of such applications are amenable to research driven reductions.

NOTES

1. Some applications of CV in Australia (for example ACIL 1997) have attempted to estimate multiple values from a single sample. The danger of this approach is that the value estimated for each option can be biased by the other options presented in the questionnaire (see Poe *et al.* 1997).
2. As CVM applications which use the dichotomous choice approach require separate sample 'splits' for each threshold value used, so CM applications require sample 'splits' to allow respondents to be exposed to the number of choice sets determined by the experimental design.

3. The question of what is an appropriate level of information to provide respondents in any stated preference application is as much a philosophical as a practical one. For instance, decision makers may choose to take a step away from a 'pure' democratic process by acting on the basis of informed public opinion. Information is thus supplied as a merit good. This necessarily involves either taking steps to inform the whole population regarding the full effects of a proposal and surveying the opinions that so form or sampling the population, informing that group and then questioning for their preferences. The latter approach carries the essence of what all stated preference techniques do.
4. See Morrison *et al.* (1996).

References

ACIL (1997), 'Economic and Financial Evaluation of Options for Sewage Treatment and Effluent Disposal from West Hornsby and Hornsby Heights Sewage treatment Plants. Final Report prepared for Sydney Water', North Sydney.

ACTEW (Australian Capital Territory Electricity and Water) (1994), *ACT Future Water Supply Strategy: Our Water Our Future*, Canberra.

Adamowicz, W., J.J. Louviere and M. Williams (1994), 'Combining Revealed and Stated Preference Methods for Valuing Environmental Amenities', *Journal of Environmental Economics and Management*, **26**, 271–292.

Adamowicz, W., J. Swait, P. Boxall, J.J. Louviere and M. Williams (1997), 'Perceptions versus Objective Measures of Environmental Quality in Combined Revealed and Stated Preference Models of Environmental Valuation', *Journal of Environmental Economics and Management*, **32**, 65–84.

Adamowicz, W., J.J. Louviere and J. Swait (1998a), 'Introduction to Attribute-based Stated Choice Methods. Final Report to Resource Valuation Branch', Damage Assessment Center, US National Oceanic and Atmospheric Administration Administration, Department of Commerce, prepared by Advanis, Inc., Edmonton, Alberta, Canada.

Adamowicz, W., P. Boxall, M. Williams and J. Louviere (1998b) 'Stated Preference Approaches for Measuring Passive Use Values: Choice Experiments and Contingent Valuation', *American Journal of Agricultural Economics*, **80**, 64–75.

Ajzen, I., T.C. Brown and L.H. Rosenthal (1996), 'Information Bias in Contingent Valuation: Effects of Personal Relevance, Quality of Information and Motivational Orientation', *Journal of Environmental Economics and Management*, **30**, 43–57.

Allenby, G. and P. Rossi (1999), 'Marketing Models of Consumer Heterogeneity', *Journal of Econometrics*, **89** (1–2), 57–78.

Anderson, D.A. and J.B. Wiley (1992), 'Efficient Choice Set Designs for Estimating Availability Cross-effects Models', *Marketing Letters*, **3**, 357–70.

Anderson, D.A., A. Borgers, D. Ettema and H. Timmermans (1995), 'Estimating Availability Effects in Travel Choice Modelling: a Stated

Choice Approach', *Transportation Research Record*, **1357**, 51–65.

Anderson, N.H. (1970), 'Functional Measurement and Psychophysical Judgement', *Psychological Review*, 77, 153–170.

Anderson, W.T. Jr and W.H. Cunningham (1972), 'The Socially Conscious Consumer', *Journal of Marketing*, 36, 23–31.

Anomymous (1991), 'Consumers: How Much Will Green Cost?', *Progressive Grocer*, September, 27–31.

Anonymous (1995), 'Consumers' True Colours', *Nation's Business*, 83, 31.

Arbuthnot, J. (1977), 'The Roles of Attitudinal and Personality Variables in the Prediction of Environmental Behaviour and Knowledge', *Environment and Behaviour*, 9, 217–232.

Arndt, J. and E. Crane (1975), 'Response Bias, Yea-saying and the Double-negative', *Journal of Marketing Research*, 12 May, 218–220.

Arrow, K.J. (1963), *Social Choice and Individual Values*, 2nd edn, New York: John Wiley.

Arrow, K., R. Solow, P. Portney, E. Leaner, R. Radner and H. Schuman (1993), 'Report of the NOAA Panel on Contingent Valuation', *Federal Register*, 58, 4601–4614.

Balderjahn, I. (1988), 'Personality Variables And Environmental Attitudes as Predictors of Ecologically Responsible Consumption Patterns', *Journal of Business Research*, 17 August, 51–56.

Batsell, R.R. and J.J. Louviere (1991), 'Experimental Analysis of Choice', *Marketing Letters*, 2, 199–214.

Ben-Akiva, M. and S.R. Lerman (1985), *Discrete Choice Analysis: Theory and Application to Travel Demand*, Cambridge, MA: MIT Press.

Ben-Akiva, M. and T. Morikawa, (1990), 'Estimation of Switching Models from Revealed Preferences and Stated Intentions', *Transportation Research A*, **24A** (6), 485–495.

Ben-Akiva, M. and T. Morikawa (1991), 'Estimation of Travel Demand Models from Multiple Data Sources', in M. Koshi (ed.) *Transportation and Traffic Theory*, Proceedings of the 11th ISTTT, Amsterdam: Elsevier.

Ben-Akiva, M., T. Morikawa and F. Shiroishi (1991), 'Analysis of the Reliability of Preference Ranking Data', *Journal of Business Research*, 24, 149–164.

Bennett, J. (1987), 'Strategic Behaviour: Some Experimental Evidence', *Journal of Public Economics*, 32, 335–368.

Bennett, J. (1996), 'Estimating the Recreation Use Values of National Parks', *Tourism Economics*, 2 (4), 303–320.

Bennett, J. (1998). 'On Values and their Estimation', paper presented to the Conference of the Australian Agricultural and Resource Economics Society, Armidale.

Bennett, J., R. Blamey and M. Morrison (1997), 'Valuing Damage to South

Australian Wetlands Using the Contingent Valuation Method', *Land and Water Resources Research and Development Corporation Occasional Chapter*, 13/97, Canberra.

Bennett, J., M. Morrison and R. Blamey (1998), 'Testing the Validity of Responses to Contingent Valuation Questioning', *Australian Journal of Agricultural and Resource Economics*, **42** (2), 131–148.

Bennett, S. (1992), 'Green Commitment: Fading Out?', *Progressive Grocer*, **71**, 4–8.

Berger, I.E. and R.M. Corbin (1992), 'Perceived Consumer Effectiveness and Faith in Others as Moderators of Environmentally Responsible Behaviours', *Journal of Public Policy And Marketing*, **112**, 79–100.

Bhat, C.R. (1995), 'A Heteroscedastic Extreme Value Model of Intercity Travel Mode Choice', *Transportation Research*, **29**, 471–483.

Bishop, R.C. (1982), 'Option Value: an Expositon and Extension', *Land Economics*, **58** (1), 1–15,

Bishop, R.C. and M.P. Welsh (1992), 'Existence Values in Benefit-Cost Analysis and Damage Assessment', *Land Economics*, **68** (4), 405–417.

Blamey, R.K. (1998), 'Decisiveness, Attitude Expression and Symbolic Responses in Contingent Valuation Surveys', *Journal of Economic Behaviour and Organization*, **34**, 577–601.

Blamey, R., M. Common and J. Quiggan (1995), 'Respondents to Contingent Valuation Surveys: Consumers or Citizens', *Australian Journal of Agricultural Economics*, **39** (3), 263–288.

Blamey, R.K., J.C. Rolfe, J.W. Bennett, and M.D. Morrison (1997), 'Environmental Choice Modelling: Issues and Qualitative Insights', Choice Modelling Research Report No. 4, School of Economics and Management, University College, University of New South Wales, Canberra.

Blamey, R.K., J.W Bennett, M.D. Morrison, J.C Rolfe and J.J. Louviere (1998a), 'Attribute Selection in Environmental Choice Modelling Studies: the Effect of Causually Prior Attributes', Choice Modelling Research Report No. 7, School of Economics and Management, University College, University of New South Wales, Canberra.

Blamey, R.K., J.W. Bennett, M.D. Morrison and J.J. Louviere (1998b), 'Divergences in Revealed and Stated Preferences and the Effect of Social Desirability Prompts: Validation of a Choice Experiment Involving Green Product Choice', paper presented to the Biennial Conference of the International Society for Ecological Economics, Santiago, Chile, 15–19 November.

Blamey, R.K., J. Gordon and R. Chapman (1999a), 'Choice Modelling: Assessing the Environmental Values of Water Supply Options', *Australian Journal of Agricultural and Resource Economics*, **43** (3), 337–

357.

Blamey, R.K., J.W, Bennett, J.J, Louviere, M.D. Morrison and J.C. Rolfe (1999b),'The Use of Policy Labels in Environmental Choice Modelling Studies', Choice Modelling Research Report No. 9, School of Economics and Management, University College, University of New South Wales, Canberra.

Blamey, R.K., J.W. Bennett and M.D. Morrison (1999c), 'Yea-saying in Contingent Valuation Surveys', *Land Economics*, 75 (1), 126–141.

Blamey, R.K., J. Gordon and R. Chapman (1999d), 'Choice Modelling: Assessing the Environmental Values of Water Supply Options', *Australian Journal of Agricultural and Resource Economics*, 43 (3), 337–357.

Blamey, R.K., J.W. Bennett, J.J. Louviere, M.D. Morrison, and J. Rolfe (2000), 'A Test of Policy Labels in Environmental Choice Modelling Studies', *Ecological Economics*, 32, 269–286.

Bohm, P. (1972), 'Estimating Demand for Public Goods: an Experiment', *European Economic Review*, 3, 111–130.

Boxall, P.C. and W.L. Adamowicz. (1999), 'Understanding Heterogeneous Preferences in Random Utility Models: the Use of Latent Class Analysis', Department of Rural Economy, Staff Chapter 99-02, p. 47.

Boxall, P., W. Adamowicz, M. Williams, J. Swait and J.J. Louviere (1996), 'A Comparison of Stated Preference Methods for Environmental Valuation', *Ecological Economics*, 18, 243–253.

Boyle, K.J. (1989), 'Commodity Specification and the Framing of Contingent-valuation Questions', *Land Economics*, 65 (1), 57–63.

Brazell, J.D. and J.J. Louviere (1998), 'Length Effects in Conjoint Choice Experiments and Surveys: an Explanation Based on Cumulative Cognitive Burden', unpublished working paper, Department of Marketing, School of Business, Faculty of Economics and Business, University of Sydney, New South Wales.

Carlson, L., S.J. Grove, N. Kangun and M.J. Polonsky, (1996), 'An International Comparison of Environmental Advertising: Substantive versus Associative Claims', *Journal of Macromarketing*, Fall 1996, 57–68.

Carson, R. (2000), 'Contingent Valuation: a User's Guide', *Environmental Sciences and Technology*, (forthcoming).

Carson, R.T. and R.C. Mitchell (1995), 'Sequencing and Nesting in Contingent Valuation Surveys', *Journal of Environmental Economics and Management*, 28, 155–173.

Carson, R.T., J.J. Louviere, D.A. Anderson, P. Arabie, D.S. Bunch, D.A. Hensher, R.M. Johnson, W.F. Kuhfeld, D. Steinberg, J. Swait, H. Timmermans, and J.B. Wiley (1994), 'Experimental Analysis of Choice',

Marketing Letters, **5**, 351–368.

Carson, R., T. Groves and M. Machina (1997), 'Information and Strategic Properties of Value Elicitation Procedures', unpublished working paper, Department of Economics, University of California, San Diego.

Carson, R., T. Groves and M. Machina (2000), 'Incentive and Informational Properties of Preference Questions', chapter presented at the Japan Forum of Environmental Valuation, Kobe, Japan, January.

Centre for International Economics (CIE) (1997), 'A Study to Assess Environmental Values Associated with Water Supply Options', report to the ACTEW Corporation, Canberra.

Champ, P.A., R.C. Bishop, T.C. Brown and D.W. McCollum (1997), 'Using Donation Mechanisms to Value Nonuse Benefits from Public Goods', *Journal of Environmental Economics and Management*, **332**, 151–162.

Chase, D. (1991), 'Pang Gets Top Marks in AA Survey', *Advertising Age*, **29**, 8–10.

Connelly, N.A. and T.L. Brown (1994), 'Effect of Social Desirability Bias and Memory Recall on Reported Contributions to a Wildlife Income Tax Check-off Program', *Leisure Sciences*, **16**, 81–91.

Couch, A. and K. Keniston (1960), 'Yeasayers and Naysayers: Agreeing Response Set as a Personality Variable', *Journal of Abnormal and Social Psychology*, **602**, 151–174.

Cronbach, L.J. (1946), 'Response Sets and Test Validity', *Education and Psychological Measurement*, **6**, 616–623.

Cronbach, L.J. (1950), 'Further Evidence on Response Sets and Test Design', *Education and Psychological Measurement*, **10**, 3–31.

CSIRO (1997), 'A Regional Landscape Perspective on Water Resource Management in the ACT', prepared for the Environmental Values Study Steering Committee and ACTEW Corporation, Canberra.

Cummings, R.G., P.T. Ganderton and T. McGuckin (1994), 'Substitution Effects in CVM Values', *American Journal of Agricultural Economics*, **76**, 205–214.

Cummings, R.G., G.W. Harrison and E.E. Rutstrom (1995), 'Homegrown Values and Hypothetical Surveys: Is the Dichotomous Choice Approach Incentive-compatible?, *American Economic Review*, **851**, 260–266.

Daganzo, C.F. and M. Kusnic (1993), 'Two Properties of the Nested Logit Model', *Transportation Science*, **27**, 395–400.

DeShazo, J.R. and G. Fermo (1999), 'Designing Choice Sets for Stated Preference Methods: the Effects of Complexity on Choice Consistency', unpublished working paper, School of Public Policy and Social Research, UCLA, January.

Diamond, P.A. and J.A. Hausman (1993), 'On Contingent Valuation Measurement of Non-use Values', in J.A. Hausman (ed.) *Contingent*

Valuation: A Critical Assessment, New York, US: Elsevier Science.

Dillman, D. (1978), *Mail and Telephone Surveys: The Total Design Method*, New York: John Wiley.

Duffield, J.W. and D.A. Patterson (1991), 'Field Testing Existence Values: Comparison of Hypothetical and Cash Transaction Values', paper presented at the Annual Meeting of the American Economic Association, New Orleans.

Edwards, A.L. (1957), *The Social Desirability Variable in Personality Assessment and Research*, New York: Dryden Press.

Einhorn, H.J. and R.M. Hogarth (1985), 'Prediction, Diagnosis and Causal Thinking in Forecasting', in D. Wright (ed.) *Behavioural Decision Making*, New York: Plenum Press, pp. 311–328.

Ellen, P.S., J.L. Wiener and C. Cobb-Walgren (1991), 'The Role of Perceived Consumer Effectiveness in Motivating Environmentally Conscious Behaviours', *Journal of Public Policy and Marketing*, **102**, 102–117.

Elrod, T. and K. Chrzan (1999), 'The Value of Extent-of-preference Information in Choice-based Conjoint Analysis', in A.A. Gustafson, Herrmann and F. Huber (eds) *Conjoint Measurement: Methods and Applications*, Berlin: Springer-Verlag, pp. 207–223.

Elrod, T., J.J. Louviere and K.S. Davey (1992), 'An Empirical Comparison of Ratings-based and Choice-based Conjoint Models', *Journal of Marketing Research*, **30**, 368–377.

Fishbein, M. and I. Ajzen (1975), *Beliefs, Attitudes, Intentions and Behaviour*, Reading, MA: Addison-Wesley.

Fraser, R. and G. Spencer (1998), 'The Value of an Ocean View: an Example of Hedonic Property Amenity Valuation', *Australian Geographic Studies*, **36** (1), 94–98.

Freeman, A. Myrick, III (1991), 'Comment: Factorial Survey Methods and Willingness to Pay for Housing Characteristics', *Journal of Environmental Economics and Management*, **20** (1), 92–96.

Frykblom, P. (1997), 'Hypothetical Question Modes and Real Willingness to Pay', *Journal of Environmental Economics and Management*, **34**, 275–287.

Gan, C. and E.J. Luzar (1993), 'Conjoint Analysis of Waterfowl Hunting in Louisiana', *Journal of Agricultural and Applied Economics*, **25**, 36–45.

Gerard, K., M. Shanahan and J.J. Louviere (1999), 'Mammography Screening: Why Do Some Women Attend?', unpublished working paper, Centre for Health Economics Research and Evaluation (CHERE), University of Sydney, Building F, Level 6, 88 Mallett St, Camperdown, NSW 2050, Australia.

Gillespie, R. and J. Bennett (1999), 'Using Contingent Valuation to Estimate

Environmental Improvements Associated with Wastewater Treatment', *Australian Journal of Environmental Management*, **6** (1), 14–21.

Granzin, K.L. and J.E. Olsen (1991), 'Characterizing Participants in Activities Protecting the Environment: a Focus on Donating, Recycling, and Conservation Behaviours', *Journal of Public Policy and Marketing*, **102**, 1–27.

Green, P.E. and V. Srinivasan (1978), 'Conjoint Analysis in Consumer Research: Issues and Outlook', *Journal of Consumer Research*, September, 103–123.

Greene, W.H. (1999), *Limdep Version 7.0: User's Manual*, Plainview, New York: Econometric Software, Inc.

Hahn, G. and S. Shapiro (1966), 'A Catalogue and Computer Program for the Design and Analysis of Orthogonal Symmetric and Asymmetric Fractional Factorial Experiments', Report No. 66-0-165, New York, General Electric Research and Development Centre.

Hanemann, W.M. (1984), 'Applied Welfare Analysis With Qualitative Response Models', Working Paper 241, University of California, Berkeley, California, USA

Hanemann, W.M. (1994), 'Valuing the Environment Through Contingent Valuation', *Journal of Economic Perspectives*, **8** (4), 19–43.

Hanley, N, R. Wright and W. Adamowicz (1998), 'Using Choice Experiments to Value the Environment', *Environment and Resource Economics*, **11** (3–4), 413–428.

Hausman, M.J. and D. McFadden (1984), 'Specification Tests for the Multinomial Logit Model', *Econometrica*, **46**, 1251–1271.

Hensher, D.A. and M. Bradley (1993), 'Using Stated Response Choice Data to Enrich Revealed Preference Discrete Choice Models', *Marketing Letters*, **4**, 139–151.

Hensher, D.A. and L.W. Johnson (1981), *Applied Discrete Choice Modelling*, New York: John Wiley.

Hensher, D., P. Barnard, F. Milthorpe and N. Smith (1989), 'Urban Tollways and the Valuation of Travel Time Savings', *Economic Record*, **66**, 146–156.

Hensher, D.A., J.J. Louviere and J. Swait (1999), Combining Sources of Preference Data', *Journal of Econometrics*, **89** (1–2), 197–221.

Hoehn, J.P. (1991), 'Valuing the Multidimensional Impacts of Environmental Policy: Theory and Methods', *American Journal of Agricultural Economics*, **73**, 289–299.

Hoehn, J.P. and J. Loomis (1993), 'Substitution Effects in the Contingent Valuation of Multiple Environmental Programs: a Maximum Likelihood Estimator and Empirical Tests', *Journal of Environmental Economics and Management*, **25**, 56–75.

Hoehn, J.P. and A. Randall (1987), 'A Satisfactory Benefit-cost Indicator from Contingent Valuation', *Journal of Environmental Economics and Management*, **14** (3), 226–247.

Horowitz, J.L. and J.L. Louviere (1995), 'What is the Role of Consideration Sets in Choice Modelling?', *International Journal of Research in Marketing*, **12**, 39–54.

Huber, J. (1997), 'What Have We Learned from 20 Years of Conjoint Research: When to Use Self-explicated, Graded Pairs, Full Profiles, or Choice Experiments', paper presented at Sawtooth Software Conference, August.

Huber, J. and J. Pinnell (1994), 'The Impact of Set Quality and Choice Difficulty on the Decision to Defer Purchase', working paper, the Fuqua School of Business, Duke University.

Huber, J. and K. Zwerina (1996), 'The Importance of Utility Balance in Efficient Choice Set Designs', *Journal of Marketing Research*, **33**, 307–317.

Huber, J., D.R. Wittink, J.A. Fiedler and R. Miller (1993), 'The Effectiveness of Alternative Preference Elicitation Procedures in Predicting Choice', *Journal of Marketing Research*, **30**, 105-114.

Imber, D., G. Stevenson and L. Wilks (1991), 'A Contingent Valuation Survey of the Kakadu Conservation Zone', Research Paper No. 3, Resource Assessment Commission, Canberra.

IPART (Independent Pricing and Regulatory Tribunal of New South Wales) (1996), 'Water Demand Management: a Framework for Option Assessment', Water Demand Management Forum, Sydney.

Jay, L. (1990), 'Green About the Tills: the Markets Discover the Eco-consumer', *Management Review*, **79**, 24–29.

Jedidi, K., R. Kohli and W.S. Desarbo (1996), 'Consideration Sets in Conjoint Analysis', *Journal of Marketing Research*, **33**, 364–372.

Jo, M.-S., J.E.Nelson and P. Kiecker (1997), 'A Model of Controlling Social Desirability Bias by Direct and Indirect Questioning', *Marketing Letters*, **8**, 429–437.

Johnson, F.R. and W.H. Desvousges (1997), 'Estimating Stated Preferences with Rated-pair Data: Environmental, Health, and Employment Effects of Energy Programs', *Journal of Environmental Economics and Management*, **34**, 79–99.

Johnson, R.F., K.E. Mathews and M.F. Bingham (2000), 'Evaluating Welfare-theoretic Consistency in Multiple-response, Stated Preference Surveys', paper presented at Japan Forum of Environmental Valuation, Conference on the Theory and Application of Environmental Valuation, Kobe, Japan, January.

Kahneman, D., J.L. Knetsch and R.H. Thaler (1991), 'Anomalies: the

Endowment Effect, Loss Aversion and Status Quo Bias', *Journal of Economic Perspectives*, **5** (1), 193–206.

Kangun, N., L. Carlson and Grove, S.J. (1991), 'Environmental Advertising Claims: a Preliminary Investigation', *Journal of Public Policy and Marketing*, **102**, 47–58.

Kelley, H. (1972), 'Causal Schemata and the Attribution Process', in E. Jones, D. Kanouse, H. Kelley, R. Nisbett, S. Valins and B. Weiner (eds) *Attribution: Perceiving Causes of Behavior*, New Jersey: General Learning Press.

Kinnear, T.C., J.R. Taylor and S.A. Ahmed (1974), 'Ecologically Concerned Consumers: Who Are They?', *Journal of Marketing*, **38**, 20–24.

Knetsch, J.L and J.A. Sinden (1984), 'Willing to Pay and Compensation Demanded: Experimental Evidence of an Unexpected Disparity in Measures of Value', *Quarterly Journal of Economics*, **94** (3), 507–521.

Kotchen, M.J. and S.D. Reiling (1999), 'Do Reminders of Substitutes and Budget Constraints Influence Contingent Valuation Estimates? Another Comment', *Land Economics*, **75** (3), 478–482.

Krantz, D.H. and A. Tversky (1971), 'Conjoint Measurement Analysis of Composition Rules in Psychology', *Psychological Review*, **78**, 151–169.

Krantz, D.H., R.D. Luce, P. Suppes and A. Tversky (1971), *Foundations of Measurement*, New York: Academic Press.

Krinsky, I. and A.L. Robb (1986), 'On Approximating the Statistical Properties of Elasticities', *Review of Economics and Statistics*, **72**, 189–190.

Krueger, R. (1988), *Focus Groups: A Practical Guide for Applied Research*, Newbury Park, CA: Sage Publications.

Kuhfeld, W.F., R.D. Tobias and M. Garrat (1994), 'Efficient Experimental Design with Marketing Research Applications', *Journal of Marketing Research*, **31**, 545–557.

Kumar, V. and G.J. Gaeth (1991), 'Attribute Order and Product Familiarity Effects in Decision Tasks Using Conjoint Analysis', *International Journal of Research in Marketing*, **8**, 113–124.

Lancaster, K. (1991), *Modern Consumer Theory*, Brookfield, US: Edward Elgar.

Lancaster, K. (1966), 'A New Approach to Consumer Theory', *Journal of Political Economy*, **74**, 132–157.

Landsberg, R.G., A.J. Ash, R.K. Shepherd and G.M. McKeon (1998), 'Learning from History to Survive in the Future: Management Evolution on Trafalgar Station, North-East Queensland', *Rangeland Journal*, **20**(1), 104–117.

Layton, D.F. (1996), 'Rank-ordered, Random Coefficients Multinomial Probit Models for Stated Preference Surveys', paper presented at the 1996

Association of Environmental and Resource Economists Workshop, Tahoe City, California, 2–4 June.

List, S.K. (1993), 'The Green Seal of Eco-approval', *American Demographics*, 15, 9–10.

Loomis, J.B., A. Gonzalez-Caban and R. Gregory (1994), 'Substitutes and Budget Constraints in Contingent Valuation', *Land Economics*, 70, 499–506.

Loomis, J., T. Brown, B. Lucero and G. Peterson (1996), 'Improving Validity Experiments of Contingent Valuation Methods: Results of Efforts to Reduce the Disparity of Hypothetical and Actual Willingness to Pay', *Land Economics*, 724, 450–461.

Louviere, J.J. (1981a), 'Laboratory Simulation vs. Revealed Preference Methods for Estimating Travel Demand Models: an Empirical Comparison', *Transportation Research Record*, 794, 42–51.

Louviere, J.J. (1981b), 'On the Use of Experimental Design Procedures to Model Judgment and Choice Behavior in Travel Choice Analysis', Proceedings, Seminar in Measuring Social Behavior in Road Research, Australian Road Research Bureau Publication, 61–73.

Louviere, J.J. (1988a), 'Analyzing Decision Making: Metric Conjoint Analysis', Sage University Papers Series in Quantitative Applications in the Social Sciences, No. 67, Newbury Park, CA: Sage.

Louviere, J.J. (1988b), *Analyzing Decision Making: Metric Conjoint Analysis,* Newbury Park, CA: Sage.

Louviere, J.J. (1988c), 'Conjoint Analysis Modelling of Stated Preferences', *Journal of Transport Economics and* Policy, 22 (1), 93–119.

Louviere, J.J. (1994), 'Conjoint Analysis',in R. Bagozzi (ed.) *Advances in Marketing Research*, Oxford: Blackwell.

Louviere, J.J. (1995), 'Relating Stated Preference Measures and Models to Choices in Real Markets: Calibration of CV Responses', in D.J. Bjornstad and J.R. Kahn (eds) *The Contingent Valuation of Environmental Resources*, Brookfield: Edward Elgar, pp. 167–188.

Louviere, J. and D. Hensher (1982), 'On the Design and Analysis of Simulated Choice or Allocation Experiments in Travel Choice Modelling', *Transportation Research Record*, 890, 11–17.

Louviere, J.J. and D.A. Hensher (2000), 'Combining Sources of Preference Data', IATBR 2000 Resource Paper, 9th International Association for Travel Behaviour Research Conference, Gold Coast, Queensland, Australia, 2–7 July.

Louviere, J.J. and D. Street (2000), 'Stated Preference Methods', in D.A. Hensher and K. Button (eds) *Handbook in Transport I: Transport Modelling*, Amsterdam: Pergamon (Elsevier Science).

Louviere, J.J. and G. Woodworth (1983), 'Design and Analysis of Simulated

Consumer Choice or Allocation Experiments: an Approach Based on Aggregate Data', *Journal of Marketing Research*, **20**, 350–367.

Louviere, J.J., H. Oppewal, H.Timmermans and T. Thomas (1993a), 'Handling Large Numbers of Attributes in Conjoint Applications: Who Says Existing Techniques Can't Be Applied? But If You Want an Alternative, How About Hierarchical Choice Experiments?', paper presented to the American Marketing Association's Advanced Research techniques Forum, Beaver Creek, CO.

Louviere, J., M. Fox and W. Moore (1993b), 'Cross-task Validity Comparisons of Stated Preference Choice Models', *Marketing Letters*, **4** (3), 205–213.

Louviere, J.J., R.J. Meyer, D.S. Bunch, R. Carson, B. Dellaert, W.M. Hanemann, D. Hensher and J. Irwin (1999a), 'Combining Sources of Preference Data for Modelling Complex Decision Processes', *Marketing Letters*, **10** (3), 187–204.

Louviere, J.J., D. Hensher and J. Swait (2000), *Stated Choice Methods: Analysis and Applications in Marketing, Transportation and Environmental Valuation*, New York: Cambridge University Press (forthcoming).

Luce, R.D. and P. Suppes (1965), 'Preference, Utility and Subjective Probability', in R. D Luce, R. R. Bush and E. Galanter (eds) *Handbook of Mathematical Psychology*, vol. III, New York: John Wiley.

Lynn, M. (1991), 'Can The Environment Survive the Recession?', *Accountancy*, September.

Mackenzie, J. (1992), 'Evaluating Recreation Trip Attributes and Travel Time via Conjoint Analysis', *Journal of Leisure Research*, **24** (2), 171–184.

Mackenzie, J. (1993), 'A Comparison of Contingent Preference Models', *American Journal of Agricultural Economics*, **75** (3), 593–603.

Manski, C. (1977), 'The Structure of Random Utility Models', *Theory and Decision*, **8**, 229–254.

Mazzotta, M.J. and J.J. Opaluch (1995), 'Decision Making When Choices are Complex: a Test of Heiner's Hypothesis', *Land Economics*, **71** (4), 500–515.

McCosker, J.C. and M.J. Cox (1996), *Central Brigalow Bioregional Conservation Strategy Report*, Canberra: Australian Nature Conservation Agency.

McFadden, D. (1974), 'Conditional Logit Analysis of Qualitative Choice Behaviour', in P. Zarembka (ed.) *Frontiers in Econometrics*, New York: Academic Press, pp. 105–142.

McFadden, D. (1981), 'Econometric Models of Probabilistic Choice', in C. Manski and D. McFadden (eds) *Structural Analysis of Discrete Data*, Cambridge, MA: MIT Press, pp. 198–272.

McFadden, D. (1986), 'The Choice Theory Approach to Marketing Research', *Marketing Science*, **5** (4), 275–297.

McFadden, D. and K. Train (1997), 'Mixed MNL Models for Discrete Response', working paper, Department of Economics, University of California, Berkeley.

McFadden, D., W. Tye, and K. Train (1977), 'An Application of Diagnostic Tests for Independence from Irrelevant Alternatives Property of the Multinomial Logit Model', *Transportation Research Record*, 534.

Mendelsohn, R. and G. Brown (1985), 'Revealed Preference Approaches to Valuing Outdoor Recreation', *Natural Resources Journal*, **23** (3), 607–618.

Miller, C. (1990), 'Use of Environmental Packaging May Take a While', *Marketing News*, **24** (18).

Mitchell, R.C. and R.T. Carson (1989) *Using Surveys to Value Public Goods: The Contingent Valuation Method*, Washington, DC: Resources for the Future.

Morikawa, T. (1994), 'Correcting State Dependence and Serial Correlation in the RP/SP Combined Estimation Method', *Transportation*, **21**, 153–165.

Morrison, M. and J. Bennett (2000), 'Choice Modelling and Tests of Benefit Transfer', *Economic Analysis and Policy*, **30** (1), 13–32.

Morrison, M., R.K. Blamey, J.W. Bennett and J.J. Louviere (1996), 'A Comparison of Stated Preference Techniques for Estimating Environmental Values', Research Report No. 1, School of Economics and Management, University College, University of New South Wales, Canberra.

Morrison, M.D., J.W. Bennett and R.K. Blamey (1997), 'Designing Choice Modelling Surveys Using Focus Groups: Results from the Macquarie Marshes and Gwydir Wetlands Case Studies', Choice Modelling Research Report No. 5, School of Economics and Management, University College, University of New South Wales, Canberra.

Morrison, M, J.W. Bennett and R.K. Blamey (1998), 'Valuing Improved Wetland Quality Using Choice Modelling', Research Report No. 6, School of Economics and Management, University College, University of New South Wales, Canberra.

Moum, T. (1988), 'Yea-saying and Mood-of-the-day Effects in Self-reported Quality of Life', *Social Indicators Research*, **20**, 117–139.

Myers, J.H. and M.I. Alpert (1968), 'Determinant Buying Attitudes: Meaning and Measurement', *Journal of Marketing* 32, 13–20.

National Land and Water Resources Audit (2000), 'Theme 6: Capacity for Change', March Newsletter, Canberra.

Natural Heritage Trust (2000), 'Building Long-term Sustainability', *Natural Heritage*, **6** (1).

Navrud, S. (1992), 'Willingness to Pay for Preservation of Species: an Experiment with Actual Payments', in S. Navrud (ed.) *Pricing the European Environment*, Oslo: Scandinavian University Press.

Neill, H.R. (1995), 'The Context for Substitutes in CVM Studies: Some Empirical Observations', *Journal of Environmental Economics and Management*, **29**, 393–397.

Nunnaly, J. (1978), *Psychometric Theory*, New York: McGraw-Hill.

Olsen, D.G. and J. Swait (1997), 'Nothing is Important', working paper, Faculty of Management, University of Calgary, Alberta, Canada.

Opaluch, J.J., S.K. Swallow, T. Weaver, C.W. Wessells and D. Wichelns (1993), 'Evaluating Impacts from Noxious Facilities: Including Public Preferences in Current Siting Mechanisms', *Journal of Environmental Economics and Management*, **24**, 41–59.

Orme, B.K. and R.M. Johnson (1995), 'How Many Questions Should You Ask in Choice-based Conjoint Studies?', paper presented to the American Marketing Association's Advanced Research Techniques Forum, Beaver Creek, Colorado, USA.

Paulhus, D.L. (1991), 'Measurement and Control of Response Bias', in J.P. Robinson, P.R. Shaver and L.S. Wrightsman (eds) *Measures of Personality and Social Psycho Attitudes*, New York: Academic Press, pp. 17–60.

Payne, J.W. and M.L. Braunstein (1978), 'Risky Choice: an Examination of Information Acquisition Behavior', *Memory and Cognition*, **6**, 554–561.

Peters, T., W.L. Adamowicz and P.C. Boxall (1995), 'Influence of Choice Set Considerations in Modelling the Benefits from Improved Water Quality', *Water Resources Research*, **31** (7), 1781–1787.

Pickett, G.M., N. Kangun and S.J. Grove (1993), 'Is There a General Conserving Consumer? A Public Policy Concern', *Journal of Public Policy and Marketing*, **122**, 234–243.

Piggott, N.E. and V. Wright (1992), 'From Consumer Choice Process to Aggregate Analysis: Marketing Insights for Models of Meat Demand', *Australian Journal of Agricultural Economics*, **36** (3), 233–248.

Poe, G.L., E.K. Severance-Lossin and M.P. Welsh (1994), 'Measuring the Difference (X-Y) of Simulated Distributions: a Convolutions Approach', *American Journal of Agricultural Economics*, **76**, 904–915.

Poe, G., M. Welsh, and P. Champ (1997), 'Measuring the Difference in Mean Willingness to Pay When Dichotomous Choice Contingent Valuation Responses are Not Independent', *Land Economics*, **73** (2), 255–267.

Polasky, S., O. Gainutdinova and J. Kerkvliet (1996), 'Comparing CV Responses with Voting Behaviour: Open Space Survey and Referendum in Corvallis, Oregon', in J. Herriges (ed.) *W-133 Benefits and Costs Transfer in Natural Resources Planning*, 9th Interim Report, Department of Economics, Iowa State University, Ames.

Portney, P. (1994), 'The Contingent Valuation Debate: Why Economists Should Care', *Journal of Economic Perspectives*, **8** (4), 3–18.

PPK (1998), *Environmental Investments - Economic Evaluation Methodology*, Nedlands: PPK Environment and Infrastructure Pty. Ltd.

Rabin, M. (1998), 'Psychology and Economics', *Journal of Economic Literature*, **36**, 11–46.

Randall, A. (1997), 'The NOAA Panel Report: a New Beginning or the End of an Era', *American Journal of Agricultural Economics*, **79**, 1489–1494.

Randall, A. and J.P. Hoehn (1996), 'Embedding in Market Demand Systems', *Journal of Environmental Economics and Management*, **30**, 369–380.

Randall, A. and J. Stoll (1983), 'Existence Value in a Total Value Framework', in R. Rowe and L. Chestnut (eds) *Managing Air Quality and Scenic Resources at National Parks and Wilderness Areas*, Boulder, CO: Westview Press.

Reber, A.S. (1985), *The Penguin Dictionary of Psychology*, Harmondsworth, Middx: Penguin Books.

Revelt, D. and K. Train (1998), 'Mixed Logit with Repeated Choices: Households' Choices of Appliance Efficiency Level', *Review of Economics and Statistics* (forthcoming).

Revelt, D. and K. Train (1999), 'Customer-specific Taste Parameters and Mixed Logit', unpublished working paper, Department of Economics, University of California, Berkeley.

Ribaux, D. (1996), 'Endorse or Perish: Do Product Endorsements Work?', *Marketing*, July, 15–21.

Rio Tinto (2000), *1999 Social and Environment Report*, London: Rio Tinto.

Roberts, J.A. (1996), 'Green Consumers in the 1990s: Profile and Implications for Advertising', *Journal of Business Research*, **36**, 217–231.

Roe, B., K.J. Boyle and M.F. Teisl (1996), 'Using Conjoint Analysis to Derive Estimates of Compensating Variation', *Journal of Environmental Economics and Management*, **31**, 145–159.

Rolfe, J. (1996), 'Why the Cost of Performing Analysis Matters for CV Practitioners', paper presented at the 40th Annual Conference of the Australian Society of Agricultural Economics, Melbourne, 11–16 February.

Rolfe, J. (1998), 'Complexities in the Valuation of Natural Resources and the Development of the Choice Modelling Technique', unpublished PhD thesis, UNSW, Canberra.

Rolfe, J. and J. Bennett (1996a), 'Valuing International Rainforests: a Choice Modelling Approach', paper presented at the 40th Annual Conference of the Australian Agricultural Economics Society, Melbourne, 11–16

February.

Rolfe J.C. and J.W. Bennett (1996b), 'Valuing International Rainforests: a Choice Modelling Approach', Vanuatu Conservation Research Report No. 12, School of Economics and Management, University College, University of New South Wales, Canberra.

Rolfe, J.C., R.K. Blamey and J.W. Bennett (1997), 'Remnant Vegetation and Broadscale Tree Clearing in the Desert Uplands Region of Queensland', Choice Modelling Research Report No. 3, School of Economics and Management, University College, University of New South Wales, Canberra.

Rossiter, J.R. and L. Percy (1997), *Advertising Communications and Promotion Management*, Sydney: McGraw Hill.

Saelensminde, K. (1998), 'Inconsistent Choices Impact on the Valuation of Travel Time in Stated Choice Studies', paper presented at the first World Congress of Environmental and Resource Economists, Venice, June.

Sagoff, M. (1988), *The Economy of the Earth*, Cambridge, MA.: Cambridge University Press.

Sawtooth Software, Inc. (1999), 'The CBC/HB Module for Hierarchical Bayes Estimation', Sawtooth Software Website: www.sawtoothsoftware .com/Techabs.htm.

Schwepker, C.H. Jr and T.B. Cornwell (1991), 'An Examination of Ecologically Concerned Consumers and Their Intention to Purchase Ecologically Packaged Products', *Journal of Public Policy and Marketing*, 102, 77–101.

Seip, K. and J. Strand (1992), 'Willingness to Pay for Environmental Goods in Norway: a Contingent Valuation Study with Real Payment', *Environmental and Resource Economics*, 21, 91–106.

Severin, V. (2000), *Comparing Statistical and Respondent Efficiency in Choice Experiments*, Unpublished PhD dissertation, Department of Marketing, The University of Sydney.

Shively, T., G. Allenby and R. Kohn (2000), 'A Nonparametric Approach To Identifying Latent Relationships in Hierarchical Models', *Marketing Science* (forthcoming).

Simmons, P. (1995), 'Green Consumerism: Blurring the Boundary Between Public and Private', in S. Edgell, S. Walklate, and G. Williams (eds) *Debating the Future of the Public Sphere,* Aldershot, UK and Brookfield, USA: Avebury.

Simon, H.A. (1955), 'A Behavioural Model of Rational Choice', *Quarterly Journal of Economics*, 69, 99–118.

Sinden, J.A. (1988), 'Empirical Tests of Hypothetical Biases in Consumers' Surplus Surveys', *Australian Journal of Agricultural Economics*, 32, 98–112.

Smith, V.K. (1985), 'The Valuation of Environmental Risks Using Hedonic Wage Models', in M. David and T. Smeeding (eds) *Horizontal Equity, Uncertainty and Economic Well-being*, Chicago: Chicago University Press.

Snowy Water Inquiry (1998), *Snowy Water Inquiry, Jointly Sponsored by the New South Wales and Victorian Governments*, Sydney: Snowy Water Inquiry.

Street, D.J., D.S. Bunch and B. Moore (1999), 'Optimal Designs for 2^k Paired Comparison Experiments', unpublished working paper, School of Mathematical Sciences, University of Technology, Sydney, Australia.

Sudman, S. and N.M. Bradburn (1974), *Response Effects in Surveys*, Chicago: Aldine.

Svenson, O. (1979), 'Process Descriptions of Decision Making', *Organizational Behavior and Human Performance*, **23**, 86–112.

Swait, J.R. (1994), 'A Structural Equation Model of Latent Segmentation and Product Choice for Cross-sectional Revealed Preference Choice Data', *Journal of Retailing and Consumer Services*, **1**, 77–89.

Swait, J. and W. Adamowicz (2001a), 'The Influence of Task Complexity on Consumer Choice: a Lafat Class Model of Decision Strategy Switching', *Journal of Consumer Research*. Forthcoming.

Swait, J. and W. Adamowicz (2001b), 'Choice Environment, Market Complexity and Consumer Behavior: a Theoretical and Empirical Approach for Incorporating Decision Complexity in Models of Consumer Choice', *Organizational Behaviour and Human Decision Processes*. Forthcoming.

Swait, J. and J. Louviere (1993), 'The Role of the Scale Parameter in the Estimation and Comparison of Multinomial Logit Models', *Journal of Marketing Research*, **30**, 305–314.

Swait, J. and J.J. Louviere, and M. Williams (1994), 'A Sequential Approach to Exploiting the Combined Strengths of SP and RP Data: Application to Freight Shipper Choice', *Transportation*, **21**, 135–152.

Swallow, S.K., T. Weaver, J.J. Opaluch and T.S. Michelman (1994), 'Heterogenous Preferences and Aggregation in Environmental Policy Analysis: a Landfill Siting Case', *American Journal of Agricultural Economics*, **76**, 431–443.

Tacconi, L. and J.W. Bennett (eds) (1997), *Protected Area Assessment and Establishment in Vanuatu: A Socioeconomic Approach*, Canberra: ACIAR.

Thomas, H. (1989), 'By Appointment to the Green Consumer', *Accountancy*, September.

Thurstone, L.L. (1927), 'A Law of Comparative Judgment', *Psychological Review*, **34**, 273–286.

Train, K. (1986), *Qualitative Choice Analysis, Theory, Econometrics and an Application to Automobile Demand*, London: MIT Press.

Train, K.E. (1998), 'Recreation Demand Models with Taste Differences Over People', *Land Economics*, **74** (2), 230–239.

Tversky, A. 1972 'Elimination by Aspects: a Theory of Choice', *Psychological Review*, **79**, 281–299.

Tversky, A. and D. Kahneman (1982), 'Causal Schemas in Judgements Under Uncertainty', in D. Kahneman, P. Slovic and A. Tversky (eds) *Judgement Under Uncertainty: Heuristics and Biases*, New York: Cambridge University Press.

Wedel, W., W. Kamakura, N. Arora, A. Bemmaor, J. Chiang, T. Elrod, R. Johnson, P. Lenk, S. Neslin and C.S. Poulsen (1999), 'Heterogeneity and Bayesian Methods in Choice Modeling', *Marketing Letters*, Special Issue on the HEC Invitational Conference on Consumer Decision-making and Choice Behaviour (forthcoming).

Whitehead, J.C. and G.C. Bloomquist (1999), 'Do Reminders of Substitutes and Budget Constraints Influence Contingent Valuation Estimates? Reply to Another Comment', *Land Economics*, **75** (3), 483–484.

Wills, I. (1997), *Economics and the Environment: A Signalling and Incentives Approach*, St Leonards: Allen and Unwin.

Zwerina, K., H. Joel and W.F. Kuhfeld (1996), 'A General Method for Constructing Efficient Choice Designs', working paper, Fuqua School of Business, Duke University.

Index